Price  11⁵˸      SKU _TAG 1016191_

Title _____

Condition - LN  (VG)  G  AC   Location _U·go——lt_

[ ] _____ Bent

[ ] _____ Bumped

[ ] _____ Creasing to Cover   [ ] _____ Edge Wear

[x] __light_____ Shelf Wear   [ ] _____ Sunned

[ ] Spine Creased  [ ] Remainder Mark

[ ] _____ Foxing

[ ] _____ Soiling

[x] No Marks in Text  [ ] _____ Underlining

[ ] Pages Yellowed   [ ] _____ Highlighting

[ ] Weak Hinge(s)    [ ] _____ Marginal Marks

[ ] _____ Tear(s) to DJ    [ ] _____ Shelf Wear to DJ

Notes _____

_____

_____

_____

*This sticker is removable.

# AFTER VATICAN II

*Trajectories and Hermeneutics*

*Edited by*

James L. Heft, S.M.

*with*

John O'Malley, S.J.

WILLIAM B. EERDMANS PUBLISHING COMPANY

GRAND RAPIDS, MICHIGAN / CAMBRIDGE, U.K.

© 2012 James L. Heft, S.M., and John O'Malley, S.J.

Published 2012 by
Wm. B. Eerdmans Publishing Co.
2140 Oak Industrial Drive N.E., Grand Rapids, Michigan 49505 /
P.O. Box 163, Cambridge CB3 9PU U.K.

Printed in the United States of America

18  17  16  15  14  13  12        7  6  5  4  3  2  1


**Library of Congress Cataloging-in-Publication Data**

After Vatican II: trajectories and hermeneutics /
    edited by James L. Heft with John O'Malley.
          p.        cm.
    Proceedings of a conference held in Feb. 2009 at the
    University of Southern California.
    Includes index.
    ISBN 978-0-8028-6731-5 (pbk.: alk. paper)
    1. Vatican Council (2nd: 1962-1965) — Congresses.  2. Catholic Church —
    Doctrines — Congresses.  3. O'Malley, John W. What happened at Vatican II —
    Congresses.  I. Heft, James.  II. O'Malley, John W.   III. Title: After Vatican 2.

    BX8301962 .A545   2012
    282.09′045 — dc23
                                                                2012004720

www.eerdmans.com

# Contents

CONTENTS

# Preface

In February 2009, a few months after the appearance of John O'Malley's *What Happened at Vatican II*, I invited in the name of the Institute for Advanced Catholic Studies a small group of scholars to gather at the University of Southern California to meet with O'Malley and carry on the conversation. Included in the group was Joseph Komonchak, who has written extensively on the council, has edited the English version of the five-volume *History of Vatican II* (Orbis/Peeters, 1995-2006), and has an extraordinary grasp of the debates, developments, and formation of the documents of the council.

O'Malley devotes the first third of his book to describing the "long nineteenth century," which he dates from the French Revolution to the fall of 1958 when Angelo Giuseppe Roncalli was elected Pope John XXIII. Without a grasp of the main historical realities that constituted the ecclesial dimensions of the Church before Vatican II, it is difficult to understand the significant changes that the bishops at the council agreed to make. The changes that the 2,400 bishops — gathered from around the world for ten weeks each fall from 1962 to 1965 — included clearly affirming religious liberty, strongly supporting ecumenical and interreligious dialogue, calling for significant changes in liturgical forms, and stating unambiguously the continuing validity of the covenant that God made with the Jews. Rather than use, as had been the custom, the language of legal decrees with "anathemas" attached, the bishops at this council wrote the sixteen documents they approved using a quite different style, a decision more important than on the surface it might suggest.

The "issues under the issues," which O'Malley had singled out in his book, were of special interest to the scholars gathered in Los Angeles.

Those issues were collegiality (the "center-periphery" issue, or the relationship between centralized and decentralized authority), change (or, how to understand the relationship between past and present teachings and practices), and style (the new literary genre that the bishops employed in all their documents). Fundamental issues are rarely, if ever, resolved once and for all time. So it is not surprising that the focus of the participants' papers picked up on O'Malley's basic issues, and traced the development of some of the most important conciliar topics beyond the council. Thus, instead of trying to describe this volume as a commentary on O'Malley's book, I think it is better described as *trajectories and hermeneutics* of Vatican II.

O'Malley's underlying issues continue to be debated. Especially over the last twenty years, those debates often address the problem of how correctly to interpret the council. The bishops at Vatican II brought about significant changes, not just for theologians involved in ecumenical and interreligious dialogue, but also for Catholics throughout the world. They had been invited to modify their attitudes and relationships, not just among themselves and within the Church, but also with other Christians and believers in other religions. Understanding what has happened *after Vatican II* provides, therefore, another important window into the ongoing debate about the proper interpretation of Vatican II. The chapters of this volume are best understood as commentary on several important developments that would have been impossible without Vatican II. That they continue to be contested should not be a surprise, especially to anyone who has read O'Malley's descriptions of both the official positions of the Church during the long nineteenth century, and the debates at the council that resulted in the decrees of Vatican II.

The Institute for Advanced Catholic Studies was founded to foster deep conversation among scholars of various disciplines so that the rich Catholic intellectual traditions might continue to develop for the benefit of the Church, other religious believers, and the world at large. The scholars at this symposium carry forward the Institute's important mission, and their papers represent the dimensions and depth of both continuity and change that mark any living tradition. I am especially grateful to John O'Malley and Joseph Komonchak for their participation in the symposium; they generously shared their knowledge and made many suggestions for the improvement of the papers. O'Malley and Komonchak respectively have also contributed framing and concluding essays for this volume. I wish to thank both John O'Malley for his editorial suggestions, and Gary

Adler, Associate Director of Research for the Institute, for his help in preparing this manuscript for publication. Finally, I wish to thank Dr. Donald Wigal for his careful preparation of the index.

JAMES L. HEFT, S.M.
*Alton Brooks Professor of Religion at the University of Southern California*
*President: Institute for Advanced Catholic Studies*

# Introduction: Trajectories and Hermeneutics

*John O'Malley, S.J.*

Even while Vatican II was still in session, publications about it began to pour off the presses. They have continued to do so up to the present, at a pace that makes it difficult even for specialists to keep up with them. They fall into a variety of categories — histories, polemics, personal memoirs, collections of conference papers, and so forth. Two categories among such publications — studies of the council's reception and commentaries on the sixteen final documents — seem to be moving into new stages, which are reflected in the studies contained in this volume.

In the symposium at the University of Southern California described above by James Heft, the participants were asked to reflect on how my book related to their research, their discipline, or their special interests. What points did I raise that resonated with them in a significant way? Our hope in posing such questions was that we might find lines of convergence that would move forward our understanding of the council and its ongoing significance. As to be expected, the scholars we gathered took off in many directions and presented us with a rich range of considerations. Nonetheless, some issues recurred in the papers and kept recurring in the discussion that followed.

This means that, although each of the contributions in this volume can stand on its own as an important study of aspects of the council, they as a group have a coherence deriving from taking my *What Happened at Vatican II* as a foil against which the authors approached the council. As it happened, the results of the process converged to a greater or lesser degree in advancing our understanding of the two categories mentioned above.

The first such category is how the council was "received," that is, how its provisions were understood and put into practice in local churches throughout the world. For scholarship on that question, the year 1985 was a turning point. From November 24 until December 8, the Extraordinary Synod of Bishops, convoked by Pope John Paul II to assess the impact and implementation of the council twenty years after its conclusion, met in the Vatican. National episcopal conferences had submitted reports on the subject in advance, and during the Synod individual bishops took it up in their oral and written interventions. Some of the reports from the conferences are available in print, and a full collection of summaries of the interventions were published in Italian the year after the Synod.[1]

The Synod was in effect a large, international symposium on the council's reception, and it is the indispensable starting point for any assessment of how the council was received. When it concluded Avery Dulles, the distinguished American Jesuit theologian, made the telling observation about what transpired: "The bishops acknowledged some difficulties and confusion, but almost all reflected enthusiasm and gratitude for the work of the council. This strong endorsement should put to rest any lingering suspicion that many bishops are unhappy about Vatican II."[2]

But scholars had already set to work. Even before John Paul II announced the Synod, Giuseppe Alberigo and his collaborators at the Istituto per le Scienze Religiose in Bologna had commissioned studies for a volume on the subject that was published in Italian and French just before the Synod opened, and was later translated into other languages, including English.[3] This volume along with the Synod itself promoted further studies, which continue to be produced up to today.[4]

---

1. For the report of the bishops from the United States, for instance, see *Origins* 15, no. 15 (26 September 1985): 225-33; from England and Wales, *Origins* 15, no. 12 (5 September 1985): 177-86. See also *Synode Extraordinaire. Célébration de Vatican II* (Paris: Cerf, 1986). For summaries of the interventions, see Gino Concetti, ed., *Il Synodo della Speranza. Documenti ufficiali della seconda assemblea straordinaria del synodo dei vescovi* (Rome: Logos, 1986)

2. Avery Dulles, "The Reception of Vatican II at the Extraordinary Synod of 1985," in *The Reception of Vatican II*, ed. Giuseppe Alberigo, Jean-Pierre Jossua, and Joseph A. Komonchak, trans. Matthew J. O'Connell (Washington, DC: Catholic University of America Press, 1987), pp. 349-63, at 349.

3. Alberigo et al., eds., *Reception of Vatican II*.

4. Among the more recent studies are Pierre-Marie Gy, *The Reception of Vatican II: Liturgical Reforms in the Life of the Church* (Milwaukee: Marquette University Press, 2003); Gilles Routhier, *Vatican II. Herméneutique et réception* (Saint-Laurent, Québec: Fides, 2006); and Ladislas M. Orsy, *Receiving the Council: Theological and Canonical Insights and Debates* (Collegeville, MN: Liturgical Press, 2009).

Reception is currently a category popular among scholars not only for Vatican II but also for the Council of Trent, whose interpretation and implementation in the sixteenth century have been the subject of many important studies, sparked to some extent by interest in the issue for Vatican II. These studies help our understanding of what happened after Vatican II by showing similarities with what happened after Trent but also by showing radical differences. In the latter regard Vatican II differs from Trent most notably in that radio, telephone, and television imbued it with an immediacy and impact for Catholic clergy and laity that was altogether lacking for Trent and that was absolutely new for a council.

Although studies in this volume could well be considered under the rubric of "reception," I suggest that "trajectory" might better catch the reality. The dictionary defines *trajectory* as the path of a moving body. We can take it here as almost a synonym for development, that is, for shifts or changes that have taken place that probably would not have done so except for the council but that cannot easily be traced to a specific provision of the council. Whereas "reception" generally indicates a direct application (or nonapplication) of explicit norms or directives, such as the revised liturgical forms, "trajectory" suggests something less obviously based on the council's norms and directives. It is related to reception, and perhaps can be considered a species of it. Introduction of it as a category of interpretation expands what we usually mean by reception.

The second category related to the council that is changing is the process by which we interpret the council's documents. Up to the present, commentaries on the documents have most commonly analyzed them as discrete units, without reckoning in any consistent fashion with how they relate to one another and are dependent upon one another. The most authoritative of the early studies along this line is the multi-authored, five-volume commentary edited by Herbert Vorgrimler and written by theologians who took part in the council, including the young Joseph Ratzinger.[5] The most recent publication of similar scope is another five-volume commentary edited by Peter Hünermann and Bernd Jochen Hilberath.[6]

In the years between the publication of these two impressive monu-

5. The English-language edition: *Commentary on the Documents of Vatican II*, 5 vols. (New York: Herder & Herder, 1967-69).

6. *Herder theologischer Kommentar zum zweiten Vatikanischen Konzil*, 5 vols. (Freiburg im Breisgau: Herder, 2004-6).

ments of scholarship, almost innumerable smaller commentaries appeared in a wide range of languages. Like these two collections, they treat the documents one by one, on an individual basis. More ambitious have been the monographs on the documents, especially those published under the inspiration of Alberto Melloni and the late Giuseppe Alberigo of the Istituto per le Scienze Religiose in Bologna.[7] These monographs are the result of careful archival research and comprehensive analysis of the genesis of the respective documents and of their course through the council.

Studies like these are of course absolutely basic and will, we hope, be amplified and updated by future scholars. They constitute a genre that will continue to be indispensable for understanding the council. Nonetheless, it seems unlikely that new data will be unearthed that will substantially change the profiles of any of the sixteen final documents as we now see them. As far as that genre is concerned, we seem to have reached a point of diminishing returns.

With that scholarship in hand, the studies in this volume suggest we are in a position to move to a further stage in interpreting the council. Instead of examining the documents in isolation from one another, we are now ready to examine them as interdependent and ready to see how that interdependence is essential for interpreting them correctly. We move to a consideration of each document as in some measure an expression of larger orientations and as an integral part of a cohesive corpus, which is a result in large part of the documents' intertextual character. Unlike the determinations of previous councils, those of Vatican II are not a grab-bag of ordinances without intrinsic relationship to one another. They implicitly but deliberately cross-reference and play off one another — in the vocabulary they employ, in the great themes to which they recur, in the core values they inculcate, and in certain basic issues that cut across them. They constitute a coherent unit and must be interpreted accordingly. In a recent article in *Theological Studies*, Massimo Faggioli provides such an interpreta-

---

7. The institution is now known as the Fondazione per le Scienze Religiose Giovanni XXIII. See, e.g., Riccardo Burigana, *La Bibbia nel concilio. La redazione della costituzione "Dei verbum" del Vaticano II* (Bologna: Il Mulino, 1998); Massimo Faggioli, *Il vescovo e il concilio. Modello episcopale e aggiornamento al Vaticano II* (Bologna: Il Mulino, 2005); Silvia Scatena, *La fatica della libertà. L'elaborazione della dichiarazione Dignitatis humanae sulla libertà religiosa del Vaticano II* (Bologna: Il Mulino, 2003); and Giovanni Turbanti, *Un concilio per il mondo moderno. La relazione della costituzione pastorale "Gaudium et spes" del Vaticano II* (Bologna: Il Mulino, 2000)

tion for *Sacrosanctum Concilium,* the constitution "On the Sacred Liturgy," and in so doing shows the fruitfulness of that method.[8]

The fact, for instance, that during the council the decree on the bishops, *Christus Dominus,* had to be substantially rewritten once the affirmation of national episcopal conferences in *Sacrosanctum Concilium* was ratified by the final vote on it, and once the collegial dimensions of *Lumen Gentium* became clear, is simply one example of an intertextuality that is pervasive. The further fact that under the up-front issues that each document treated as its remit lurk deeper issues that cut across a number of the documents manifests this intertextuality at one of its profoundest levels. I singled out four such issues — how to deal with change, how to deal with the implications of a truly world church, with the relationship between center and periphery, and with the style in which the church conducts its mission. These four are intimately related to one another, and to touch one is to some degree to touch the others.

The last of them, the style in which the church conducts its business, finds expression in the new literary genre the council adopted and the new vocabulary that goes with it. Style here is not superficial ornamentation but the vehicle for conveying a significant shift in values and priorities. Whereas earlier it was a value to hold other Christian churches and other religions in contempt, it was now a value to find common ground with them. Whereas formerly it was a priority in evangelization to import with it Western culture, it was now a priority to adapt to indigenous cultures. Such shifts in values and priorities touched upon the very personality of the church and of the individual Catholic.

Since the genre and the vocabulary were common, in varying degrees, to all the documents, they conditioned the character of the other three issues, which is yet another indication that to grasp the full import of any single document of the council, that document must be considered in its relationship to the others. What emerges from this approach is the fact that Vatican Council II enjoys a literary and thematic unity that is unique in the annals of Christian councils.

This means the council had certain basic orientations that, while based on individual documents, transcend them. These orientations are coherent or consonant with one another, and they thus allow us to rehabilitate the expression "the spirit of the council." Yes, that expression has been abused

---

8. See Massimo Faggioli, "*Quaestio Disputata. Sacrosanctum Concilium* and the Meaning of Vatican II," *Theological Studies* 71 (2010): 437-52.

to justify interpretations that can hardly be verified in the texts. Yes, it lacks technical precision. But the distinction between letter and spirit in interpreting difficult texts enjoys a venerable place in Catholic traditions of exegesis. Moreover, the Extraordinary Synod of Bishops, 1985, called to assess implementation of the council, itself made use of the distinction by insisting that the spirit of the council had to depend upon the letter.[9]

From such considerations emerges, I believe, the necessity to construct and apply a hermeneutic that takes full account of the inviolable integrity of the full corpus of the documents, especially of the four constitutions — *Sacrosanctum Concilium, Lumen Gentium, Dei Verbum,* and *Gaudium et Spes* — but as well as of two documents particularly hotly debated in the council — *Nostra Aetate* and *Dignitatis Humanae.* Such a hermeneutic implies that it is not possible to deconstruct one of the documents without distorting the meaning of the others. It is not possible to "reform" one of them without violating the integrity of the entire corpus and setting in motion a process of dismantlement that reduces the council to an inconsequential blip on the ecclesiastical radar screen. At the council itself neither the majority nor the minority thought its decisions inconsequential. The minority in particular fought some of them with all the forces it could muster, almost as if they were life-and-death issues.

In sum, such a hermeneutic will take account of at least four features: first, the new literary genre that frames the documents; second, the new vocabulary the genre employs; third, the great issues that cut across the documents in either explicit or implicit form, such as the problems posed by the new "world-church" situation, the problems posed by our new consciousness of historical change, the problems of the relationship in the church between center and periphery; and, finally, as a consequence of all the above, takes into account the intertextual character of the documents and the consequent inviolable integrity of the corpus as such. With this in place, we can legitimately speak of "the spirit of the council." It is an expression that plays a considerable role and elicits a great deal of discussion in the contributions to this volume.

By calling attention to the council's trajectories, the studies in this volume *ipso facto* deal with hermeneutics. They call attention to the fact that the council was not essentially a collection of documents, fundamental though those documents are, but an event in the long history of the church

9. See "The Final Report: Synod of Bishops," *Origins* 15 (19 December 1985): 444-50, at 445-46.

that had a beginning, an actualization, and an ongoing impact. For understanding the council and interpreting it, that impact must be taken into account. Trajectories and hermeneutics intersect.

\*       \*       \*

Surely, one of the most interesting phenomena in the Catholic Church since Vatican II has been the development of "movements" such as Opus Dei, Communion and Liberation, and the Community of St. Egidio. These institutions, even those whose origins antedate the council, identify themselves as "the fruit of Vatican II" and claim legitimacy on the basis of the council — if not in the "letter" of its documents certainly in their "spirit." Despite the importance of the movements and the publicity they enjoy in more popular media, they have not received from scholars the attention they deserve. Aside from the book edited by Michael A. Hayes a few years ago, there have been virtually no comparative studies of them and, within that comparative perspective, no close analysis against the intentions and orientations of the council.

Massimo Faggioli provides below precisely such an analysis. He acknowledges that the movements have a relationship to the council but questions its nature. Just how, for instance, are they in accord with the "letter" and the "spirit" of the council? In addressing this question, Faggioli is led into a consideration of hermeneutics. He shows quite convincingly that, if by "spirit" we mean fundamental orientations that cut through the documents of Vatican II and give them coherence among themselves, the movements run counter to at least one of the most important of the council's orientations, the attempt to restore a due measure of authority to the episcopacy and to the local church. He deals, therefore, with the center-periphery issue.

Faggioli shows that the movements, like every other entity in the church, "received" the council in ways peculiar to themselves. They received and took hold of the council's empowerment of the laity especially as expressed in the decree on the lay apostolate, *Apostolicam Actuositatem*. But in their appeal to the center for grants of independence from the episcopacy, they in at least one crucial regard went beyond both the letter and the spirit of the council and even against it. In so doing they begin to look more like trajectories from the council than as instantiations of its reception.

Darlene Fozard Weaver and M. Cathleen Kaveny write as moral theologians. They note two things about Vatican II: first, the council issued no document specifically devoted to moral theology, and, second, it nonetheless had a huge impact on the field. After the council Catholic moral theologians, therefore, did not try to implement a directive of the council regarding the character of their discipline but drew consequences from the council's teachings that in fact resulted in a significant reorientation of it. This reorientation seems better described as a trajectory than what we ordinarily mean by a reception.

Weaver begins by describing the character of moral theology before the council, which was determined almost exclusively by the "manuals," that is, seminary textbooks. This theology was directed exclusively to seminarians and priests and was constructed principally as an aid to appropriate confessional practice. It operated apart from other theological disciplines and was focused on sin rather than on the breadth of the moral life.

How did Vatican II help change things? Not by explicitly mandating a new moral theology. How then? Weaver takes up the theme of the council as a language-event, and in the implications of that theme she discovers the basis for the new style that moral theology adopted after the council, a style that correlates with the implications of the new style of discourse the council adopted.

That style allowed the emergence, for the first time in a council, of the great theme of the universal call to holiness. That theme presaged and promoted the turn moral theology took after the council to a broader scope in which morality and spirituality coalesce. Moral theology, though of course still concerned with individual actions, now situates the moral life in a person's continuing endeavor to grow in the love of God and neighbor and to take upon oneself the appropriate measure of responsibility for the common good. Weaver bases her analysis on the letter of the documents but in a way that leads her beyond prooftexting to get to more basic orientations.

M. Cathleen Kaveny also reviews how moral theology moved from the perspectives of the manuals before the council to notably different ones afterwards. In describing the character of earlier moral theology, however, she shows that official teaching was broader than what the manuals suggest, due principally to the social encyclicals of the popes, beginning in 1891 with Leo XIII's *Rerum Novarum*. The encyclicals were as much concerned with the protection of rights as with the avoidance of evil and as much concerned with corporate action to deal with social problems as with the action of individuals. These encyclicals provided an important impetus leading to *Gaudium et Spes*, which placed the church and individual Christians firmly in the present, firmly in "the modern world," where they would act as agents for peace, justice, and the advancement of all aspects of the common good.

After the council, as moral theology began to develop in new ways, the influence of papal encyclicals upon it grew even stronger than before. Among those encyclicals Kaveny singles out Pope John Paul II's *Veritatis Splendor* for special consideration because it addresses the topic of fundamental moral theology, "dealing with such questions as how we are to think about our obligations to pursue good and avoid evil." Although sometimes criticized for being a conservative document, it according to Kaveny partakes of many of the qualities embodied in the style of moral theology that developed after the council. The pope insisted that he conceived his teaching in *Veritatis Splendor* in relationship to Vatican II. When Kaveny analyzes the encyclical against the great issues-under-the-issues of the council, she thereby judges it against "the spirit of the council." By applying this hermeneutic, she in the main finds the pope's contention justified.

Francis Sullivan directly engages an extraordinarily important and quite specific trajectory or development: official teaching on the salvation of non-Christians. He traces the teaching on the subject as first explicitly addressed in modern times by Pius IX, through the council's handling of it in several key documents, to its further elaboration in official documents up to the present. In this process the council was crucial as a privileged matrix in which the question was addressed from a variety of angles. In analyzing the council's teaching, Sullivan provides a good example of an issue that cut across several crucial documents of the council, and he thus highlights the documents' intertextual character. Especially important, moreover, is the fact that the council's teaching did not signify a definitive coda to the subject but served, rather, as a launching pad for further development.

In the ongoing evolution of the church's teaching on the subject, we see exemplified in a relatively unambiguous way a "development of doctrine" in its most straightforward sense. That is, we see further elaborations in a given direction. In this case, that direction is ever more positive in its assessment of other religions. It is thereby ever more inclusive by taking account not only of the God-given impulse in those religions to observe the natural law but also in taking account of the divine inspiration of elements of their religious belief and practice.

Of course, no truly Christian teaching can be without *ressourcement*. It must "return to the sources," especially Scripture, to validate its claims. Nonetheless, in this case we easily perceive an ongoing trajectory that for a century and a half has moved, not without some occasional detours, in the same direction. In that regard, it differs very much from the problem John Courtenay Murray and others faced at the council with their approach to the church-state problem, which seemed to their critics to be just the opposite of a development or trajectory and more like a dangerous and illegitimate abandonment of the true course for a new and forbidden one.

John Connelly takes up a subject closely related to Sullivan's, the church's relationship to the Jews. Does the church have an obligation to work for their salvation? If so, why so? If not, why not? The code expression for this issue is "mission to the Jews," meaning mission to convert. Connelly like Sullivan is able to trace a trajectory that began before the council, that in *Nostra Aetate* found crucial expression, and that has continued to be a live and controversial reality in the church (and in the world beyond the church!) up to the present.

Symptomatic of the direction the trajectory has taken is how Msgr. John M. Oesterreicher over the course of years turned from insistently advocating conversion to a quite different position. Oesterreicher is significant not only because he himself converted to Catholicism from Judaism and became a Catholic priest, but because during the council he was a member of the Secretariat for Christian Unity that drafted *Nostra Aetate*. He plays an illuminating and deservedly important role in Connelly's analysis of the issue.

One of the merits of Connelly's study is to show that mission was an issue dominating the several other issues that made *Nostra Aetate* so problematic during the council. The debate on the document, among the most bitter in the whole council, breached the walls of the basilica to engage not only public opinion on a large scale but even to become for the Vatican a major diplomatic problem. Mission continues as a hot issue today.

Unlike Sullivan's trajectory, therefore, which has followed a more or less straight course, this one has not only zigzagged since the council but at times seems to have reversed itself. As Connelly shows, the sometimes erratic course of the trajectory has made mission the sticking point in Jewish-Catholic dialogue ever since the council. When in 2007 Pope Benedict XVI revised the prayer of the Good Friday liturgy to implore "that God our Lord illuminate their hearts, so that they will recognize Jesus Christ, the Savior of all men," he raised the issue again in an authoritative and dramatic fashion. He made front-page news and sent bloggers into a frenzy. He, moreover, made mission to the Jews an undertaking for whose success every Catholic who goes to church on Good Friday must pray.

There is a profound irony in all this. If we do not count the first few generations of Christians and situations as in Spain and Portugal in the fifteenth and sixteenth centuries where Jews were threatened with banishment unless they gave up their faith, conversions have been few. Even more telling, as Connelly points out, is that, despite the seriousness of mission as a theological issue, the Catholic Church as such has never had a concerted program for the conversion of the Jews or on an official level established an institution for that purpose. In terms of the actual practice of the church, therefore, the issue has floated in the heavens of speculation and never touched down to earth.

In Henri de Lubac, Robin Darling Young deals with a thinker who based his career on *ressourcement.* When Pope John XXIII appointed de Lubac to the Preparatory Theological Commission whose remit was to formulate documents for action at the council, the act was interpreted as a dramatic rehabilitation of de Lubac and of the *nouvelle théologie* of which he was a principal architect. De Lubac continued throughout the council as an official *peritus.* Although we now know that his direct role was small in the drafting of *Lumen Gentium* and *Gaudium et Spes,* the two documents for which he is often given credit, his indirect influence on them was in fact considerable due to the impact his writings had had on theologians in the decades prior to the council. During the council, therefore, he became for many people almost an icon of what the council stood for and what it was trying to accomplish.

Yet, as is well known, after the council he expressed his disillusionment with the directions the church seemed to be taking. Nor in such feelings was he alone among major figures at the council. The causes for him and for others were, we must assume, surely complex and due at least in part to social and cultural upheavals of the late 1960s and early 1970s that had little to do with the council. Nonetheless, Young puts her finger on two causes that lie within de Lubac's intellectual enterprise. They are extremely important.

The first is de Lubac's conviction that a misunderstanding of the true character of the relationship between nature and grace that had crept into Catholic theology with the scholastics and persisted up the present was in good measure responsible for many of the problems in the contemporary church. This was an intellectual's intellectual analysis of a complex issue much more rooted in the social and political reality of the church than in a theological misunderstanding.

The second cause is the character of his *ressourcement* itself, the character of his recovery of the patristic sources upon which he based his vision of the church and his hope for its renewal. It is related to the first but even more important in explaining what happened to de Lubac after the council. As Young shows, de Lubac's return *ad fontes* was a highly selective process in which he turned a blind eye to aspects of his sources that did not fit his idealized and somewhat romantic reconstruction of them. Among those aspects were not only the bitter theological conflicts that divided the early writers among themselves but also the political machinations and social upheavals that were a defining part of the religious reality. Had he attended to those aspects, Young suggests, he would have been less shocked and disillusioned with the aftermath of Vatican II.

Joseph A. Komonchak, the most widely recognized American scholar on Vatican II, graciously agreed to write a conclusion to our volume. In it he takes up the volume's themes of trajectory and hermeneutics, which he develops in several revealing ways. He pays special attention to Joseph Ratzinger's many statements about how the council is properly to be interpreted and analyzes them from historical and theological perspectives. As is well known, Ratzinger, both as theologian and now as Pope Benedict XVI, made the disjunction between continuity and discontinuity the hermeneutical tool that scholars and polemicists seized upon for interpreting the council and for separating the wheat from the chaff.

By addressing that disjunction, Komonchak goes, therefore, to the heart of the controversies today over how to interpret the council. He shows the valid aspects of the disjunction and shows the ways Ratzinger developed it. More emphatically, however, he shows its inadequacy when applied without taking into account that the council was not simply a corpus of documents but a historical event. The council, like the church, was not a reality "floating off somewhere in the ether with no human beings in it." The council took place in time and space. It happened "in the modern world."

Komonchak has elsewhere written eloquently about the council as event, which he defines as a happening that unfolds, a happening that has a plot — a happening in which something happens. In an event, what happens is a break with routine. Contemporaries are aware of the break, but the event's full implications are generally not realized until later. An aspect of the event that contemporaries deem critical may turn out to have been a tempest in a teapot, whereas an aspect seemingly trivial may have important repercussions. Events, in other words, have trajectories. To fully comprehend the event one must take those trajectories into account. In so doing one constructs a hermeneutic based on the status quo before the event, on the event itself, and on the event's further unfolding. Trajectories and hermeneutics are inseparable.

\* \* \*

As the studies in this volume make clear, Vatican II continues to be a reality very much alive in the church today. It in various ways conditions every aspect of Catholic life, some few of which are described and analyzed here. The council was an extraordinarily complex phenomenon. It is no wonder, therefore, that opinions vary widely as to its significance. Nonetheless, nearly fifty years after its close, we are able with the benefit of a half-century of remarkable scholarship to understand it at a deeper level than ever and, indeed, to rescue it from simplistic labels, such as liberal and conservative, that especially in the United States have so much confused discussion of it. This volume is meant as a contribution to that important and ongoing scholarly enterprise.

# Between Documents and Spirit:
# The Case of the "New Catholic Movements"

*Massimo Faggioli*

The central place of the "new Catholic movements" (such as Communion and Liberation, the Community of St. Egidio, Focolare, Neocathecumenal Way, Cursillos de Cristiandad, Legionaries of Christ) in the contemporary Catholic Church needs to be addressed from the point of view of their historical origins and relationship with Vatican II. It is indeed common language within the Catholic Church to define these new movements as the fruit of the council, also because they tend to define themselves as, precisely that, "the fruit of Vatican II."

It is not an easy task to define these movements. It is clear, however, that both the auto-definitions and descriptions of the Catholic movements in the *Code of Canon Law* can be of little help. The minimum common denominator of the new Catholic movements is a group of Catholics that have "a charismatic founder, a particular charism, some form of ecclesial reality or expression, a predominantly lay membership, a radical commitment to the Gospel, a form of teaching or training closely linked to its charism, a specific focus and a commitment to bringing its own emphasis or understanding into the life of the Church."[1]

These new movements, which presuppose a stable commitment and a rule to follow, which may be written or habit, have often been described as integralist, fundamentalist, ultramontane, and sectarian. Hard feelings are often the source of biased judgments in the debate on these new Catholic movements. But as many of these new Catholic movements were founded

---

1. See Charles Whitehead, "The Role of Ecclesial Movements and New Communities in the Life of the Church," in *New Religious Movements in the Catholic Church*, ed. Michael A. Hayes (London/New York: Burns & Oates, 2005), p. 18.

after Vatican II, they clearly are part of the outcome of the council and, therefore, are an integral part of the face of "post–Vatican II Catholicism."

The question is thus not whether there is a relationship between the movements and Vatican II, but rather what kind of Vatican II they claim to be the fruit of: the literal meaning of the documents of Vatican II or the "spirit of Vatican II"? Indeed, it is necessary to investigate the relationship between the new Catholic movements and the allegedly distorting appeal to the "spirit of Vatican II"[2] in order to explain and defend their success and role in the post–Vatican II Catholic Church. This brief study will help us to understand that post–Vatican II Catholicism, as well as the battle for control of the council's legacy, are based on the narrative of the documents and their interpretation, given that "it is not the documents that reveal how hot the issue was but the narrative of the battles for control of the council itself."[3]

## From the "Long Nineteenth Century" to Vatican II

A decisive element of the passage between the "long nineteenth century,"[4] Vatican II, and the "new Catholic movements" was the contribution of the "revival movements" of the early twentieth century. The biblical movement, the patristic revival and *ressourcement,* the liturgical renewal, and the ecumenical movement based in Europe and North America had survived the modernist crisis at the beginning of the twentieth century[5] and

2. For the polemics about the "spirit of Vatican II" see Camillo Cardinal Ruini (vicar for the Diocese of Rome), in Rome, 17 June 2005, presenting Agostino Marchetto's *Il concilio ecumenico Vaticano II. Contrappunto per la sua storia* (Vatican City: Libreria Editrice Vaticana, 2005): private audio recording. From Cardinal Ruini see also the introduction to Karol Wojtyla, *Alle fonti del rinnovamento. Studio sull'attuazione del Concilio Vaticano II,* ed. Flavio Felice (Polish edition 1972, 1981; first Italian edition Città del Vaticano, 2001, published by Libreria Editrice Vaticana), foreword by Camillo Cardinal Ruini (Soveria Mannelli: Fondazione Novae Terrae, Rubbettino, 2007), pp. v-ix. Similar opinions are evident in Matthew L. Lamb and Matthew Levering, "Introduction," in *Vatican II: Renewal within Tradition,* ed. Matthew L. Lamb and Matthew Levering (Oxford/New York: Oxford University Press, 2008), pp. 4-7. On the other side, see Alberto Melloni, "Concili, ecumenicità e storia. Note di discussione," *Cristianesimo nella Storia* 28, no. 3 (2007): 509-42, and "Council Vatican II: Bibliographical Overview 2005-2007," *Cristianesimo nella Storia* 29, no. 2 (2008): 567-610.

3. See John W. O'Malley, *What Happened at Vatican II* (Cambridge, MA, and London: Belknap/Harvard University Press, 2008), p. 304.

4. See O'Malley, *What Happened at Vatican II,* pp. 53-92.

5. See Émile Poulat, *Histoire, dogme et critique dans la crise moderniste* (Paris: Casterman, 1962).

the condemnations of Pius XII and managed to bring to the fathers and *periti* of Vatican II the core of their historical-theological reflections for the *aggiornamento* of the Catholic Church.[6]

The *biblical revival* introduced into the Catholic Church the drive for direct access to the Bible for all Catholics, with emphasis on the importance of the historical-critical method for biblical scholarship, in order to give every faithful the opportunity to reach the Word of God in the Scripture and thus nourish their spiritual life.[7] The *liturgical renewal* stressed the need to reset the balance of the life of the Church around the liturgy and to renew the liturgical language in order to strengthen the connection between spiritual life and the sources of liturgy, with liturgy as a source.[8] The *ecumenical movement* had suffered some severe setbacks from Rome from the 1920s on, but at the local level it had slowly broken the taboo of official relations between Catholics, Protestants, and Orthodox Christians.[9] The *patristic renewal* had advocated the return to the great tradition of the fathers of the Church.[10]

The Catholic Church arrived at the end of Pius XII's pontificate and on the eve of Vatican II in a complex situation: on the one hand, an extremely Rome-centered and Curia-controlled theology officially still based on Thomas Aquinas's guidelines for theological and spiritual identity, and

6. For the pre–Vatican II "reform movements" see Étienne Fouilloux, "I movimenti di riforma nel pensiero cattolica del XIX e XX secolo," in *I movimenti nella storia del cristianesimo. Caratteristiche, variazioni, continuità*, ed. Giuseppe Alberigo and Massimo Faggioli, Cristianesimo nella Storia 24 (2003), pp. 659-76. About the movements before and after Vatican II see Massimo Faggioli, *Breve storia dei movimenti cattolici* (Rome: Carocci, 2008; Spanish translation, Madrid: PPC, forthcoming); Massimo Faggioli, "The New Catholic Movements, Vatican II and Freedom in the Catholic Church," *The Japan Mission Journal* 62, no. 2 (Summer 2008): 75-84; for the United States, James M. O'Toole, *The Faithful: A History of Catholics in America* (Cambridge, MA, and London: Belknap/Harvard University Press, 2008), esp. pp. 144-265.

7. See François Laplanche, *La crise de l'origine. La science catholique des Évangiles et l'histoire au XXe siècle* (Paris: Albin Michel, 2006); Bernard Montagnes, *Père Lagrange, 1855-1938: The Story of Father Marie-Joseph Lagrange, Founder of Modern Catholic Bible Study* (New York: Paulist, 2006).

8. See Annibale Bugnini, *The Reform of the Liturgy, 1948-1975* (Collegeville, MN: Liturgical Press, 1990); Keith F. Pecklers, *The Unread Vision: The Liturgical Movement in the United States of America, 1926-1955* (Collegeville, MN: Liturgical Press, 1998).

9. See Yves Congar, *Chrétiens désunis. Principes d'un "œcuménisme" catholique* (Paris: Cerf, 1937).

10. See Étienne Fouilloux, *La Collection "Sources chrétiennes." Editer les Pères de l'Eglise au XXe siècle* (Paris: Cerf, 1995).

on the other hand the "revival" or "renewal movements" were gaining audience in the theological and ecclesiastical milieu. These "revival movements" directly or indirectly contributed to the council debate on ecclesiology, which became the main issue debated at Vatican II.

Nevertheless, the issue of the "Catholic movements" did not become center stage at Vatican II, neither from a theological nor a canonical point of view.

## The Event of Vatican II and the Catholic Movements

The new Catholic movements identify themselves as the real "fruit" of Vatican II,[11] encouraged by John Paul II who repeatedly affirmed the relationship between the movements and Vatican II.[12] As a matter of fact, the event of Vatican II had a profound impact on the history of the organizations and movements of the Catholic laity, but the relationship between the council and the identity of the new movements is far from direct and unequivocal.

John XXIII announced Vatican II on January 25, 1959, after Pius XII's long pontificate which had confirmed and exalted, in continuity with Pius XI's intuition, Catholic Action as *the* organization of the Catholic laity in a still Europe-centered Catholicism.[13] Although the fortune of

11. See Joseph Cardinal Ratzinger, "I movimenti ecclesiali e la loro collocazione teologica," in Pontificium Consilium pro Laicis, *I movimenti nella Chiesa. Atti del Congresso mondiale dei movimenti ecclesiali (Roma, 27-29 maggio 1998)* (Vatican City: Libreria Editrice Vaticana, 1999), pp. 23-51 (in English: *Movements in the Church: Proceedings of the World Congress of the Ecclesial Movements, Rome, 27-29 May 1998* [Vatican City: Pontificium Consilium pro Laicis, 1999]); John Paul II, homily at the Mass of Pentecost with the Catholic Movements (Rome, 31 May 2000); Joseph Cardinal Ratzinger (Pope Benedict XVI), *New Outpourings of the Spirit: Movements in the Church* (San Francisco: Ignatius, 2007). See also the address of the secretary of the Pontifical Council for the Laity at the international conference for the bishops organized by the Pontifical Council (Rocca di Papa, 15-17 May 2008), Joseph Clemens, "Papa Ratzinger e i movimenti," *Il Regno-documenti* 13 (2008): 441-49, and Pontificium Consilium pro Laicis, *The Beauty of Being a Christian: Movements in the Church* (Vatican City: Libreria Editrice Vaticana, 2007).

12. The movements "represent one of the most significant fruits of that springtime in the Church which was foretold by the Second Vatican Council" (John Paul II, *Message*, 27 May 1998), in Pontificium Consilium pro Laicis, *Movements in the Church: Proceedings of the World Congress of the Ecclesial Movements* (Vatican City: Libreria Editrice Vaticana, 1999), p. 16.

13. See Liliana Ferrari, *Una storia dell'Azione cattolica. Gli ordinamenti statutari da*

Catholic Action was different in the United States,[14] it was crucial in other parts of the Catholic world, such as continental and Western Europe, where it was the matrix of twentieth-century Catholic laity. Pius XI's and Pius XII's strategic options for the presence of the Catholic Church in the European countries at the crossroads between nationalistic ideologies (fascism in Italy, nazism in Germany) and communist threat (in Eastern Europe) was the creation of a "Catholic Action" based on the roots of the late nineteenth-century "social Catholicism," but more closely controlled by the pope, bishops, and clergy in every single group and community. In the Catholic Church of the first half of the century, there was officially no room for autonomy for Catholics in the political sphere, nor for the theological insights of the renewal movements (biblical, ecumenical, liturgical). Within European Catholicism of the 1920s-1940s, Catholic Action was supposed to educate the lay faithful, to "protect" them from the bad influences of the modern ideologies (both socialist-communist and nationalist-fascist) and to control every possible social, political, and theological "motion" of the *ecclesia discens* — the "learning Church" – carefully guided by the "teaching Church" and its supreme leader, the pope.

Within the walls of official Catholicism, however, Catholic Action managed to contain some seeds of the theological renewal movements as well as of the future leaders and insights of the new Catholic movements. The council developed some aspects of the "theology of the laity" born in Europe in the 1940s,[15] and Vatican II witnessed the flourishing of the new movements, whose growth was due also to the identity crisis of Catholic Action. But the connection between Vatican II, its debates, and final texts on one side and the new Catholic movements on the other, is complex.

If we look at the history of Vatican II and the final outcomes of the debates, it is clear that the council did not address the issue of the newborn

---

*Pio XI a Pio XII* (Genoa: Marietti, 1989); Angelica Steinmaus-Pollak, *Das als katholische Aktion organisierte Laienapostolat. Geschichte seiner Theorie und seiner kirchenrechtlichen Praxis in Deutschland* (Würzburg: Echter, 1988); Leo R. Ward, *Catholic Life, U.S.A. Contemporary Lay Movements* (St. Louis: Herder, 1959); David O'Brien, *Public Catholicism* (New York: Macmillan; London: Collier Macmillan, 1989).

14. See O'Malley, *What Happened at Vatican II*, pp. 229-30; and O'Toole, *The Faithful*, pp. 145-98.

15. See especially Yves Congar, *Lay People in the Church: A Study for a Theology of the Laity* (Westminster, MD: Newman Press, 1957).

"movements."[16] On one side, Vatican II debated some aspects of the life of the "Catholic associations" and of Catholic Action in particular, trying to revitalize the old cradles of Catholic lay elites with some injection of the French "theology of the laity." On the other side, Vatican II benefited from the experience of the "reform movements" (biblical, liturgical, ecumenical, patristic renewal), but the profound culture of those "old renewal movements" did not reach the core theological and spiritual identity of the "new Catholic movements."

The documents of Vatican II provide the new movements with a general legitimacy for a new central place for the laity in the Church: especially the decree *Apostolicam Actuositatem* about the lay apostolate, chapter 4 of the constitution *Lumen Gentium* about the laity, the pastoral constitution *Gaudium et Spes* about the Church and the modern world (paragraph 43), and the decree *Presbyterorum Ordinis* (paragraph 8). Only *Apostolicam Actuositatem* directly addressed the issue of the organizations of the laity, mentioning no "movement" but Catholic Action.

The approach of Vatican II to the issue of the lay apostolate was purely theological, with no attention given to the juridical, canonical, or institutional aspects of the organized movements supporting the new central position of the Catholic laity.[17] The debate on the floor and the commission of Vatican II about the schema *De apostolatu laicorum* focused on the need to define clearly the theological identity of the laity, that is, the rights, duties, and opportunities for the activity of the laity in the Church. The debate never went beyond the boundaries of a concept of the apostolate as "animation of temporal realities" in communion with the hierarchy of the Church.[18]

Chapter 4 of *Apostolicam Actuositatem*, whose title reads "The various forms of the apostolate," specifies in paragraphs 18-21 and especially in paragraph 20 the variety of the forms of the organized apostolate, the need for such an apostolate, and the risk of a dissipation of the lay apostolate's human resources. Paragraph 18 of the decree describes the possibility to be apostles "both in their family communities and in their parishes and dioceses, which themselves express the community nature of the apostolate, as well as in the informal groups which they decide to form among them-

16. The Opus Dei (a rather particular "movement") was created in 1928, but most of the other Catholic movements were founded between the end of World War II and the 1970s.

17. See Barbara Zadra, *I movimenti ecclesiali e i loro statuti* (Rome: Pontificia Università Gregoriana, 1997).

18. See *History of Vatican II*, ed. Giuseppe Alberigo, English version ed. Joseph A. Komonchak, esp. vol. 4 (Maryknoll, NY: Orbis, 2004).

selves." Paragraph 20 makes reference to Catholic Action, presented as the typical form of organized apostolate, and does not mention other kinds of associations and movements, even though it leaves some room for other forms: "Organizations in which, in the opinion of the hierarchy, the ensemble of these characteristics is realized, must be considered to be Catholic Action even though they take on various forms and titles because of the needs of different regions and peoples." In particular, *Apostolicam Actuositatem* tried to collect under Pius XI's ideal type of apostolate, that is, Catholic Action, a variety of associations and groups that were never able or willing to unite in a unique association:

> Whether these forms of the apostolate have the name of "Catholic Action" or some other title, they exercise an apostolate of great value for our times and consist in the combination and simultaneous possession of the following characteristics:
> a) The immediate aim of organizations of this kind is the Church's apostolic aim, that is, the evangelization and sanctification of men and the formation of a Christian conscience among them so that they can infuse the spirit of the Gospel into various communities and departments of life.
> b) Cooperating with the hierarchy in their own way, the laity contribute the benefit of their experience to, and assume responsibility for the direction of these organizations, the consideration of the conditions in which the pastoral activity of the Church is to be conducted, and the elaboration and execution of the plan of things to be done.
> c) The laity act together in the manner of an organic body so that the community of the Church is more fittingly symbolized and the apostolate rendered more effective.
> d) Whether they offer themselves spontaneously or are invited to action and direct cooperation with the apostolate of the hierarchy, the laity function under the higher direction of the hierarchy itself, and the latter can sanction this cooperation by an explicit mandate.[19]

---

19. Vatican II's decree, *Apostolicam Actuositatem* 20. Those four criteria — apostolic aim, cooperation with the hierarchy, unity of the laity, and mandate of the hierarchy — would be subsequently developed by John Paul II's apostolic exhortation *Christifideles Laici* (1988). See Guido Bausenhart, "Theologischer Kommentar zum Dekret über das Apostolat des Laien," in *Herders Theologischer Kommentar zum Zweiten Vatikanischen Konzil,* ed. Hans Jochen Hilberath and Peter Hünermann, vol. 4 (Freiburg im Breisgau: Herder, 2005), pp. 5-123.

It is easy to see how the documents of Vatican II maintained the concept of a lay apostolate next to the ideal of Catholic Action, slightly more independent from the ecclesiastical hierarchy but still in need of a "mandate" coming from the hierarchy and faithful to the teaching of the Church. This element would soon fade in the post–Vatican II praxis of the Catholic movements, featuring a growing organizational independence (especially towards the bishops and dioceses where they are active) and an increasingly advertised obedience to the pontifical *magisterium*. But also in the constitution *Lumen Gentium,* the final draft of which opened with a chapter on the mystery of the Church, chapter 2 on "the people of God" stressed once again the relationship between the charisms and the judgment of the "appointed leaders of the Church":

> The Holy Spirit . . . distributes special graces among the faithful of every rank. By these gifts He makes them fit and ready to undertake the various tasks and offices which contribute toward the renewal and building up of the Church, according to the words of the Apostle: "The manifestation of the Spirit is given to everyone for profit." These charisms, whether they be the more outstanding or the more simple and widely diffused, are to be received with thanksgiving and consolation for they are perfectly suited to and useful for the needs of the Church. Extraordinary gifts are not to be sought after, nor are the fruits of apostolic labor to be presumptuously expected from their use; but judgment as to their genuineness and proper use belongs to those who are appointed leaders in the Church, to whose special competence it belongs, not indeed to extinguish the Spirit, but to test all things and hold fast to that which is good.[20]

In chapter 4 *Lumen Gentium* presented the mission of the laity, framing it into a notion still tied to the traditional concept of "Catholic action in society":

> Besides this apostolate which certainly pertains to all Christians, the laity can also be called in various ways to a more direct form of cooperation in the apostolate of the Hierarchy. This was the way certain men and women assisted Paul the Apostle in the Gospel, laboring much in the Lord. Further, they have the capacity to assume from the Hierarchy certain ecclesiastical functions, which are to be performed for a spiritual purpose.[21]

20. Vatican Council II, constitution *Lumen Gentium* 12.
21. Vatican Council II, constitution *Lumen Gentium* 33. See Gérard Philips, *La Chiesa e*

Through a rather "ecclesiastical" and not at all "movementist" view of the history of early Christianity as presented in the New Testament, *Lumen Gentium* described the role of the laity as strictly tied to the hierarchy both for its aim and its form — that is, as a "complement" of the role of the ecclesiastical hierarchy. Vatican II never addressed the fundamental issue of the institutional and canonical setting of the organized laity. Nor did the council debate the issue of the canonical and theological consequences of the "ecclesiology of the people of God," that is, a new regime of relationship between hierarchy and clergy on one side and organized laity on the other. The established subjection of Catholic Action to the hierarchy, as Pius XI and Pius XII had institutionalized it, remained the backdrop for the "debate on the laity" that took place at Vatican II. Moreover, the debate on how the laity might be organized never took place also because the juridical aspects of the Church of Vatican II were postponed, to be treated in the new "Code of Canon Law" (promulgated by John Paul II only in 1983). This delay served as an alibi for the Roman Curia to put off the debate on the juridical consequences of the ecclesiology of Vatican II.[22]

The letter of *Gaudium et Spes* recalled the concept of "animation of temporal realities," although it did not make any progress in exploring the responsibilities of the organizations of lay Catholics toward the Church and the modern world:

> Secular duties and activities belong properly although not exclusively to laymen. Therefore, acting as citizens in the world, whether individually or socially, they will keep the laws proper to each discipline and labor to equip themselves with a genuine expertise in their various fields. They will gladly work with men seeking the same goals. Acknowledging the demands of faith and endowed with its force, they will unhesitatingly devise new enterprises, where they are appropriate, and put them into action. Laymen should also know that it is generally the function of their well-formed Christian conscience to see that the divine law is in-

---

*il suo mistero nel Concilio Vaticano II. Storia, testo e commento della Costituzione Lumen Gentium* (Milan: Jaca Book, 1969), vol. 2, pp. 30-62.

22. The 1983 *Code of Canon Law* addressed the issue of the organizations of the laity, even if in a way that did not please the supporters of the new lay apostolate; see Eugenio Corecco, "Aspects of the Reception of Vatican II in the Code of Canon Law," in *The Reception of Vatican II*, ed. Giuseppe Alberigo, Jean-Pierre Jossua, and Joseph A. Komonchak (Washington, DC: Catholic University of America Press, 1987), pp. 249-96.

scribed in the life of the earthly city; from priests they may look for spiritual light and nourishment.[23]

It was a rather classical division of duties between laypeople on one side and clergy on the other: rather classical, if we consider the situation inside the post–Vatican II Catholic movements, where roles of the laity and clergy have intertwined in a way that makes it difficult to return to the letter of the council documents. It is well known that in the mainstream new movements the laity have taken on duties traditionally typical of the clergy (preaching, teaching of theology, relationship with the bishops and the Roman Curia).

It is fair to say that the council documents prepared the ground for the post–Vatican II movements; but the post–Vatican II movements can and do find a rationale in Vatican II or post–Vatican II "spirit" far more than in its documents.[24]

It is to be noted that the documents of Vatican II about the laity were still firmly within the pre–Vatican II "theology of the laity," according to which the laity were supposed to support and cooperate with the hierarchy. Very little room was granted the laity to play a leading role in the Church; therefore, a literal interpretation of these texts would have given no room to the flourishing variety of new movements within the Catholic Church. This "theology of the laity" was also directed to a laity still integrated in local churches, and its newness was more in the "characters" than in the "script" of Catholicism: the "theology of the laity" was alien to the quest for Church reform for new forms of Christian life in spirituality, the catechumenate, liturgy, or religious education.

We must read the documents of Vatican II on the lay apostolate in a framework of dualism between hierarchy and laity, which would have been overcome in the 1980s and 1990s through a silent yet epoch-making shift in the Vatican policy towards the movements. That shift came from John Paul II's plan for a "new evangelization" in Europe and in the Western world.[25]

23. Vatican Council II, constitution *Gaudium et Spes* 43. For the history of the constitution see Norman P. Tanner, *The Church and the World: Gaudium et spes, Inter mirifica* (Mahwah, NJ: Paulist Press, 2005).

24. See Franco Giulio Brambilla, "Le aggregazioni ecclesiali nei documenti del magistero dal concilio fino ad oggi," *La Scuola Cattolica* 116 (1988): 461-511.

25. See Bruno Forte, "Associazioni, movimenti e missione nella chiesa locale," *Il Regno-documenti* 1 (1983): 29-34.

In the Vatican II documents we cannot find a description of the way to organize the communion of laypersons: the faithful have a right to organize their apostolate as long as it is in communion with the hierarchy. *Apostolicam Actuositatem* 15-22 expressed, in theological language, "mobilization" as a key element of the twentieth-century Western sociopolitical history, but a mobilization under the control of the ecclesiastical hierarchy. In the history of the Catholic Church between Pius XI and Pius XII, especially in Europe, Catholic Action worked both as the engine and brakes for the lay commitment in the Church and in society at large. The letter of Vatican II confirmed both the institutional framework and ecclesial centrality of Catholic Action for the future of the Church. But the theological context — the "spirit" given by the council debates and other documents and the end of a Europe-centered Church — provided Catholicism with a new set of opportunities for the creation of movements.

The "letter" of Vatican II therefore set a different perspective from the one pursued by the new movements. On one side, the council documents affirmed the importance of the lay organizations, trying to tie them to Catholic Action; on the other, the variety of lay organizations somehow recognized by Vatican II should be inserted into the ecclesiology of Vatican II, an ecclesiology of *ressourcement,* with its emphasis on the bishop and the local Church, as well as on the proclaimed need for a more *ressourced* and thus "participatory" Church (parish councils, diocesan councils).[26]

From a literal reading of the documents of Vatican II, we can describe the endorsement given by the council to the new Catholic movements as an approval *e silentio,* as it is to be found in the "spirit" of post–Vatican II doctrinal policy more than in Vatican II debates and final documents. The post–Vatican II biographical and theological path of Cardinal Suenens illustrates the complexity of the relationship between the Vatican II drive for "reform" and the flourishing of the Catholic movements. A few years

---

26. See Fernand Boulard, "La curie et les conseils diocésains," in *La charge pastorale des évêques. Texte, traduction et commentaires* (Paris: Cerf, 1969), pp. 241-74; Georg Kretschmar, *Das bischöfliche Amt. Kirchengeschichtliche und ökumenische Studien zur Frage des kirchlichen Amtes,* ed. Dorothea Wendebourg (Göttingen: Vandenhoeck & Ruprecht, 1999); Massimo Faggioli, *Il vescovo e il concilio. Modello episcopale e aggiornamento al Vaticano II* (Bologna: Il Mulino, 2005); Massimo Faggioli, "Institutions of Episcopal *Synodality*-Collegiality after Vatican II: the Decree 'Christus Dominus' and the Agenda for Synodality-Collegiality in the 21st Century," in Proceedings of the Peter and Paul Seminar (Georgetown University, April 15-17, 2004), *The Jurist* 64, no. 2 (2004): 224-46.

after being one of the most active and vocal advocates of reform and collegiality in the Church on the floor of St. Peter during the council and immediately after the council, he gave a major endorsement to the Catholic Charismatic Renewal.[27]

## From Vatican II to the "New Catholic Movements"

Even though the new Catholic movements, their leaders, and the profound reasons beneath these movements were completely absent from the floor of the council and from the texts debated and approved between 1960 and 1965, Vatican II represents, in the official biography of the new Catholic movements, a crucial moment: the movements' birth certificate, evidence of their orthodoxy, and shield from every possible criticism moved against them.

This direct link between Vatican II and the movements may be theologically acceptable, but, from a historical point of view, it has to be discussed. On one hand, the metamorphosis of the organized Catholic laity started between World War II and Vatican II through a dissemination of new and different groups created by leaders coming from Catholic Action. This dissemination gave the new groups some inspiration taken from the "reform movements" of the late nineteenth and early twentieth century (but without the emphasis on "reform" as the outcome of scholarly and intellectual work that was a marker of the biblical, liturgical, patristic, and ecumenical movements), from the need to reorganize the Catholic laity on a more participative (if not "democratic") basis, and as an outreach beyond the cultural boundaries of Tridentine Catholicism. The Catholic sociology of the *pastorale d'ensemble* and the new way of clustering Catholic Action into new associations gathering the Catholic laity along the generational and professional belonging were two sides of the same "updating" of the laity in European Catholicism.[28]

On the other hand, the real flourishing of the "new Catholic movements" started only after Vatican II and through an implicit denial of some basic markers of the brief season of the pre–Vatican II and Vatican II Catholic Action.

A first decisive element in this transition was the change of paradigm

27. See Leo Jozef Suenens, *A New Pentecost?* (London: Darton, Longman & Todd, 1974).
28. See Joseph Debès and Émile Poulat, *L'appel de la JOC. 1926-1928* (Paris: Cerf, 1986).

in Catholic ecclesiology.[29] Besides the ecclesiology of *Lumen Gentium* and *Gaudium et Spes* and its institutional reception, the post–Vatican II emphasis on the laity made not only the classical distinction between the *duo genera christianorum* — clergy and laity — look old, but also reconfigured the carefully worded "balance of power" within the Church between pope and bishops. The new Catholic movements took that window of opportunity in order to protect their own "community ecclesiology," thus neglecting the local dimension of the communion of the Church and choosing the universal Church and its symbol, the pope, as the first and last controller of their catholicity — just as did the mendicant orders in the Middle Ages.[30] In that process the movements were one of the winners of the post–Vatican II power struggle in the Catholic Church, whose final results were the undermining of the bishops' authority and the despair of the "unorganized laity" in some local churches.

A second factor, linked to the new ecclesiology, was the crisis of Catholic Action, of its identity and membership, as the unique container of the exuberance of the Catholic laity. On one side, as the Catholic Church opened itself to the world, Catholic Action lost a great deal of its original mission to educate the faithful and preserve the Catholic laity from the attacks coming from the liberal ideologies and totalitarian regimes in Europe. On the other, in a politically and socially less hostile environment, the end of the political and social "Catholic ghetto" meant that Catholic Action was not as needed as it was before World War II.

Between the 1960s and the end of Paul VI's pontificate, the flourishing of the Catholic movements was marked by a slow series of steps taken by different and sometimes antagonistic movements. Far from being an organized plot to take over the Church, every single movement walked its own way according to its own Catholic identity, theological options, and cultural background. The common pattern was not a common ideology, theology, or spirituality, but a common struggle to survive in an "ecclesiastically" hostile environment, such as the post–Vatican II Catholic Church and its local and universal leadership. The movements that survived the decade after the end of Vatican II had faced the difficulty of obtaining recognition of their existence within the Catholic communion from the insti-

---

29. See Richard P. McBrien, *The Church: The Evolution of Catholicism* (New York: Harper, 2008), pp. 182-92; about the new movements, pp. 345-49.

30. See Giovanni Miccoli, *Chiesa gregoriana. Ricerche sulla riforma del secolo XI* (Rome: Edizioni di Storia e Letteratura, 1999), pp. 1-58.

tutional Church. That period of time produced the scars of the untold suffering of the new Catholic movements, which soon turned their early experience of the Church's lack of understanding of their religious experience into self-promotion within the ranks of John Paul II's Church.[31]

From the beginning of John Paul II's pontificate on, the "new Catholic movements" experienced a time of success and endorsement by the official teaching authority of the Church and especially by the pope himself.[32] Organizations and movements such as Opus Dei, Focolare, Neocatechumenal Way, and the Catholic Charismatic Renewal managed to make themselves trustworthy, mostly by distancing themselves as far as possible from the experience of the "Catholic dissent" fringe movements and through expressing loyalty to the Holy See and personally to the pope as their ultimate virtue — sometimes at the cost of making enemies among the national bishops' conferences or among the bishops in whose dioceses they were active.[33]

In some cases the post–Vatican II period was the time to launch a new type of movement deeply influenced by the council; in other cases, post–Vatican II provided some older organizations the opportunity to obtain an institutional acknowledgment previously denied.[34] In any case, the success or failure of a new movement depended greatly on its ability to connect with the top part of the ecclesiastical institution and its theological agenda towards the global Church.

## The New Catholic Movements and the Center-Periphery Issue

The spectacular development of these movements has flourished and yet has been rife with problems and inner tensions within the Church and

31. On the support experienced during John Paul II's pontificate by Opus Dei, Legion of Christ, Communion and Liberation, The Neo-Catechumenate, Focolare, and the Community of St. Egidio, see McBrien, *The Church*, pp. 345-47. On the movements and the government of the Church under John Paul II see Thomas J. Reese, *Inside the Vatican: The Politics and Organization of the Catholic Church* (Cambridge, MA: Harvard University Press, 1998).

32. See Giancarlo Rocca, *L'Opus Dei. Appunti e documenti per una storia* (Milan: Paoline, 1985).

33. For case of Italy, see Massimo Faggioli, "Tra referendum sul divorzio e revisione del Concordato. Enrico Bartoletti segretario della CEI (1972-1976)," *Contemporanea* 2 (2001): 255-80.

34. Opus Dei is obviously the most important case.

among the movements themselves. After the transitional "theology of the laity" worded by Vatican II, the "new Catholic movements" had a hard time finding their way during the troublesome period between the end of Vatican II, 1968, and the beginning of the tensions within the Catholic Church, on how to interpret the council and combine Christian faith and political commitment.[35]

It has indeed been acknowledged that the phenomenon of the new movements has much more to do with post–Vatican II than with the council as such: "One of the most striking developments in Catholic life since the council ended has been the flourishing of 'movements' such as Opus Dei, the Neo-Catechumenate, Communion and Liberation, and so on."[36] But the movements' claim of the legacy of Vatican II raises the issue of the reception of Vatican II and especially of the reception of the core message of the council, that is, the main issues of the most important event in the history of modern Catholicism.[37]

In the conclusions to his book, John O'Malley emphasizes the three "issues under the issues" of the council:[38] (1) Vatican II as a *language-event;* (2) the possibility of *change* in the Church; and (3) the *relationship between center and periphery.* The importance of these three issues appears even more striking if we try to understand the relations between the council and one of the most spectacular phenomena of post–Vatican II, such as the "new Catholic movements." The most important among these issues, in order to understand the importance of the relationship between the new Catholic movements and Vatican II, is the relationship between center and periphery.

In his conclusion, John O'Malley emphasizes the importance of the center-periphery issue and its relationship to collegiality, making the case for the link between ecclesiology, *ressourcement,* and new role of the bishops in Vatican II Catholicism.[39] From that point of view, the history of the

35. See, for example, Massimo Faggioli, "Catholic Movements after 1968: Shaping a New Catholic Elite in Italy," in the Proceedings of the International Conference "1968 en Europe: Héritage d'un évènement, 1968-2008" (Université de Paris X — Nanterre), 30-31 May 2008 (forthcoming).

36. Nicholas Lash, *Theology for Pilgrims* (Notre Dame: University of Notre Dame Press, 2008), p. 236.

37. See, for example, Gianfranco Calabrese, "Quaestiones Disputatae: Chiesa come 'popolo di Dio' o Chiesa come 'comunione'? Ermeneutica e recezione della Lumen Gentium," *Rassegna di teologia* 5 (2005): 695-718.

38. See O'Malley, *What Happened at Vatican II,* pp. 298-313.

39. See O'Malley, *What Happened at Vatican II,* pp. 302-5.

post–Vatican II Catholic movements proves problematic, given the fact that there is more than a coincidence between the dramatic crisis of the bishops' authority in the Church and the flourishing of the movements.

According to Nicholas Lash, "there are, at present, few more urgent tasks facing the Church than that of realizing the as-yet unrealized program of Vatican II by throwing into reverse the centralization of power which accrued during the twentieth century, and restoring episcopal authority to the episcopate."[40] It is a fact that the new movements tend to describe themselves as the twentieth-century equivalent of the mendicant orders in the Middle Ages or the Jesuits in the Tridentine Church. Even if this description were true, such an attempt to explain their flourishing in the Catholic Church proves the ecclesiological inclinations of the new movements. Despite the differences between the movements' ecclesiologies (for example, between Opus Dei and the Catholic Charismatic Renewal), their success comes at the expense of the ecclesiology of the local Church, thus helping to undermine the quest for a new balance between center and periphery in modern-world Catholicism.

Although some of the new Catholic movements have received and enriched the "modernity" of the Church and some important issues of the social teaching of the Church,[41] their development and growth within the Catholic Church have so far been largely marked by scant awareness of the relationship between collegiality and the bishops' role (if we look at the relationship between some movements and the bishops in their local churches), and by a nonsynodal model of governance within their communities (if we look at the role of the leaders and the founders in some of the most successful movements).

The success of the movements, in that regard, proves to be a failure, or at least has created significant difficulty for the local Church's ecclesiology between the end of the twentieth century and the beginning of the twenty-first century.[42] The direct appeal to the papacy coupled with the bypassing of the local bishops could have been justified in past centuries by the

---

40. Lash, *Theology for Pilgrims,* p. 234.

41. See Marvin L. Krier Mich, *Catholic Social Teaching and Movements* (Mystic, CT: Twenty-Third Publications, 1998).

42. See Joseph Ratzinger, "L'ecclesiologia della Costituzione 'Lumen Gentium,'" in *Il Concilio Vaticano II. Recezione e attualità alla luce del Giubileo,* ed. Rino Fisichella (São Paolo: Cinisello B., 2000), pp. 66-81; Walter Kasper, "Das Verhältnis von Universalkirche und Ortskirche. Freundschaftliche Auseinandersetzung mit der Kritik von Joseph Kardinal Ratzinger," *Stimmen der Zeit* 12 (2000): 795-804.

"threats" of Conciliarism in the fifteenth century or by the moral corruption of noble bishops in sixteenth-century European Catholicism.[43] But given the Catholicism of Vatican II, such an "ecclesial praxis" is hardly justifiable from an ecclesiological point of view, especially when one considers the results of the rise of these movements in the "state of communion" with some local churches.[44] The rejection of the ecclesiology of the local Church *(communion)* in favor of an ecclesiology of the group *(community)* means not only a rejection of the "*ressourcement* ecclesiology" of Vatican II, but also a substantial refusal to acknowledge the center-periphery issue.[45]

The epoch-making shift made possible by Vatican II from a hierarchical, institutional ecclesiology to one centered on *communio* implies a new pattern of relationship between pope, bishops, clergy, and laity, and between Rome and the local churches. At the local level, the new ecclesiology of Vatican II means not only the resurgence of synods, provincial councils, and plenary councils, the need of which had been ignored for four centuries, but also the actual engagement in the new councils and boards created by Vatican II at the diocesan and parish level.[46]

In the mind of the bishops at Vatican II, these new institutions were supposed to redress the balance of power within the local Church, stressing the ordinary powers of bishops alongside the pope's extraordinary powers in the government of dioceses. They were meant to enable the participation of laity in the life of local churches, not just through liturgy and social action, but also by taking part in the theological reception of Vatican II.[47] In the last three decades the practical ecclesiology of the movements has initiated the end of the local Church led by the bishop and the

43. See Klaus Ganzer, "Gesamtkirche und Ortskirche auf dem Konzil von Trient," *Römische Quartalschrift* 95, nos. 3-4 (2000): 167-78; Massimo Faggioli, "Chiese locali ed ecclesiologia prima e dopo il concilio di Trento," in *Storia della Chiesa in Europa tra ordinamento politico-amministrativo e strutture ecclesiastiche*, Proceedings of the Conference organized by Fondazione Ambrosiana Paolo VI and École Française de Rome (Gazzada, Italy, 18-20 October 2001), ed. Luciano Vaccaro (Brescia: Morcelliana, 2005), pp. 197-213.

44. See, for example, the case involving the local bishops and the "Redemptoris Mater Seminary" that the Neocatechumenal Way runs in Japan.

45. See Jean-Marie R. Tillard, *L'église locale. Ecclésiologie de communion et catholicité* (Paris: Cerf, 1995), pp. 250-71 and 397-410.

46. For some examples of the everlasting life of the idea of a "synodal Church," see *Synod and Synodality: Theology, History, Canon Law and Ecumenism in New Contact*, International Colloquium Bruges 2003, ed. Alberto Melloni and Silvia Scatena (Münster: LIT, 2005).

47. See Massimo Faggioli, *Il vescovo e il concilio. Modello episcopale e aggiornamento al Vaticano II* (Bologna: Il Mulino, 2005).

clergy. These movements have not gone in the direction of a more participatory local Church, given the problematic relationship between the new
Catholic movements on one side and the parish pastoral council, the diocesan pastoral councils, and the diocesan synods on the other.[48] From this
point of view, if we can define "synodality" as the capability of the Church
to hear the voices of all the faithful — through liturgy, through parish experience, through participation in the visible Church structures as pastoral
councils and diocesan synods — then the contribution of the new Catholic movements, while multifaceted and diverse, have actually often presented a "ticket mentality" typical of a "closed-community Catholicism"
more than the synodal face of "Church as communion." The movements
have replaced the participatory model with a more leader-driven model of
Christian community, where inner diversity is paradoxically far less present and less welcome than in the past.[49]

Of course we can identify important differences between the movements. It is possible to divide the movements with respect to their mod-
els of governance: *revanche-driven* movements with a strong anti-liberal
political and religious culture (Opus Dei, Communion and Liberation,
Legionaries of Christ, Neo-Catechumenal Way); more open pentecostal-
charismatic movements (Charismatic Renewal, Cursillos, Focolare);
Catholic elites active in the neomonastic communities or movements
close to the *ressourcement;* and the ecumenical *rapprochement* (Communities of St. Egidio).[50] But they all seem to share a "neo-universalist
ecclesiology," which is at the core of some of the new movements' identity and "ecclesial praxis," and which acts as an undeclared disowning of
Vatican II collegiality, going far beyond Vatican I-style infallibility.[51]

48. See Jacques Palard, "L'istitution catholique en recherches. L'acteur, le théologien et
le sociologue," in Jacques Palard (ed.), *Le gouvernement de l'église catholique. Synodes et
exercice du pouvoir* (Paris: Cerf, 1997), pp. 7-57; Ghislain Lafont, *Imaginer l'église catholique*
(Paris: Cerf, 1995) (in English: *Imagining the Catholic Church: Structured Communion in the
Spirit* [Collegeville, MN: Liturgical Press, 2000]).

49. For the "ticket mentality" in small-community life see Theodor W. Adorno et al.,
*The Authoritarian Personality* (New York: Harper, 1950).

50. For some tentative classifications of the new Catholic movements see Massimo
Faggioli, *Breve storia dei movimenti cattolici* (Rome: Carocci, 2008), pp. 119-20; Alberto
Melloni, "Movimenti. De significatione verborum," *Concilium* 3 (2003); *I movimenti nella
chiesa*, ed. Alberto Melloni, pp. 13-34.

51. See Hermann J. Pottmeyer, *Towards a Papacy in Communion: Perspectives from Vatican Councils I and II* (New York: Crossroad, 1998); John R. Quinn, *The Reform of the Papacy*
(New York: Crossroad, 2000).

Their "political" option for an ecclesiology based almost exclusively on obedience to the pope, applied through an intense communitarianism that almost completely bypasses communion with the local churches (their bishops and parishes), has serious implications for the issue of freedom in the Church. The twentieth-century struggle to rediscover the ancient patristic, conciliar, and synodal tradition in the Church seems to have had a short life. The post–Vatican II anti-modern anguish embodied by the movements has contributed to the present difficulties of the conciliar and synodal institutions in the Church and to the loss of subsidiarity in the relations between Rome and the local churches.[52]

From this point of view, the success of the new Catholic movements in the Church of John Paul II is directly proportional to the capability of some of those movements to undermine the call for a more synodal and less centralized Church. If it is true that Vatican II pushed for a new balance between center and periphery in the Church through a new discovery of collegiality thanks to "a process of *ressourcement*,"[53] the practical ecclesiology of many of the new Catholic movements has been leaning towards a "modern" or "postmodern" model of one-man infallible leadership, much more than towards a first-millennium *ressourcement* ecclesiology of collegiality.

The post–Vatican II history of the reform of ecclesiastical institutions has shown that the council affirmations on collegiality did not touch the shape and form of the power of the bishop of Rome. From a "church politics" point of view, the difficult implementation of collegiality in the 1970s left the new movements untouched, and the movements played a role, especially from the 1980s on, giving the Catholic Church a new face that cheerfully complied with the doctrinal policy of John Paul II. From an ecclesiological point of view, the shortcomings of the Vatican II ecclesiology of the local Church[54] received some serious blows when some of the most "media-savvy" movements (such as Opus Dei, Communion and Liberation, Neo-Catechumenal Way) deliberately bypassed the authority of the local bishops and sought protection directly from the Holy See,

---

52. See Massimo Faggioli, "Prassi e norme relative alle conferenze episcopali tra concilio Vaticano II e post-concilio (1959-1998)," in *Synod and Synodality*, ed. Melloni and Scatena, pp. 265-96.

53. O'Malley, *What Happened at Vatican II*, pp. 302-3.

54. See Gilles Routhier, "Beyond Collegiality: The Local Church Left Behind by the Second Vatican Council," in Jonathan Y. Tan (ed.), *The Catholic Theological Society of America, Proceedings of the Sixty-second Annual Convention, 2007*, pp. 1-15.

whose "doctrinal focus" (on issues like moral theology and theology of liberation) was much more in harmony with the movements than with the bishops and the national bishops' conferences at that time. As unpopular as some bishops might be (especially in some countries), this "takeover" of the collegial voice of the bishops and the national bishops' conferences has hardly improved the relationship between center and periphery in the post–Vatican II Catholic Church.

The movements' "church politics" has reduced the already very limited breathing room for collegiality in the post–Vatican II period, and has played a role not unlike that played by some new religious orders (together with the Roman Curia of Catholic reform) in undermining the role of the bishops that was restored and reformed at Trent.[55] But the main difference between the post-Trent new religious orders and the post–Vatican II movements is their contribution to the culture of Catholicism. The new Catholic movements defined themselves, or were defined, as the fruit of Vatican II because of their support of John Paul II's implementation of the council, despite their scant contribution to the theological debate in the post–Vatican II Church.

## Discerning the Spirits of Vatican II: Conclusions

From a first analysis of the mainstream new Catholic movements' reception of the council's "issues under the issues," the complexity of the relationship between the movements and Vatican II is clear. The movements have absorbed Vatican II not in the literal meaning of its final documents, but rather have appealed to its "spirit," being repeatedly encouraged to do so by John Paul II's teaching and doctrinal policy towards them. John Paul II wanted to give the movements new spaces for action in a highly institutionalized Catholic Church. It is time to go beyond the "fictional history" of the relationship between Vatican II and the new Catholic movements. The movements as such had no role among the participants at Vatican II, nor in the final documents of the Council, but from the 1980s on they turned to the often-repudiated "spirit of Vatican II," as they had no opportunity to find much support in conciliar texts themselves.[56]

55. See Hubert Jedin, "Delegatus Sedis Apostolicae und bischöfliche Gewalt auf dem Konzil von Trient," in *Die Kirche und ihre Ämter und Stände. Festgabe Joseph Kardinal Frings* (Cologne: Bachem, 1960), pp. 462-75.

56. See Barbara Zadra, *I movimenti ecclesiali e i loro statuti* (Rome: Pontificia Università

In this critical moment of the reception of Vatican II, the issue of the spirit of the council is more important than ever. Pottmeyer already called for a discernment of spirits in the 1980s:

> The reception of the Council as a movement is an equally unfinished business. This aspect of the Council is sometimes referred to as its "spirit"; what is meant is the intellectual and spiritual impulse toward renewal that animated the work of the Council itself and that emanates from it. "Spirit" is also a theologically appropriate description. . . . [H]ere the task confronting a hermeneutic of the Council goes far beyond an objective interpretation of the texts. Something more is needed: a *discretio spirituum,* a recognition and distinction or discernment of spirits.[57]

More recently, and with a historically more secure awareness of "what happened at Vatican II," John O'Malley has addressed the issue of the spirit of the council:

> [F]or the first time in history, a council would take care self-consciously to infuse its documents with vocabulary and themes that cut across them all. In that sense Vatican II conveyed a "spirit." . . . In revealing the spirit it reveals not a momentary effervescence but a consistent and verifiable reorientation.[58]

This general reorientation was articulated in a characteristic vocabulary and a "style of Church,"[59] and originated from the set of new urgencies, sensibilities, and proposals generated by the meeting of the universal episcopate especially from the point of view of the center-periphery issue: "the centralized 'implementation' . . . that had followed the Council of Trent belonged to a type of council and a cultural stage now completely of the past."[60]

Gregoriana, 1997), pp. 7-21; *History of Council Vatican II*, vol. 4: *Church as Communion - Third Period and Intersession, September 1964–September 1965*, ed. Giuseppe Alberigo and Joseph Komonchak (Maryknoll, NY: Orbis, 2004).

57. Hermann J. Pottmeyer, "Interpretation of the Council," in *The Reception of Vatican II*, ed. Giuseppe Alberigo, Jean-Pierre Jossua, and Joseph A. Komonchak (Washington, DC: Catholic University of America Press, 1987), pp. 27-43, esp. p. 41.

58. O'Malley, *What Happened at Vatican II*, p. 310.

59. See John W. O'Malley, "Trent and Vatican II: Two Styles of Church," in *From Trent to Vatican II: Historical and Theological Investigations*, ed. Raymond F. Bulman and Frederick J. Parrella (New York: Oxford University Press, 2006), pp. 301-20.

60. See Giuseppe Alberigo, "The New Shape of the Council," in *History of Vatican II*,

For that reason, it is time to reframe the debate on Vatican II and its spirit and try to "discern the spirits" of Vatican II in relation to some new form of Western Catholicism, such as the new Catholic movements. While some elements of their reception of Vatican II are susceptible to being presented as reception of the council teaching (new centrality of the laity in the groups' and communities' spiritual leadership, engagement in public-policy issues, biblical and patristic renewal in their cultural identity), other elements seem far more problematic if we consider both the documents and the debate on the floor of St. Peter at Vatican II (universalist ecclesiology and disregard of the authority of the local bishops; anti-synodal attitude; "ticket mentality" in their relationship toward the modern world).

In the near future, the successes and setbacks of the new movements and the studies on this phenomenon will provide new elements for the debate on Vatican II Catholicism. For the time being, however, it is clear that in the last twenty-five years the "spirit of Vatican II" has been used in the Catholic Church in different ways: some of the interpreters of this spirit have been praised for embodying a creative way to be faithful to the real Vatican II, while others have been harshly criticized for provoking a theological debate that promotes a distorted reading of the council.

Therefore, it is not an overstatement to see a double standard in this attitude toward the "spirit of Vatican II": as if the spirit, that is, the "gust" of Vatican II, were good for the Catholic movements and bad for the global hermeneutic of Vatican II debated by historians and theologians. Looking at the example of the relationship between Vatican II, the movements, and present Catholicism, any attempt to ban the "spirit of Vatican II" from the language of historical and theological debate on the council seems hazardous and unproductive, but most of all inconsistent.

---

ed. Giuseppe Alberigo, English version edited by Joseph A. Komonchak, vol. 3 (Maryknoll, NY: Orbis, 2000), p. 505.

# Vatican II and Moral Theology

*Darlene Fozard Weaver*

Two initial reviews of John O'Malley's book, *What Happened at Vatican II*, provide a helpful point of entry for this essay.[1] Both reviews examine O'Malley's volume in light of, and in judgment upon, some forty years of disagreement whether Vatican II is in continuity with, or significantly departs from, the Catholic tradition that preceded it. In his *New York Times* review, Peter Steinfels writes that "O'Malley's superb history demonstrates why any effort to shuffle the cards of continuity and discontinuity so as to minimize the profound reorientation wrought by the council borders on the ludicrous."[2] A review by the late Richard John Neuhaus, written shortly before his death, compares O'Malley's book with another recent volume, *Vatican II: Renewal Within Tradition*.[3] Neuhaus contends that the volumes respectively illustrate the two most prominent interpretations of the council. O'Malley's volume, writes Neuhaus, exemplifies the "hermeneutic of discontinuity and rupture" that Pope Benedict XVI spoke against in his 2005 Christmas address to the Roman Curia.[4] Seen through the lens

1 Portions of this chapter are condensed versions of an argument I develop in chapter one of my book, *The Acting Person and Christian Moral Life: Involvements with God and Goods* (Washington, DC: Georgetown University Press, 2011). See also John W. O'Malley, *What Happened at Vatican II* (Cambridge, MA, and London: Belknap/Harvard University Press, 2008).

2. Peter Steinfels, "New Book Reaffirms Depth of Change Wrought by Vatican II," *New York Times*, 19 December 2008, available online at http://www.nytimes.com/2008/12/20/us/20beliefs.html. Last accessed 14 January 2009.

3. Matthew Lamb and Matthew Levering, eds., *Vatican II: Renewal Within Tradition* (Oxford: Oxford University Press, 2008).

4. Pope Benedict XVI, "Address of His Holiness Pope Benedict XVI to the Roman Curia Offering Them His Christmas Greetings," 22 December 2005. Available online at: http://

of this hermeneutic, the council is all about *aggiornamento,* or updating. The other hermeneutic Benedict invokes, and in this case commends as proper, is the "'hermeneutic of reform,' of renewal in the continuity of the one subject-Church which the Lord has given to us."[5] According to Neuhaus, although O'Malley's book appeals to the spirit of *aggiornamento* to interpret the council as ushering in a new epoch in Catholicism, *Vatican II: Renewal Within Tradition,* offering theological commentary on the sixteen documents the council approved, exemplifies and argues for the continuity of Vatican II with earlier Catholic tradition. In short, for Neuhaus, O'Malley looks to the council's "spirit," which in the hands of "liberals" covers a multitude of sins, whereas *Vatican II: Renewal Within Tradition* looks at what the council actually said.

What Neuhaus notes but doesn't fully reckon with is the force of O'Malley's argument that Vatican II was a "language event." Steinfels grasps the importance of this insight for the "spirit vs. letter" debate over the council's meaning: "Ultimately, the council deliberately chose language, tone and themes conveying a reorientation that Father O'Malley believes can legitimately be described as 'the spirit of the council'"; O'Malley's history "makes it impossible . . . to deny that this reorientation is no less rooted in the documents of Vatican II than in the story of how they came to be written, debated, voted and promulgated."[6]

What might all this mean for understanding the significance of Vatican II with regard to Catholic moral tradition? It is easy to speak of moral theology *before* Vatican II, although the way this is done generally focuses narrowly on the development of penitential and manualist moral theology to the exclusion of other aspects of Catholic moral tradition. It is also easy to speak of moral theology *after* Vatican II, which is marked by particular emphases, new *loci,* and, of course, heated debate. Indeed, the conflict between those who appeal to the council's spirit and those who insist on its letter is perhaps most visible when it comes to Catholic moral teaching. Is there a moral theology "of" Vatican II? Where would one look to find such a thing? As M. Cathleen Kaveny notes in her contribution to this volume, the council did not produce a distinct text addressing the field of moral theology. The moral theology *of* Vatican II is something to be gleaned from spe-

www.vatican.va/holy_father/benedict_xvi/speeches/2005/december/documents/hf_ben_xvi_spe_20051222_roman-curia_en.html. Last accessed 14 January 2009.

5. Pope Benedict XVI, "Address of His Holiness Pope Benedict XVI to the Roman Curia Offering Them His Christmas Greetings."

6. Steinfels, "New Book Reaffirms Depth of Change Wrought by Vatican II."

cific conciliar documents that touch on moral issues along with a larger sense of the council's character and aims.

This chapter takes its lead from O'Malley's contention that Vatican II was a "language event." Because the process of drafting and approving the documents is inseparable from the process of determining their focus, tone, and terminology, we may say that the council endorsed and fueled a shift already underway, one from an emphasis on analyzing particular moral actions, particularly sins to be confessed, to an emphasis on the whole person as a moral subject and agent. One way to focus and appreciate this shift in the moral theology of Vatican II is the issue of freedom of conscience. It was a charged issue on the eve of the council and figures in two conciliar documents *(Gaudium et Spes* and *Dignitatis Humanae).* This issue also provides a way to appreciate the larger landscape of postconciliar moral theology as a contest between appeals to the spirit and letter of the council. I will conclude with some remarks about moving beyond these debates and the future of Catholic theological ethics.

## Preconciliar Moral Theology

Vatican II called for a renewal of theology in general and made special mention of moral theology. The "Decree on Priestly Training" *(Optatum Totius)* urges a "perfecting of moral theology" by means of scriptural nourishment and by integrating theological disciplines more fully.[7] Moral theology, animated by the personalism that characterizes the council's theology, was to illuminate the loftiness of the faithful's calling and their obligation to bear fruit in charity for the life of the world.[8] It is worth noting that this renewal, while taking for granted that the discipline of moral theology is yoked to a seminary context and priestly formation, ultimately aims at assisting all the faithful. Moreover, rather than fix on determining the moral status of particular actions so as to avoid sin, moral theology has a more positive task, to show the nobility of the calling of the faithful. Following *Lumen Gentium* we may say that this call is to nothing short of holiness.[9] Finally, moral theology is to show the moral life as principally a matter of positive obligations, the duty to do good, to bear fruit, to build up the world in the work of love.

7. *Optatum Totius* 16.
8. *Optatum Totius* 16.
9. See *Lumen Gentium* V. I discuss the universal call to holiness below.

Why call for the improvement of moral theology? On the eve of the council, moral theology was dominated by manuals (textbooks) used for training priests in seminaries. The manuals were developed in the late sixteenth century and dominated moral theology until the time of Vatican II. Over these four centuries the manuals did evolve, but as John Gallagher notes, certain structural and substantive features remained constant.[10] Structurally, the manuals treated general moral theology (the nature of the human act, conscience, law, sin), special moral theology (particular sins, identified either as violations of the Decalogue or as acts contrary to the virtues), and canon law requirements regarding the sacraments.[11] Substantively, the manuals were deeply indebted to the theology of Thomas Aquinas, yet their theological scope was more narrowly concerned with what was relevant for assisting priests in resolving cases of conscience. Hence, although the manuals undeniably affirm that the moral life concerns the person's relation to her natural and supernatural ends, their focus falls on conduct and actions contrary to these ends, that is, sins.[12]

Complaints about manualist moral theology are now standard. According to James Keenan, as the Vatican came to exercise more control over moral teaching, manualists became translators of that teaching rather than scholars offering informed opinions.[13] The manualists resisted theological innovation as well as integrating their discipline with other theological disciplines. Moral reflection was thus cut off from biblical studies, dogmatic theology, and spiritual theology. Finally, the manuals display a narrow and reductive understanding of morality. Manualists paid far more attention to certain areas of moral life and to intrachurch concerns than to global moral issues. Says Keenan, "One has only to see that girls' dresses and sperm received more attention than atomic weapons to appreciate how distant the manualists were from the world as it emerged out of the rubble of the Second World War and faced the possibility of nuclear

10. John A. Gallagher, *Time Past, Time Future: An Historical Study of Catholic Moral Theology* (New York: Paulist, 1990).

11. Gallagher, *Time Past, Time Future*, p. 30.

12. John Mahoney's influential book, *The Making of Moral Theology* (Oxford: Oxford University Press, 1989), details the profound importance of the sacrament of confession/reconciliation for the development of moral theology.

13. James F. Keenan, *A History of Catholic Moral Theology in the Twentieth Century: From Confessing Sins to Liberating Consciences* (London and New York: Continuum, 2010). See also his "Virtue Ethics," in Bernard Hoose, ed., *Christian Ethics: An Introduction* (Collegeville, MN: Liturgical Press, 1998), p. 30.

war."[14] Moreover, rather than treat the totality of the person, the breadth and history of her moral life, and the character traits and dispositions that comprise her identity, the manualists focused on the morality of individual acts, particularly understood as a violation of divine law.[15] Further, they tended to excerpt specific actions from the social and personal contexts in which they figure morally. They inflated their moral significance, thereby reducing the full breadth and depth of sin to sins, which often are understood in terms of wrongdoing.[16] Moreover, manualists tended to regard penitents as incompetent agents. Keenan grants that pastoral compassion for sinners probably motivated manualists to consider factors that prevent penitents from discerning and executing right courses of action.[17] But even aside from such compassion, the manualists understood moral theology as a highly specialized taxonomy of moral pathology, an expertise into which priests needed to be tutored.[18] The manualists thus implied that the average layperson's conscience is seriously impaired. Although morality is grounded in natural law, in principle knowable to all persons of good will, in order that they might form and rightly exercise conscience, such laypersons needed to be instructed by clergy. That moral instruction chiefly concerned itself with the identification and avoidance of sins.

Catholic moral tradition includes other forms of disseminating church teaching, from papal encyclicals to homilies offered in local parishes, along with a wide variety of practices that express, instantiate, and cultivate Catholic values — devotions, spiritual reading — as well as artistic expressions of Catholic moral vision and commitments, and the many forms of service and social activism conducted by the institutional Church and by the Catholic faithful. Nonetheless, there is a great deal of truth in the going story about Vatican II and moral theology. It suggests that moral theology essentially developed as a discipline done by priests and for priests, that it was focused more on sinful actions than on the whole person as a recipient of divine grace, and, moreover, that sin was understood largely in legal terms and with a view to determining how culpable of sin a penitent might be.

In the years leading up to Vatican II, however, a number of alternative approaches to moral theology began to emerge. For instance, Bernard

14. Keenan, "Virtue Ethics," p. 30.

15. See Gallagher, *Time Past, Time Future*, p. 85, and Mahoney, *The Making of Moral Theology*, pp. 225-27.

16. See Mahoney, *The Making of Moral Theology*, p. 32.

17. Keenan, "Virtue Ethics," p. 27.

18. Keenan, "Virtue Ethics," pp. 20-21.

Häring's *The Law of Christ* was a thoroughly Christocentric approach that construed the moral life in terms of the person's encounter with Christ. It emphasized the moral centrality of love, the person's awareness of values, and the priority of grace over the law.[19] The characteristics of works like Häring's — their attention to Scripture, their broader focus on the person, their emphasis on love and the virtues rather than sin and the law — signal the moral reorientation that the council both called for and itself enacted.

## The Moral Theology of Vatican II

As I noted above, John O'Malley describes Vatican II as a "language event." He writes, "For the first time in history, a council would take care self-consciously to infuse its documents with vocabulary and themes that cut across them all. In that sense Vatican II conveyed a 'spirit.' When properly examined, 'the letter' (form and vocabulary) reveals 'the spirit.'"[20] O'Malley shows that the council adopted a style that differs from previous councils. The council was not primarily doctrinal but pastoral. In his opening address Pope John XXIII set a positive tone for the council. The address indicates, according to O'Malley, the pope's intention that the council "should look forward; it should not be afraid to make changes in the church wherever appropriate; it should not feel constrained to stay within the old methods and forms, as if hermetically sealed off from modern thought; it should look to human unity, which suggested an approach that emphasized commonalities rather than differences; it should encourage cooperation with others; it should see its task as pastoral."[21] O'Malley notes that the council deliberately spoke in words that conveyed and evoked equality or fraternity and sorority among the faithful, words of reciprocity, humility, change, and interiority. These words signal particular values, and their deliberate use enacts a commitment to a mode of exercising authority, fulfilling responsibilities, and sharing gifts that is compatible with such values. According to O'Malley, a comparison of the language used in Vatican II with that of previous councils

19. See Bernard Häring, *The Law of Christ*, 3 vols., trans. Edwin G. Kasper, C.PP.S. (Westminster, MD: Newman Press, 1966). See also Dom Odon Lottin, *Principes de Morale*, 2 vols. (Louvain: Éditions de l'Abbaye de Mont César, 1947), and Gerard Gilleman, S.J., *The Primacy of Charity in Moral Theology* (Westminster, MD: Newman Press, 1959).

20. O'Malley, *What Happened at Vatican II*, p. 310.

21. O'Malley, *What Happened at Vatican II*, p. 96.

suggests, indeed, that at stake were almost two different visions of Catholicism: from commands to invitations, from laws to ideals, from definition to mystery, from threats to persuasion, from coercion to conscience, from monologue to dialogue, from ruling to serving, from withdrawn to integrated, from vertical to horizontal, from exclusion to inclusion, from hostility to friendship, from rivalry to partnership, from suspicion to trust, from static to ongoing, from passive acceptance to active engagement, from fault-finding to appreciation, from prescriptive to principles, from behavior modification to inner appropriation.[22]

If we were to construct a similar parallel to compare the manualist moral theology that dominated Catholic moral tradition prior to the council and the moral theology of the council, we might say that at stake were almost two different visions of morality: from isolated acts to whole persons, from sin to holiness, from laws to love. Saying as much need not commit oneself to interpreting the council with a hermeneutic of rupture and discontinuity. Postconciliar moral theology actually draws on aspects of Catholic tradition — particularly Scripture and spirituality — that actually belong to Catholic moral tradition going back centuries, but simply do not figure largely in the usual tale of preconciliar moral theology. Moreover, as we will see, it is not as though moral theology in the wake of Vatican II eschews attention to particular acts, or sin, or laws. Indeed, these issues continue to occupy moral theologians, albeit in new ways. But first let us get some purchase on the moral theology discernible in the council texts.

Crucial to understanding the moral theology of Vatican II is the universal call to holiness. The call to holiness occurs in *Lumen Gentium*, the Dogmatic Constitution on the Church:

> All Christians in any state or walk of life are called to the fullness of Christian life and to the perfection of love, and by this holiness a more human manner of life is fostered also in earthly society. In order to reach this perfection the faithful should use the strength dealt out to them by Christ's gift, so that, following in his footsteps and conformed to his image, doing the will of God in everything, they may wholeheartedly devote themselves to the glory of God and to the service of their neighbor. Thus the holiness of the People of God will grow in fruitful abundance.[23]

22. O'Malley, *What Happened at Vatican II*, p. 307.
23. *Lumen Gentium*, no. 40, quoted from *Vatican Council II: The Conciliar and Post*

Several points deserve to be drawn out of this remarkable passage. To begin, the council rejects a two-level ethic that would reserve holiness for a certain class of Christians, such as clergy and religious, and leave some ordinary goodness to the masses. All Christians are called to holiness, whatever their station in life, and precisely in those diverse stations. Holiness is not something set or sought apart from the concrete details of daily life but wrought within them (see also *Gaudium et Spes* 38). In these details we can appropriate Christ's gift of himself so that our lives become an imitation of his, so that we become an image of him. The call to holiness presents an approach to the moral life that is simultaneously exacting and life-giving. Moral goodness does not consist in a denial of our humanity or a flight from the world; rather, holiness is fullness of life, abundance, a realization of our humanity, and a benefit to earthly society. The call to holiness means that the moral life and spiritual life are not two separable realities. As an ethics of perfection, the call to holiness clearly enlarges morality beyond concern with particular actions or moments of decision (though surely these are not unimportant) and casts the moral life as an ongoing endeavor to grow in love for God and neighbor, to become holy in an ever-deeper and more faithful obedience to God's will. Holiness is, then, the work of a lifetime. It demands that one give oneself over unreservedly to the will of God and in love for him and for one's neighbors.

The call to holiness did not appear in the original schema, *De Ecclesia*, which became *Lumen Gentium*. Between the first period of the council and the second, O'Malley describes how the text changed in ways that facilitated the articulation of a universal call to holiness. The revised version drew more heavily on scriptural and patristic sources and identified the church in a more horizontal rather than vertical fashion as "the People of God."

> The new chapter on the call to holiness imbued *Lumen Gentium* with its finality by saying explicitly, forcefully, and for the first time ever in a council that holiness is what the church is all about, what human life is all about. By presenting the church as more than a guardian of orthodoxy and an enforcer of good behavior, this crucial document helped move the council . . . to a new modality. From this point forward, in fact,

---

Conciliar Documents, New Revised Edition, ed. Austin Flannery (Northport, NY: Costello, 1992).

the holiness theme began to find a place in the documents of the council by the time they appeared on the floor [for deliberation].[24]

O'Malley rightly perceives that the rhetoric and style deliberately adopted by the council is "values-expressive."[25] It instantiates morally freighted commitments to be a particular sort of ecclesial community, one that has implications for the internal life of the church and for the church in relation to the modern world.

The call to holiness presupposes a particular moral theological anthropology, one that is discernible across the conciliar documents but is especially visible in *Gaudium et Spes*.[26] The person is made by and meant for God. As a creature the person reflects the divine, and as an image of God he possesses an inviolable dignity and irreducible value.[27] The person is a unity of body and soul. He is therefore "obliged to regard his body as good and hold it in honor," yet "by his power to know himself in the depths of his being he rises above the whole universe of mere objects."[28] The person is endowed with intelligence and made to know the truth.[29] The person is irreducibly social. He comes into being through a union of persons, and his fulfillment as a person only comes in relationships with others.[30]

The person is created free; he is responsible for himself. "When he is drawn to think about his real self he turns to those deep recesses of his being where God who proves the heart awaits him, and where he himself decides his own destiny in the sight of God" (*GS* 14). He is interiorly divided by sin, which affects every facet of his life so that he experiences it as a struggle between good and evil. "But the Lord himself came to free and strengthen man, renewing him inwardly and casting out the 'prince of this world' (Jn. 12:31), who held him in the bondage of sin" (*GS* 13). As a mortal, the person suffers in his awareness that death awaits him, but faith that Christ frees us from death and offers eternal life answers the anxieties of our hearts and provides us hope. Taken together, the person's freedom, re-

24. O'Malley, *What Happened at Vatican II*, p. 174.

25. O'Malley, *What Happened at Vatican II*, p. 308.

26. Here I follow the discussion of Paulinus Ikechukwu Odozor, C.S. Sp., *Moral Theology in an Age of Renewal* (Notre Dame: University of Notre Dame Press, 2003), pp. 27-31.

27. *Gaudium et Spes* 12.

28. *Gaudium et Spes* 14.

29. *Gaudium et Spes* 15.

30. *Gaudium et Spes* 12.

sponsibility for himself, and helplessness with regard to sin describe the human situation in a way that allows the divergent moral emphases one sees in the wake of the council. On the one hand, the council affirms both real human freedom to decide about oneself before God and, on the other hand, real dependence upon God to choose God instead of perdition (*GS* 17).

The council's depiction of conscience expresses this freedom-in-dependence. *Gaudium et Spes* describes conscience this way:

> In the depths of his conscience, man detects a law which he does not impose upon himself, but which holds him to obedience. Always summoning him to love good and avoid evil, the voice of conscience when necessary speaks to his heart: do this, shun that. For man has in his heart a law written by God; to obey it is the very dignity of man; according to it he will be judged. (*GS* 16)

Conscience is here depicted as responsive — it detects a moral law not of one's own making but already given and exercising a normative pull. Moreover, as "the secret core or sanctuary of a man," where "he is alone with God," conscience refers to the person's encounter with God in the depths of his being and captures the council's understanding of the moral life as a response to God's self-offer (*GS* 16).

A little more than a century before, Pope Gregory XVI had denounced freedom of conscience in his encyclical *Mirari Vos*. But now "the council affirmed that in the last analysis the moral norm that everybody is obliged to obey is their own conscience, which is not a vague feeling of right and wrong but a moral judgment."[31] The council affirmed that individuals have a responsibility to form and exercise their conscience, and then are obliged to obey their conscience:

> For God has willed that man remain "under the control of his own decisions," so that he can seek his Creator spontaneously, and come freely to utter and blissful perfection through loyalty to Him. Hence man's dignity demands that he act according to a knowing and free choice that is personally motivated and prompted from within, not under blind internal impulse, nor by mere external pressure. Man achieves such dignity when, emancipating himself from all captivity to passion, he pursues his

---

31. O'Malley, *What Happened at Vatican II*, p. 296.

goal in a spontaneous choice of what is good, and procures for himself through effective and skilful action, apt helps to that end. (*GS* 17)

Freedom of conscience does not mean that persons are morally permitted to do as they like, to decide *what* is good. The dignity of conscience consists in the free choice of what *is* good. Put differently, a person enjoys freedom when her choices are ordered to her human and the common good, when an interior conformity of her will to the objective moral order issues in rightly executed outward actions. Freedom of conscience, then, does not amount to an intuition or vague feeling of right and wrong, but a judgment of right reason. The person enjoys political rights associated with the free exercise of conscience because faith is born in free human response to grace. Judgments that spring from servility, fear, oppression, or passion are unhinged from reason. Though the encyclical *Pacem in Terris* affirmed a human right to worship God according to the dictates of conscience (*PT* 14), the position was highly controversial. O'Malley describes the difficult process the bishops went through drafting, deliberating, and then finally approving the document on religious liberty, *Dignitatis Humanae*. Those opposed to *Dignitatis Humanae* emphasized the relation of conscience to the truth, argued that "error has no rights," and worried, among other things, that conciliar approval of religious liberty would encourage relativism and religious indifferentism.[32]

Although the council clearly affirms the dignity of individual conscience, it also stresses that the individual's conscience is not isolated, unfettered, or immune from sin. Loyalty to conscience joins Christians to others in pursuit of the truth and right moral solutions (*GS* 16). Moreover, the council repeatedly describes conscience as a law that is not of man's own making but is instead inscribed on his heart by God. Conscience, then, testifies to objective moral requirements that man is obliged to obey. Conscience may err through a nonculpable ignorance, but the council warns against a culpable failure properly to inform conscience (*GS* 16).

In addition to the council's morally freighted orientation, its discernible moral theological anthropology, and its noticeably higher regard for individual conscience, the council offers some explicit moral principles and addresses several specific moral issues. *Gaudium et Spes* identifies a number of principles, values, and commitments that, taken together, begin

---

32. See O'Malley, pp. 211-18 and pp. 254-58. In the end the council approved *Dignitatis Humanae* overwhelmingly. See O'Malley, *What Happened at Vatican II*, p. 287.

to flesh out the task *Optatum Totius* no. 16 gave to moral theology — namely, to illuminate the loftiness of the faithful's calling and their obligation to bear fruit in charity for the life of the world. *Gaudium et Spes* urges respect for the person, but insists on the person's sociality and interdependence. Accordingly, the pastoral constitution also stresses human solidarity, the common good, and principles of responsibility and participation.[33] "Here then is the norm for human activity — to harmonize with the authentic interests of the human race, in accordance with God's will and design, and to enable men as individuals and as members of society to pursue and fulfill their total vocation."[34] This norm is later specified with reference to the Paschal mystery, which provides the example *par excellence* of the love we are obligated to exercise in our love for the world.[35] The council affirms the daily work of the laity as crucial to the service the Church yields the world; it acknowledges the rightful autonomy of earthly affairs (36) yet encourages the laity to cultivate informed consciences so as "to impress the divine law on the affairs of the earthly city" (43). Moreover, the council acknowledges that pastors do not possess answers to all the problems the laity might confront: "[T]his is not the role of the clergy: it is rather up to the laymen to shoulder their responsibilities under the guidance of Christian wisdom and with eager attention to the teaching authority of the Church" (43). This attitude toward the laity differs markedly from the tendency of preconciliar manuals of moral theology to regard lay penitents as incompetent moral agents.

Finally, the moral theology of Vatican II is visible in the council's attention to specific "urgent problems" in the world. In the second part of *Gaudium et Spes,* the council addresses marriage and the family, the proper development of culture, economic and social life, the political community, and the need to foster peace among nations. The council generally treats these issues in keeping with its emphasis on the person. For instance, the council states that developing nations should be firmly convinced that their aim is "the total human development of their citizens" (86). The section on marriage and family speaks of their dignity and their importance for the well-being and sanctification of their members and society at large. The council affirms traditional teaching that conjugal love has two ends, procreative and unitive, but addresses the latter first and makes it clear that

---

33. See *Gaudium et Spes* 23-39.
34. *Gaudium et Spes* 35.
35. *Gaudium et Spes* 38.

conjugal love is good in itself. At several points the council insists on the married couple's moral responsibilities regarding procreation. The responsible transmission of life is not simply a matter of sincere intentions but "objective criteria." These criteria are "drawn from the nature of the human person and human action, criteria which respect the total meaning of mutual self-giving and human procreation in the context of true love" (51).

The moral theology of Vatican II is not reducible to a "spirit" capable of being invoked apart from the conciliar documents. The documents communicate a discernible, if unsystematic and general, moral theology centered on the human person. The council considers the person as a creature made by God and for love and knowledge of him in communion with others. The moral life is accordingly envisioned in terms of the person's free response to God. This response is made in the depths of the individual yet is wrought in the details of daily life. Indeed, one cannot respond affirmatively to God's self-offer apart from loving service to others in the world. When the council does speak of particular moral actions rather than human activity more generally, it emphasizes the need to order them to the human and common good and to the person's final end. In other words, particular moral actions fall under objective standards or obligations that are derived from the person's good integrally considered. Hence, the council can speak against

> all offenses against life itself, such as murder, genocide, abortion, euthanasia and willful suicide; all violations of the integrity of the human person, such as mutilation, physical and mental torture, undue psychological pressures; all offenses against human dignity, such as subhuman living conditions, arbitrary imprisonment, deportation, slavery, prostitution, the selling of women and children, degrading working conditions where men are treated as mere tools for profit rather than free and responsible persons; all these and the like are criminal: they poison civilization; and they debase the perpetrators more than the victims and militate against the honor of the creator.[36]

The council both reiterates traditional moral teaching and fundamentally reorients moral theology by shifting its tone, emphases, and purview.

Although preconciliar moral theology includes moments of heightened concern to liberate consciences in cases where the binding force of

36. *Gaudium et Spes* 27.

some particular moral norm was in doubt or in the absence of definitive ecclesial judgment about a moral matter, the weight of the tradition prior to the council lay decidedly on the side of viewing freedom of conscience as a dangerous error that would spawn a host of ills. The particular issue of freedom of conscience highlights differences between manualist moral theology and that of the council. The latter gives laypersons more respect as moral agents and regards the person more wholly. Conscience is free because God wills a personal response to the divine offer of grace; human dignity is compromised by blind obedience. The clergy are not experts on every moral matter. At no point, however, does the council forget that moral life is grounded in an objective moral order. The right formation of conscience, then, requires attentiveness to the church's moral teaching. The church witnesses to and authentically interprets moral norms that bind conscience. Conscience thus has both objective and subjective dimensions. It consists of more than a faculty by which eternal, ahistorical norms are applied to concrete circumstances. Conscience captures the heart of the individual's free and responsible decision to, about whom, and how to be in response to God and others. This decision is unavoidably indexed to features of human existence — the natural moral law — and wrought within economies of sin and grace.

## Postconciliar Moral Theology

Thus far we have considered the profound shift (which is not to say rupture) from Catholic moral tradition's focus on particular moral actions to the council's moral focus on the person. Now we will consider, albeit briefly, the way postconciliar moral theology has grappled with this shift. Postconciliar moral theology does not break with earlier moral tradition but, retaining key elements of traditional teaching, engages neglected aspects of Catholic moral tradition, which is far broader than the manualist moral theology discussed earlier.

Nowhere is the shift from actions to persons more evident than in the vigorous Catholic retrieval of virtue ethics. Virtue ethicists, says James Keenan, "are not primarily interested in particular actions. We do not ask 'Is this action right?' 'What are the circumstances around an action?' or 'What are the consequences of an action?' We are simply interested in persons." Keenan goes on to say that virtue ethics instead asks three related questions: "Who am I?" "Who ought I to become?" "How am I to get there?"[37] Keenan rightly notes that virtue ethics asks more fundamental and enduring questions than one finds in ethics that focus on moral dilemmas or quandaries like abortion, euthanasia, and capital punishment. This is not to say that virtue ethics isn't practical. To answer truthfully the question "Who am I?" one must consider one's behavior. The question "Who ought I to become?" involves developing a vision of who we ought to be and striving to attain it. The third question, "How am I to get there?" is a matter of prudence. Prudence is the virtue that determines and directs the other virtues. The cultivation of prudence is a lifelong task. It requires setting realistic goals for oneself and regularly asking whether one is behaving in ways that habituate oneself in the virtues. Keenan thus describes virtue ethics in a way that highlights its consideration of human agency, yet contrasts it to approaches that reduce ethics to the analysis of quandaries or actions isolated from the questions that virtue ethics poses.

Notwithstanding the rise of virtue ethics, postconciliar moral theology remains deeply concerned with particular actions, sin, and law; yet the character and significance of each becomes highly contested. These issues were brewing during the council and boiled over upon the publication of *Humanae Vitae*. It is well known that Pope John XXIII formed a commission in 1963 to consider overpopulation, which was later expanded by Paul VI to consider Church teaching on birth control.[38] Equally well known is that the commission issued a majority report recommending the approval of recourse to artificial contraception under some circumstances. A "minority report" was also presented to Paul VI urging the continuation of Church teaching against contraception, both because changing it would imply the magisterium had been mistaken about a gravely important matter and because the moral character of contraception rested finally on the Church's theological understanding of sexuality.[39] Paul VI reserved the final decision to himself — a move that at least some bishops thought departed from Vatican II's position on collegiality — and in 1968 he upheld Church teaching against contraception in *Humanae Vitae*.

The encyclical met with spirited responses from those inside and outside the Church and from around the world. In the United States a group of theologians openly dissented from the teaching of *Humanae Vitae*.

37. Keenan, "Virtue Ethics," p. 84.

38. See John T. Noonan, Jr., *Contraception: A History of Its Treatment by the Catholic Theologians and Canonists* (Cambridge, MA: Belknap, 1986).

39. See the discussion of *Humanae Vitae* in Odozor, Mahoney, Mark Graham, *Josef Fuchs on Natural Law* (Washington, DC: Georgetown University Press, 2002).

They, and others, identified the grounds of their dissent in terms of the encyclical's ecclesiology and methodology. For many, *Humanae Vitae* seemed a step backwards from Vatican II. Not only does it raise questions about the teaching authority of the magisterium, the encyclical appears to favor a biological over a more integral understanding of the person, and conjugal acts over the totality of marriage. In much subsequent work on Catholic sexual ethics, revisionist and traditionalist positions continue to turn on the issues of how to understand the moral significance of human embodiment (with revisionists charging that traditionalists privilege biology over personhood and traditionalists charging that revisionists neglect the body's significance) and the question whether or not the procreative and unitive values of human sexuality must be inseparably joined in each and every act.[40]

Disagreements about *Humanae Vitae* unfolded into larger postconciliar debates regarding moral norms, intrinsically evil actions, the character of human freedom, and its expression in or determination by the choice of concrete moral actions. Pope John Paul II's 1993 encyclical *Veritatis Splendor,* and replies to it, captures these debates well.

## *Veritatis Splendor* and Postconciliar Moral Theology

*Veritatis Splendor* expressed Pope John Paul II's grave disapproval of much postconciliar moral theology. John Paul argues that much moral theology since the council is marked by false understandings of human freedom and conscience, consequentialism and moral subjectivism, and the denial of intrinsically evil acts and absolute moral norms. The pope criticizes "some theologians," by which he seems to mean certain moral theologians working in the academy, for tendencies that appear to run away with the spirit of Vatican II. In sum, those tendencies undermine conviction in an objective moral order established by God. Specifically, John Paul II criticizes what he calls a "creative" understanding of conscience. The worry is that a creative understanding of conscience makes conscience the arbiter of right and wrong. Morality would therefore be subjective rather than

40. See, for example, Christine E. Gudorf, *Body, Sex, and Pleasure* (Cleveland: Pilgrim, 1994). More recently, see Margaret Farley, *Just Love: A Framework for Christian Sexual Ethics* (London: Continuum, 2008), and Todd A. Salzman and Michael G. Lawler, *The Sexual Person: Toward a Renewed Catholic Anthropology* (Washington, DC: Georgetown University Press, 2008).

grounded in an objective order established by God, linked to aspects of the natural world, and already writ within conscience.

The reason a "creative" understanding of conscience undermines conviction in an objective moral order is because, according to John Paul II, it attenuates the relations between conscience and law, freedom and truth. The revisionist theologians criticized in *Veritatis Splendor,* for example, are said to believe that moral norms are not objectively binding on conscience but simply specifications of a moral perspective that orient the person's moral deliberation. They have this more provisional character out of necessity, since specific moral norms are inevitably insufficient given the complexity of moral life. Moral norms cannot account for unique circumstances, personal histories, and as-yet unknown developments in human history, knowledge, and technology. What truly and unconditionally obliges persons morally lies at some existential level that may or may not cohere with the particular doctrinal requirements proposed by the Church. John Paul II criticizes these ways of qualifying moral norms by saying, "a separation, or even an opposition, is thus established in some cases between the teaching of the precept, which is valid in general, and the norm of the individual conscience, which would in fact make the final decision about what is good and what is evil" (*VS* 56). For John Paul II a creative conscience implies that human freedom is not dependent upon the truth. The pope charges that the moral theologians he criticizes enlist a creative understanding of conscience to justify "pastoral" exemptions to moral rules and excuse moral actions that are contrary to the teaching of the magisterium.

Conciliar deliberations regarding religious freedom and liberty of conscience met with opposition from a largely conservative-leaning minority, at least some of whom worried that these principles would threaten the Church's position in secular cultures. Decades later conservative leaning bishops and laypersons now invoke freedom of conscience and religious liberty protectively on behalf of the Church. Recently, bishops have invoked these principles in response to several legislative developments in the United States and Great Britain. In Boston, Massachusetts, Catholic Charities closed the adoption program it had run for over one hundred years because state law required them to allow same-sex couples to adopt available children. Legal battles have erupted in states like California, New York, and Wisconsin over whether church-related organizations like hospitals, schools, and social-service agencies are subject to state laws that require employers to provide contraceptive insurance coverage. For example, in 2004 the California Supreme Court ended a legal battle to exempt Catholic charities from the Women's Contraceptive Equality Act, a law that requires employers who provide their employees with insurance coverage for prescriptions to include contraceptive coverage. The law includes an exemption for religious employers, but the state Supreme Court upheld an earlier decision that Catholic Charities did not qualify as a religious employer because they provide secular services available to persons regardless of religious belief. Finally, Pope Benedict XVI recently spoke against Great Britain's proposed Equality Bill, saying it would require private organizations like the Church to hire openly gay and transgendered individuals. In an address to bishops of England and Wales the pope said, "Your country is well known for its firm commitment to equality of opportunity for all members of society. Yet as you have rightly pointed out, the effect of some of the legislation designed to achieve this goal has been to impose unjust limitations on the freedom of religious communities to act in accordance with their beliefs."[41] Lest someone counter by asking how a defense of religious liberty and freedom of conscience squares with discriminatory hiring practices, Pope Benedict echoes the charge that "error has no rights" by invoking a natural law justification for the church's position:

> In some respects it actually violates the natural law upon which the equality of all human beings is grounded and by which it is guaranteed. I urge you as Pastors to ensure that the Church's moral teaching be always presented in its entirety and convincingly defended. Fidelity to the Gospel in no way restricts the freedom of others; on the contrary, it serves their freedom by offering them the truth.[42]

## Conclusion: The Future of Catholic Theological Ethics

Vatican II, like any council, will continue to be received and appropriated. Traditions live through ongoing processes of negotiating with the past in response to present circumstances and with a view to the future. Moral

41. "Benedict XVI to the Bishops of England and Wales on their 'ad Limina' visit," 1 February 2010. See the 3 February 2010 issue of *L'Osservatore Romano* for the text, available at http://www.vatican.va/news_services/or/or_eng/index.html#top. Last accessed 7 February 2010.

42. "Benedict XVI to the Bishops of England and Wales on their 'ad Limina' visit."

traditions inevitably include conservative and progressive impulses with regard to the inheritance of earlier tradition. Catholic moral tradition will continue to exhibit tensions between self-consciously traditionalist and revisionist camps. Yet Vatican II will inevitably mean something different for scholars who did not live through it, whose own practice of Catholic faith did not undergo the significant changes of the late twentieth century.[43] Generational differences are already making themselves felt between moral theologians whose careers were underway or soon followed the council and successive generations whose training and scholarship are chronologically and substantively born decades into the council's aftermath. Emerging scholars will bring the perspectives and concerns of their own generations to the fore in ways that, God willing, will destabilize the boundary lines drawn over the last several decades and will allow acrimony and mistrust to give way to productive, charitable, yet nonetheless spirited exchanges.

Indeed, the locus of moral theology — where it is done and who does it — bears importantly on its substance and aims. Catholic moral tradition will continue to diversify, to become a more "worldly" enterprise as moral theologians from the global South figure more prominently in Catholic theological ethics and, one hopes, in the leadership of the bishops. In 2006 the first known international gathering of moral theologians convened in Padova, Italy.[44] Efforts made there and elsewhere to engage, disseminate, and learn from the work of scholars in the global South will enrich Catholic moral tradition and, in a helpful way, de-center it as scholars in the global North become more accountable to the world church.

Finally, Catholic moral reflection is, at least in some quarters, becoming more "participatory." I borrow the idea of "participatory ethics" from Lisa Sowle Cahill. In her recent volume, *Theological Bioethics*, Cahill describes participatory bioethics as a concerted reflection on and engagement with social action for change.[45] Rather than reserve bioethics to theoretical inquiry undertaken in the classroom, participatory bioethics

43. See William C. Mattison, *New Wine, New Wineskins: A Next Generation Reflects on Key Issues in Catholic Moral Theology* (New York: Sheed & Ward, 2005).

44. The conference ran from July 8-11, 2006. See *Catholic Theological Ethics in the World Church: The Plenary Papers from the First Cross-cultural Conference on Catholic Theological Ethics*, ed. James Keenan (London: Continuum, 2007), and *Applied Ethics in a World Church: The Padua Conference*, ed. Linda Hogan (Maryknoll, NY: Orbis, 2008).

45. Lisa Sowle Cahill, *Theological Bioethics: Participation, Justice, and Change* (Washington, DC: Georgetown University Press, 2005).

better appreciates the relationship between theory and praxis, the "doing" of ethics in, say, grassroots organization and in practices of caregiving. A more participatory form of Catholic social teaching would certainly capitalize on the history, presence, and expertise of so many Catholic organizations, such as Catholic Relief Services, to hear better the needs and perspectives of underserved populations and those service providers who live with and minister to them. Catholic moral teaching about sex, marriage, and family is also benefiting from more participatory approaches, as moral theologians draw on the experience of negotiating marital relations and parenting to develop theologies of sex, marriage, and family that extend beyond the magisterial focus on responsible procreation.[46] Moral theology undertaken in a more participatory fashion would require greater versatility on the part of scholars, who would have to learn to listen, develop skills for teaching effectively in diverse contexts, and acquire new methodologies that respond to the knowledge yielded in acting with others for social change. In this way moral theology can continue the renewal initiated by Vatican II, better to illuminate our obligation to bear fruit in charity for the life of the world.

---

46. See, for instance, Julie Hanlon Rubio, *A Christian Theology of Marriage and Family* (New York: Paulist, 2003).

# The Spirit of Vatican II and Moral Theology:
## *Evangelium Vitae* as a Case Study

*M. Cathleen Kaveny*

The spirit of Vatican II is a contested concept in the church today. Pointing to the developments of doctrine, sensibility, and practice that took place in the Second Vatican Council (1962-1965), so-called progressives call upon that spirit as a basis for further departures from past practices in the Catholic Church. Over the years, it has been invoked to demand a more inclusive role for women, sometimes including their ordination as priests. It has also been invoked to demand a more collegial structure of governance, which would emphasize the priesthood of all believers as much as or more than the ordained priesthood in the life of the "People of God." Correlatively, it has been used to justify increased sensitivity on the part of the church to aspects of the contemporary world, both positively and negatively. For example, the "spirit" of Vatican II has been used to justify incorporating contemporary elements such as folk music in celebrations of the Eucharist, and to reach out across boundaries to other Christians in ecumenical endeavors ranging from joint soup kitchens to joint worship services. It has also been used to justify political activism against the great threats to human life on this earth, such as nuclear weapons, terrorism, and increasingly, global warming.

So-called "traditionalists," however, view the "spirit" of Vatican II with suspicion. They worry about the developments that the progressives advocate, believing them to be illegitimate extrapolations from the council designed to advance political agendas imported into the church from the broader world, such as feminism, political liberalism, and a commitment to world government. Consequently, they urge renewed attention to the "letter of the Council," to the actual texts of its documents, as the only way to ensure fidelity both to the council and to the larger tradition of which it forms a part. Following Pope Benedict XVI, they propose a "hermeneutic of reform," which highlights the way in which Vatican II remains continuous with past teaching and practices of the church, rather than a "hermeneutic of rupture," which sharply divides the church into two eras, before and after the council. They argue that careful attention to the "letter" of the council, to the texts themselves, supports their approach.[1]

Whatever its merits, the shift in focus from the "spirit" to the "letter" of Vatican II is arguably a workable strategy in a number of theological disciplines. It is, however, simply not a viable option in the field of moral theology. There is no distinct conciliar document dedicated to the field, as there is to the fields of biblical studies *(Dei Verbum)*, ecclesiology *(Lumen Gentium)*, liturgy *(Sacrosanctum Concilium)*, or ecumenism *(Unitatis Redintegratio)*. There is, in other words, little or no "letter of Vatican II" with respect to moral theology.

The council did, of course, produce several documents that bear more or less directly on questions taken up by the field of moral theology. Most notably, *Gaudium et Spes,* the pastoral constitution on the church and the modern world, addresses broad questions of human meaning and human flourishing in contemporary times. *Dignitatis Humanae,* the declaration on religious liberty, makes important statements on the dignity of the human person and the respect due to individual conscience in fundamental matters such as religious belief. *Lumen Gentium,* the dogmatic constitution on the church, describes the nature and purpose of the church as the body of Christ, and outlines the various responsibilities of laypersons and members of the clergy in building up the kingdom of God. *Dei Verbum,* the constitution on divine revelation, offers guidance on how to interpret Scripture, including its ethical implications. Lacking a distinct document addressed to them, moral theologians have no choice but to draw upon the insights and themes of the foregoing conciliar documents, along with a

---

1. In a recent vivid expression of this thought, R. Walker Nickless, the bishop of Sioux City, Iowa, writes in a pastoral letter: "[T]he Holy Father . . . explains that the 'spirit of Vatican II' must be found only in the letter of the documents themselves. The so-called 'spirit' of the Council has no authoritative interpretation. It is a ghost or demon that must be exorcized if we are to proceed with the Lord's work." R. Walker Nickless, "*Ecclesia Semper Reformanda* (The Church Is Always in Need of Renewal)," 15 October 2009, p. 4; http://www.scdiocese.org/files/Pastoral_Letter_updated100809.pdf; retrieved 1 November 2009. He is referring to Pope Benedict XVI, "Address of His Holiness Benedict XVI to the Roman Curia Offering Them His Christmas Greetings," 22 December 2005, http://www.vatican.va/holy_father/benedict_xvi/speeches/2005/december/documents/hf_ben_xvi_spe_20051222_roman-curia_en.html.

general understanding of the council's nature and purpose, in order to reform their discipline to reflect the teaching of Vatican II.

Catholic moralists, in other words, have no option other than to draw upon the "spirit of Vatican II" and its general themes in order to produce moral theology that is influenced by the council. But what exactly is the spirit of Vatican II? How, systematically, should we understand the council's nature and purpose? The lack of a clear, comprehensive answer to these questions has hampered the ability of Catholic moralists to gauge the effect of the council upon their field. Accordingly, Catholic moralists owe John J. O'Malley, S.J., a debt of gratitude for providing such an answer in *What Happened at Vatican II*.[2] Not only does he offer a history of the council that is both readable and detailed, he also provides an analytical framework that allows us to appreciate its central themes and questions. As useful as that framework is for evaluating the topics that received explicit attention at Vatican II, its assistance is even more crucial for gauging the impact of the council on fields of study that did not receive such attention, such as moral theology.

More specifically, O'Malley argues that the three fundamental issues permeating conciliar debates are: (1) *Change and Continuity*, which focuses on the "circumstances under which change in the church is appropriate and the arguments with which it can be justified"; (2) *Center and Periphery*, which is concerned with "how authority is properly distributed between the papacy, including the Congregations (departments or bureaus) of the Vatican Curia, and the rest of the church"; and (3) *Rhetoric and Style*, which refers to the "style or model according to which that authority should be exercised."[3] O'Malley contends that "[t]hese three issues-under-the-issues . . . provide lenses for interpreting the Council. They are a first step toward a hermeneutic that transcends an often myopic, sometimes almost proof-texting approach to the Council that focuses on the wording of the documents without regard for contexts, without regard for before and after, and without regard for vocabulary and literary form."[4]

By drawing upon O'Malley's analytical framework, we can not only understand the council itself in a more holistic manner, we can also appreciate more accurately the council's tremendous impact on the field of

---

2. John O'Malley, S.J., *What Happened at Vatican II* (Cambridge, MA, and London: Belknap/Harvard University Press, 2008).

3. O'Malley, *What Happened at Vatican II*, p. 8.

4. O'Malley, *What Happened at Vatican II*, p. 12.

moral theology, despite the fact that no conciliar document was dedicated to the topic. My task is to flesh out this claim. In another essay in this volume, Darlene Weaver focuses her attention on the work of academic moral theologians. My concentration here will be upon magisterial teaching, and in particular upon the most important encyclical in moral theology to appear after the council: Pope John Paul II's *Evangelium Vitae* (*The Gospel of Life*, 1995).

*Evangelium Vitae* is as controversial as it is important, because it has been almost thoroughly absorbed into polarizations of the contemporary church. Noting that it reaffirms traditional teaching on contraception as well as abortion and euthanasia, progressives and traditionalists alike have painted it as an effort to tamp down the progressive "spirit of Vatican II." In the United States, *Evangelium Vitae*'s prophetic language of the "culture of life" versus the "culture of death" has been drafted to play a role in political controversies, largely by Republicans who oppose legalized abortion.

In my judgment, it is a mistake to consign (or concede) *Evangelium Vitae* to the forces in the church and the society that are opposed to the full implementation of the Second Vatican Council. Building upon O'Malley's insights, I will argue that *Evangelium Vitae* is a thoroughly postconciliar document. In fact, it is a model of magisterial moral theology done in the "spirit of Vatican II." My argument does not imply, of course, that one cannot criticize specific arguments made or conclusions reached in the encyclical, or that calls for further reform ought to be stifled or muted. But such criticisms and calls ought to take clearly into account the degree to which *Evangelium Vitae* presupposes and confirms the developments of the Second Vatican Council.

## Moral Theology before and after Vatican II

For many centuries, Catholic moral theology was articulated, defended, and developed in the course of producing "manuals" for confessors to use in identifying and evaluating the sins confessed to them by penitents seeking absolution in the Sacrament of Penance.[5] The manuals grew in importance after the Council of Trent, which emphasized the necessity of confes-

---

5. The best overview of the history is John Mahoney, *The Making of Moral Theology* (Oxford: Clarendon, 1987), ch. 1. As he details, there were confessors' manuals before the Council of Trent. There were also other forms of penitential books.

sion for the forgiveness of sins. The practical stakes were high, because the confessors were concerned not only with the temporal well-being of the penitents, but also and primarily with their eternal well-being.

The method employed by the manuals followed from their purpose. Because penitents were obligated to confess each and every sinful act, along with the number of times they committed that act, the manuals created a detailed taxonomy that allowed confessors to evaluate the kind of sin that was involved and its objective seriousness. They also incorporated elaborate analysis that allowed confessors to distinguish sinful acts from acts that were, in close cases, not sinful. It is this sort of analysis, including the drawing of fine distinctions, that merited the name "casuistry" for the manualist genre.

The manualists, who were priests themselves, saw their task as facilitating the pastoral work of the church by enabling their brethren to become good confessors. They did not, generally, see themselves as making original contributions to scholarship in the manner so prized in contemporary academia. This does not mean, however, that there was no room for creativity or groundbreaking analytic rigor in their work. There was such room, in the realm of discussing and debating controverted cases of moral decision-making. Never far removed from the implications of their work for ordinary Catholics, the manualists developed and applied important distinctions such as that between ordinary and extraordinary means of life-prolonging medical treatment. This distinction continues to be helpful to this day.[6]

Yet, there were significant drawbacks to much moral theology produced before the Second Vatican Council, many of which were due to the limitation of the genre of confessors' manuals. First, the manuals were focused primarily on sin and wrongdoing, not the positive features of life as a member of the body of Christ. Reading through the manuals, one could easily get the impression that the ideal life of a Catholic Christian consisted solely in avoiding a clearly defined set of wrongful acts, rather than positively pursuing a calling of faithfulness to God's will.

Second, the manuals were generally focused on the wrongdoing of in-

---

6. One is obliged to use "ordinary" means to preserve one's life, but not to use "extraordinary" means. See the United States Conference of Catholic Bishops, *Ethical and Religious Directives for Catholic Health Care Services* (4th ed.), directives 56 and 57, http://www.usccb.org/bishops/directives.shtml#partfive; retrieved 1 November 2009. For a concise history of the distinction, see Kevin Wildes, S.J., "Ordinary and Extraordinary Means and the Quality of Life," *Theological Studies* 57, no. 3 (1996): 500-512.

dividuals rather than that of corporate agents such as families, churches, or communities. Individuals, after all, were the primary moral agents, the ones who presented themselves for the sacrament of penance. It was their deeds — or misdeeds — that would occupy the attention of the confessor. This is not to say that role-related obligations of responsible individuals were never considered by the manuals; they were. But those obligations were of interest only to the extent that they overlapped with the specific moral duties of a potential penitent.

Third, the manuals tended to describe actions from an external perspective, rather than from the perspective of the acting agent. In traditional moral theology, the most important aspect of an action was its "object" or immediate end. Some manualists tended to describe the object from an external perspective that focused on the physical results of an action, rather than from the perspective of the acting agent herself. This could lead to a mechanistic, or physicalist, account of human action, rather than an account that placed at its center an agent's purposeful causality. It also led to obvious deficiencies. From an external perspective, a serial killer and a surgeon might make an initial cut into an unconscious person's chest in the same way. But the object of their actions could not be more different. The object of the former's act is described as a lethal "knifing," while the object of the latter's act is described as a life-saving "surgical incision."

Finally, the manuals tended to focus on actions described in an isolated and abstract manner. The abstraction is triple. First, the actions in question were not generally presented in relationship to the penitent's overall character. It is important to acknowledge, of course, that the relationship of act to character is not entirely straightforward. It is true that a morally good person can commit a sinful act, and a person of morally dubious character can act uprightly on occasion, or even in one entire sphere of his or her life. Nonetheless, it is also true that one of the most significant long-term effects of actions is the manner in which they shape the character of the person who performs them. An act, if repeated often enough, can become a habit, and a habit is a constitutive part of a person's way of being or responding in the world.

Moreover, the actions in question tend to be presented in a manner abstracted from broader social or personal pressures. The motive and circumstances under which an act was committed are relevant, but not as decisive as the object. Consequently, manualists devoted more time to clarifying the object of an action in controverted cases than they did to reflecting upon the motives and circumstances that would lead an agent to commit such an action. So, for example, it would be important for a manualist to clarify that giving a patient with terminal cancer narcotics would not be euthanasia, because the object of the act was to relieve pain, not to shorten the patient's life. It would be less important to reflect upon the pressures that might tempt a patient or his family members to seek euthanasia, or the social structures that would need to be in place to alleviate such temptations.

In addition, and relatedly, the actions were generally from a timeless, ahistorical perspective. In Catholic manualist moral theology, the core of the natural moral law was seen to be eternal, unchanging, and clearly separable from historically and socially contingent norms of various cultures and societies. It was this unchanging core that drew most of the interest of the manualists, who saw themselves as training priest-confessors for the universal church. Accordingly, they devoted much of their attention to matters of sex (humanity's nature as male and female was decreed by God from the beginning of time) and homicide (the moral law against intentionally killing the innocent was also so decreed, as the story of Cain and Abel shows). While positive duties in connection to procreation and protection of life could vary from culture to culture, the negative duties, the set of acts that it was always wrong to engage in, no matter what the culture or context, remained constant. These were always objectively sinful acts.

Much moral theology before the council was, in short, focused on identifying, classifying, and distinguishing the sinful acts of individuals.[7] For those who have not had the opportunity to peruse the manuals, sufficient sense of their flavor can be gained by a snapshot of a segment of one. One of the most important manualists of the first half of the twentieth century was Marcellino Zalba, S.J., a professor at the Gregorian University in Rome, who produced a manual in three volumes in Latin. Typical of the genre, it moves systematically from general topics, to more particular topics, to ever-finer distinctions between sinful acts and those that are morally permissible. The second volume, dealing with particular moral questions, is organized according to the Ten Commandments, and structured to con-

---

7. There were exceptions, which were harbingers of the changes to come. In the 1950s Gerard Gilleman wrote *The Primacy of Charity in Moral Theology* (Westminster, MD: Newman Press, 1959). A few years later, Bernard Häring wrote *The Law of Christ,* a two-volume manual that attempted to recast moral theology in a more Christocentric direction (Westminster, MD: Newman Press, 1961-63).

sider the acts that violate each commandment. For example, the section on the fifth commandment has four chapters, on dominion over life and suicide, homicide, dueling, and war. The first chapter has two "articles" or subsections, one on dominion over human life and the other on suicide, mutilation, and the proper care for life. The second subsection of that chapter defines suicide, and divides it into categories of "direct" and "indirect." Direct (i.e., intentional) suicide is always illicit, while indirect (i.e., an act committed while the agent foresees but does not intend to cut short his or her life) is sometimes permissible (or even required), sometimes not. Under the treatment of indirect suicide there are five applications to different factual circumstances. Among these are whether it is ever permissible or even required for a doctor, nurse, or priest to expose themselves to risk of death by visiting contagious patients (yes to both questions), and whether a virgin is permitted to kill herself in order to avoid rape (no).[8]

If one only looked at the manuals, one could easily reach the conclusion that the focus of Catholic moral reflection was narrow, negative, and individualistic *in toto*.[9] Happily, that conclusion would be mistaken. Developing along a different track from "moral theology" was Catholic social teaching, which considered the nature and purposes of human society, as well as the rights and obligations of its constitutive members, ranging from government itself, through intermediary associations such as corporations, trade unions, churches, and families, and reaching down to individuals themselves.

Whereas moral theology was developed largely by seminary professors preparing confessor manuals, the magisterium claimed the lion's share of influence in the development of Catholic social thought. Its modern articulation is usually dated to 1891, when Pope Leo XIII issued *Rerum Novarum,* which affirmed the rights of workers to a living wage against the demands of an uncontrolled capitalism. Before the advent of the Second Vatican Council, Pope Pius XI and Pope John XXIII made important contributions to the development of modern Catholic social theory, issuing *Quadragesimo Anno* (1931) and *Mater et Magistra* (1961), respectively.

While the manuals of moral theology focused on the duties of individ-

---

8. Marcellino Zalba, S.J., *Theologiae Moralis Summa,* vol. 2: *Theologia Moralis Specialis. Tractatus de Mandatis Dei et Ecclesiae* (Madrid: Bibliotecha de Autores Cristianos, 1953).

9. Let me also add that I see many positive features in the manualist tradition, despite its obvious deficiencies. See M. Cathleen Kaveny, "Retrieving and Reframing Catholic Casuistry," in *The Crisis of Authority in Catholic Modernity,* ed. Michael Lacey and Francis Oakley (Oxford: Oxford University Press, 2011).

uals (largely negative duties), Catholic social teaching examined the actions not only of individual agents, but also of corporate agents. Moreover, its focus was largely positive, focusing not only on the avoidance of wrongs, but upon the protections of rights *(jus, jura)* in the course of constructing a just society. Moreover, Catholic social teaching was not written from a timeless, eternal perspective; it engaged the particular social challenges and threats of the times to which it was addressed. Of necessity, therefore, it grappled with contingencies, assessments of the causes and social problems, and predictions of the course of actions that would exacerbate or ameliorate them. Popes could call attention to broadly worrying social trends, but were not policy experts capable of offering solutions to all the world's problems.

The Second Vatican Council confirmed Catholic social teaching, strengthening and broadening its appeal. *Gaudium et Spes,* the pastoral constitution on the church and the modern world, built upon prior magisterial documents, and generated further reflections on the social order by popes and bishops in its wake. It also awakened widespread scholarly interest in Catholic social teaching, which was functionally conceived as a subfield distinct from moral theology. For example, theorists such as David Hollenbach, S.J., John Haughey, S.J., and John Coleman, S.J., worked out a social ethics of rights and obligations that scarcely overlapped with the concerns of manualist moral theology, concerned as it was with the casuistry of individual cases.

What happened to the discipline of moral theology? As O'Malley details, the participants in the council were directed by Pope Paul VI to prescind from the question of artificial birth control, a topic of central concern to the manualist tradition.[10] After the conclusion of the council, however, a papal commission continued to study the question; that commission recommended a development in the teaching to permit the responsible use of birth control by married couples. Against their advice, Paul VI reaffirmed the ban, extending it to encompass the use of the newly developed "birth control pill." His encyclical *Humanae Vitae* (1968) set off a firestorm of controversy within the church, on two grounds. First, many Catholics disagreed with the encyclical's judgment that birth control was

---

10. O'Malley, *What Happened at Vatican II,* p. 6, pp. 236-38. O'Malley's account, however, reveals harbingers of Paul VI's ultimate rejection of birth control in his actions at the council, including a last-minute "counsel" to include a definitive prohibition in *Gaudium et Spes,* which he did not insist upon in the end; see pp. 284-85.

always impermissible because it was an "intrinsically evil act." Second, the fact that the pope refused to take the advice of his own commission dashed the hope of many progressives for a more broadly consultative church sensitive to the lived experience of the faithful laity. In contrast, a cadre of traditionalists defended *Humanae Vitae* on both grounds. Battle lines were quickly hardened.

In my judgment, the field of moral theology was badly fractured, perhaps irreparably, in the wake of *Humanae Vitae*. What were the lines of the break? Because of space constraints, my focus will be on the North American scene. That focus is necessarily limited. The Catholic Church is global in scope; issues vary in importance from continent to continent and even country to country.

The first and most obvious fissure was the between the reformists, such as Richard McCormick, S.J., and Charles Curran, and the traditionalists, such as Germain Grisez and John Ford, S.J. The manualists judged contracepted sexual acts to be prohibited because the *object* of such acts was morally impermissible: its immediate aim or "end" was to remove the procreative purpose of the act of sexual intercourse. According to Curran and McCormick, the focus of the manualists on the object of an action was both distorted (in that it understood the object in a physicalist manner) and constricted (in that it did not take into account the circumstances or motives of the contracepting couple). So they advocated a "proportionalist" approach to moral theology, which argued that contraception could be justified in particular cases, given sufficiently grave circumstances and motives. While some traditionalists (e.g., Grisez) also proposed revisions to the manualist approach (including a critique of a physicalist account of action), they did not believe those revisions permitted or required a change in church teaching on contraception.

Whatever their differences, and they could be sharp, the proportionalists and their opponents were all still working within the same normative universe, dominated by the act analysis proffered by the manualist tradition. Other developments left that tradition (and the proportionalist debate) behind entirely, by adopting a different framework for moral analysis. Indisputably, these developments were due to new forms of openness made possible, at least in part, by the Second Vatican Council. Not only did Catholic laypersons begin studying theology, they also began doing so in ecumenical settings, which did not place a high priority on studying confessors' manuals written in Latin. Consequently, an emerging generation of moralists began to adopt methods of moral analysis influenced by

Protestant thought, as well as newer trends in secular philosophy, such as rights theory, feminism, and Marxist-influenced liberationist theology.[11] This new group of lay moral theologians had neither the training in the manualist tradition nor the inclination to devote themselves to highly technical and increasingly bitter debates.

Yet this did not mean they were not interested in Catholic tradition. In addition to a program of *aggiornamento* (updating the discipline to take into account new developments in cognate disciplines) there was also a program of *ressourcement* (attempting to go deeper into the Catholic tradition to retrieve important but overlooked resources), to borrow two words that are commonly used to refer to different themes of the council. Many of those with interests in moral theology began to return to the work of St. Thomas Aquinas, not primarily with the intent of revisiting his treatise on human acts, but instead with the purpose of recovering his version of Aristotelian virtue theory. Their efforts in this regard were encouraged not only by virtue-centered Catholic theologians such as Servais Pinckaers, O.P., but also by Protestant thinkers such as Stanley Hauerwas and analytic philosophers such as Alasdair MacIntyre.[12]

Some of the more radical approaches offered new ways of integrating questions of personal morality taken up by the manualists with larger social concerns. However, while the bridge between moral theology and social ethics was beginning to be visible, it was not often crossed in the first three decades after the council. In the academic realm, Catholic social theory and fundamental moral theology tended to operate in distinct spheres of thought.[13]

---

11. See, e.g., Lisa Sowle Cahill's *Between the Sexes: Foundations for a Christian Ethics of Sexuality* (Philadelphia: Fortress, 1985), which employs a method resembling the Wesleyan "quadrilateral" (Scripture, tradition, reason, and experience) to address questions in sexual ethics. In interpreting the tradition, she draws not only on the work of Thomas Aquinas, but also upon that of Martin Luther.

12. Alasdair MacIntyre's groundbreaking *After Virtue* (Notre Dame: University of Notre Dame Press, 1981) gave new impetus to this movement. See also Stanley Hauerwas, *Character and the Christian Life: A Study in Christian Theological Ethics* (San Antonio: Trinity University Press, 1975); and Servais Pinckaers, *The Sources of Christian Ethics*, 3rd ed. (New York: Continuum/T. & T. Clark, 1995).

13. The reader might fruitfully compare my account of changes in the field to that produced two decades ago by the eminent Jesuit moralist Richard A. McCormick, S.J., who for a period of twenty years wrote the annual "Notes on Moral Theology" section of the journal *Theological Studies*. See Richard A. McCormick, S.J., "Moral Theology: An Overview," *Theological Studies* 50, no. 1 (1989): 3-24. In my judgment, McCormick's list stands the test of

What about in the magisterial realm? In America, the United States Conference of Catholic Bishops was galvanized both by the issue of abortion and by questions of war and economic equity. In 1973, the U.S. Supreme Court declared that the constitutional right to privacy protects a woman's right to choose to obtain an abortion.[14] Shocked, the American bishops organized to protest the decision and advocate for legal protection for unborn life. At the same time, they demonstrated firm commitment to issues of social justice, which culminated in the pastoral letters on nuclear deterrence and the economy produced in the mid-1980s.[15] Yet, as several observers in the American Catholic scene have recently pointed out, it is telling that the pro-life and the social justice wings of the church have separate offices, and often distinct concerns, not only on the national level, but also on the diocesan level.[16] Efforts to bring them closer together, such as Cardinal Joseph Bernardin's proposal of a "consistent ethic of life," have not met with widespread success. Cardinal Bernard Law and other prominent clerics rejected Bernardin's "seamless garment" approach on the grounds that it undermined the primacy of the issue of abortion.[17]

By far the greatest magisterial influence on moral theology in the years since the Second Vatican Council has been the writing of Pope John Paul II. A moral philosopher by training, he released a prodigious number of letters, encyclicals, and other teaching documents during the twenty-seven years of his papacy. Of his thirteen encyclicals, three deal with Catholic social teaching (*Laborem Exercens*, 1981, *Sollicitudo Rei Socialis*, 1987, and *Centesimus Annus*, 1991). Two encyclicals are particularly important for

---

time, although he might have given more weight than he did to the "restorationist" tendency he identified.

14. *Roe v. Wade*, 410 U.S. 113 (1973).

15. United States Conference of Catholic Bishops, "The Challenge of Peace: God's Promise and Our Response" (1983), http://www.usccb.org/sdwp/international/TheChallenge ofPeace.pdf; and "Economic Justice for All" (1986), http://www.usccb.org/sdwp/international/ EconomicJusticeforAll.pdf.

16. See George Wesolek, "American Catholic Structural Polarization," *Catholic San Francisco*, 5 July 2009, p. 1.

17. See Joseph Cardinal Bernardin, *Consistent Ethic of Life*, ed. Thomas G. Fuechtmann (Kansas City, MO: Sheed & Ward, 1988), for a collection of Cardinal Bernardin's writings on the topic, as well as scholarly essays. For an account of clerical criticisms, see Margaret Ross Sammon, "The Politics of the U.S. Catholic Bishops: The Centrality of Abortion," in *Catholics and Politics: The Dynamic Tension Between Faith and Power*, ed. Kristin E. Heyer, Mark J. Rozell, and Michael J. Genovese (Washington, DC: Georgetown University Press, 2008), pp. 18-21.

moral theology, *Veritatis Splendor* (1993)[18] and *Evangelium Vitae* (1995).[19] Moreover, because the two encyclicals are integrally related, it is necessary to say a few words about the former before moving on to focused consideration of the latter.

*Veritatis Splendor* addresses the topic of fundamental moral theology, dealing with such questions as how we are to think about our obligation to pursue good and avoid evil. Pope John Paul II devotes a substantial amount of attention to contemporary moral theories that he views as deeply mistaken. One such theory is a purely constructivist approach to ethics, which depicts human conscience as creating the norms of the moral order, rather than discerning them. Also mistaken is any theory that incorporates thoroughgoing cultural relativism; while John Paul II recognizes that "man always exists in a particular culture," he maintains that "man is not exhaustively defined by that culture." Human nature is the "measure of culture and the condition ensuring that man does not become the prisoner of any of his cultures, but asserts his personal dignity by living in accordance with the profound truth of his being" (*VS* 53).

Among those profound truths are the truths of the natural moral law; the encyclical reasserts the magisterium's claim to special competence to interpret those truths to the extent they bear upon questions of salvation. In this context, Pope John Paul II rejects the idea that one's fundamental option for or against God is all that matters; instead, he insists (along with the tradition) that we work out our relationship with God through our particular acts. Consequently, he reaffirms the distinction between venial sins and mortal sins, the commission of which with requisite mental state could separate a person permanently from God.

In addition, Pope John Paul II rejects proportionalism, which he understands to be a moral theory that assesses the moral acceptability of a particular action according to its consequences.[20] In so doing, he also reaf-

18. *Veritatis Splendor* (1993). All quotations are taken from the official English edition at the Vatican website, http://www.vatican.va/holy_father/john_paul_ii/encyclicals/documents/hf_jp-ii_enc_06081993_veritatis-splendor_en.html.

19. *Evangelium Vitae* (1995). All quotations are taken from the official English edition at the Vatican website, http://www.vatican.va/holy_father/john_paul_ii/encyclicals/documents/hf_jp-ii_enc_25031995_evangelium-vitae_en.html, except for the material described in note 35.

20. It should be pointed out that some of those who identified themselves as proportionalists did not recognize themselves in the account of the theory given in *Veritatis Splendor*. See the essays in Charles E. Curran and Richard A. McCormick, eds., *John Paul II and Moral Theology*, Readings in Moral Theology No. 10 (Mahwah, NJ: Paulist, 1998).

firms the traditional framework used by the manualists to assess human action. More specifically, he reasserts that an action takes its moral species from its object. There are some actions — intrinsically evil actions — that are always wrong, because the choice of their object is always incompatible with human flourishing. While an agent's motive and the other circumstances may mitigate the wrongfulness of an intrinsically evil action, they cannot eliminate it.

*Veritatis Splendor* can therefore be called conservative, because it reaffirms the basic framework (found in St. Thomas) in which the church has analyzed human actions for centuries. At the same time, it is important to recognize that it is not simply reinstituting a regime of manualist theology — far from it. John Paul II takes care to emphasize, for example, that the object of the act is not to be determined solely by looking at its immediate physical results, but must be identified from "the perspective of the acting person."[21] While focusing on the importance of recognizing that it is never permissible to violate absolute negative norms, the pope takes care to indicate that they do not exhaust Catholic morality, but are the foundation for positive acts of love and justice.

Finally, and most significantly for my upcoming discussion of *Evangelium Vitae, Veritatis Splendor* attempts to move beyond the relevance of absolute negative moral prohibitions for the salvation of the individual agent to consider their role in protecting the common good. He writes:

> By protecting the inviolable personal dignity of every human being they help to preserve the human social fabric and its proper and fruitful development. The commandments of the second table of the Decalogue in particular, those which Jesus quoted to the young man of the Gospel (cf. Mt 19:19), constitute the indispensable rules of all social life. (*VS* 97)

*Veritatis Splendor,* then, begins the task of knitting together the (revised) act analysis found in the manuals with the Catholic social ethics tradition.

---

21. "By the object of a given moral act, then, one cannot mean a process or an event of the merely physical order, to be assessed on the basis of its ability to bring about a given state of affairs in the outside world. Rather, that object is the proximate end of a deliberate decision which determines the act of willing on the part of the acting person" (*VS* 78).

## *Evangelium Vitae* and Vatican II: Applying O'Malley's Framework

Pope John Paul II released *Evangelium Vitae (The Gospel of Life)*, in 1995, two years after *Veritatis Splendor*. As its name suggests, the central concern of the encyclical is to affirm the transcendent dignity and value of each and every human life. Building upon the fundamental theology developed in *Veritatis Splendor*, *Evangelium Vitae* is a work in applied or "special" moral theology; its focus is on abortion, infanticide, euthanasia, and to a lesser extent, contraception. These are a subset of the intrinsically evil acts that were identified and defined in *Veritatis Splendor;* they are also a subject to which the traditional manuals in moral theology devoted significant attention.

The fact that John Paul II conceived the encyclical in strong relationship with Vatican II is clear in the introduction, in which he cites a famous passage from *Gaudium et Spes*. He writes:

> The Second Vatican Council, in a passage which retains all its relevance today, forcefully condemned a number of crimes and attacks against human life. Thirty years later, taking up the words of the council and with the same forcefulness I repeat that condemnation in the name of the whole Church, certain that I am interpreting the genuine sentiment of every upright conscience: "Whatever is opposed to life itself, such as any type of murder, genocide, abortion, euthanasia, or wilful self-destruction; whatever violates the integrity of the human person, such as mutilation, torments inflicted on body or mind, attempts to coerce the will itself; whatever insults human dignity, such as subhuman living conditions, arbitrary imprisonment, deportation, slavery, prostitution, the selling of women and children; as well as disgraceful working conditions, where people are treated as mere instruments of gain rather than as free and responsible persons; all these things and others like them are infamies indeed. They poison human society, and they do more harm to those who practice them than to those who suffer from the injury. Moreover, they are a supreme dishonour to the Creator. (*EV* 3)[22]

---

22. Pope John Paul II cites this well-known passage from *Gaudium et Spes* (27) in *Veritatis Splendor* (80), in order to illustrate his claim that there are intrinsically evil acts. However, *Gaudium et Spes* does not refer to them as "intrinsically evil," but as "disgraces" or "infamies." (*[H]aec omnia et alia huiusmodi probra quidem sunt, ac dum civilizationem humanam inficiunt, magis eos inquinant qui sic se gerunt, quam eos qui iniuriam patiuntur et Creatoris honori maxime contradicunt.*) It is not clear how each and every act listed in

Nonetheless, to quote one document from the Second Vatican Council, however important, does not demonstrate a pervasive influence, much less reveal the manner in which the influence has exerted itself. How does one systematically assess the degree to which *Evangelium Vitae* is in fact influenced by the themes of Vatican II in its reconfiguration of moral theology? How does one discern whether the invocation of Vatican II reveals a genuine intellectual debt, or nothing more than mere prooftexting? It is in answering these questions that O'Malley's tripartite framework is immensely helpful.

## Continuity and Change

A crucial conciliar theme identified by O'Malley is the tension between continuity and change. As he perceptively notes, continuity is an important value in the church: "By its own definition the Christian church is a conservative society whose essential mission is to pass on by word and deed a message received long ago."[23] At the same time, the church's salvific message has to be communicated effectively in changing historical circumstances, a fact that Vatican II explicitly acknowledged. Vatican II was a unique council in that it explicitly attended to the challenges involved in proclaiming the word of God in changing times.

As O'Malley identifies, time can relate to the proclamation of the gospel message in three ways. We can update the message in a process of *aggiornamento*, as Pope John XXIII described one purpose of the council. Although the message stays the same, the manner in which it is communicated or set forth might need to be altered to reflect contemporary needs. Moreover, through the assistance of the Holy Spirit, the church might come to deeper insights into other truths it already holds.

The tacit premise of the concept of *aggiornamento* is that human beings are historical beings, embedded in time and culture. That premise is also a basic assumption of *Evangelium Vitae,* and indeed a primary moti-

---

*Gaudium et Spes* 27 qualifies as an intrinsically evil act according to the technical definition. For example, "subhuman living conditions" are a state, not an action, and "arbitrary imprisonment" would seem to be a wrong by virtue of circumstances rather than by the object of the act. The official Latin text of Gaudium et Spes can be found at: http://www.vatican.va/archive/hist_councils/ii_vatican_council/documents/vat-ii_cons_19651207_gaudium-et-spes_lt.html.

23. O'Malley, *What Happened at Vatican II,* p. 299.

vation for writing it. John Paul II wants to call attention to "the extraordinary increase and gravity of threats to the life of individuals and peoples, especially where life is weak and defenseless" (*EV* 3). Both the introduction and the first chapter of the encyclical make clear that the pope deplores a wide array of contemporary threats to human life and dignity, from poverty and malnutrition to armed conflict and the drug trade (*EV* 10). Why, then, is he concentrating on abortion and euthanasia? It is because "in generalized opinion these attacks tend no longer to be considered as 'crimes'; paradoxically they assume the nature of 'rights,' to the point that the State is called upon to give them legal recognition and to make them available through the free services of health-care personnel" (*EV* 11). Quite simply, the pope is shocked, not primarily by the fact that abortion and euthanasia are committed, but by the contemporary world's attempt to justify them.

In my view, the failure to pay sufficient attention to the historical-cultural context of the pope's message in *Evangelium Vitae* leads to a distorted reading of the encyclical. For example, in the context of the American culture wars, Catholic pro-lifers often use the encyclical to justify the claim that we need to prioritize abortion over questions of war and poverty because it is a more serious evil, a "non-negotiable" evil, or an "intrinsic evil."[24] The pope is saying none of these things; he is not making a transcultural, transhistorical claim. Instead, his fundamental assertion is that the threat of abortion and euthanasia is greater in the contemporary contexts, because wide swaths of people don't recognize these practices as morally wrong.

O'Malley suggests that the second key point on the continuity/change axis is that of *ressourcement*, retrieval of aspects of our two-thousand-year-old tradition that have been occluded by our immediate past. As he points out, an important focus of the impetus for *ressourcement* had to do with the church's approach to Scripture, which Vatican II worked out in *Dei Verbum*. O'Malley notes that the council's majority "wanted to recapture modes of thinking that . . . encouraged the reading of Scripture as the primary source of Christian piety."[25] Even a cursory comparison of *Evangelium Vitae* to the preconciliar manuals of moral theology demonstrates that John Paul II has

---

24. See, e.g., the voting guide produced by the apologetics group Catholic Answers, http://www.caaction.com/pdf/Voters-Guide-Catholic-English-1p.pdf.

25. O'Malley, *What Happened at Vatican II,* p. 301. See John Henry Newman, *An Essay on the Development of Christian Doctrine* (New York: Cosimo Classics, 2007).

thoroughly internalized this approach to Scripture. Whereas the manuals tended to draw upon biblical passages for prooftexts or abbreviated illustrations, John Paul II draws from them extended meditations on the relationship of human beings to one another in light of their overarching relationship with God. In chapter 1 of the encyclical, the roots of human violence are considered in the context of the story of Cain and Abel contained in the Book of Genesis. Chapter 2 works out the implications of the "Gospel of Life" extensively in terms of the Good News of Jesus Christ, who is proclaimed as the fulfillment of the message that Yahweh delivered to Israel through the priests and the prophets. Throughout the text, the pope presents Scripture as an invitation to his readers to find echoes of their own hopes and fears therein. While this strategy is no doubt due in part to the heavy influence of Christian personalism on his thought, it also reflects the retrieval of an older form of reading Scripture that is highly commended by the Second Vatican Council.

The third key point on O'Malley's axis of continuity and change is the notion of development. As O'Malley observes, the term "development" is often used as a synonym for change. Nonetheless, in part due to the legacy of John Henry Newman, it gestured toward a particular account of change, "an unfolding of something already present implicitly or in germ."[26] Not every move of the council could easily be accommodated within the rubric of "development." It was a challenge, as O'Malley notes, to fit the label of "development" on the about-face that the declaration on religious liberty seemed to involve. *Evangelium Vitae,* however, involves no such difficulties. In fact, it offers a clear and important example of development, by fully integrating the church's pro-life position into a larger framework of social justice.

As I indicated above, the manualist tradition tended to present abortion and euthanasia as the isolated acts of an individual penitent, most often the woman who sought the procedure and on occasion the physician who performed it. While *Evangelium Vitae* does not in any way deny the wrongfulness of these acts, it takes care to situate them more broadly, in two ways. First, it looks at the social context in which individuals seek such procedures. John Paul II explicitly notes, for example, that women can be tempted to abortion because of the tragic circumstances in which a baby will be born, including a situation that threatens the ability of the family to feed and clothe older brothers and sisters. He recognizes the pressure to

26. Newman, *An Essay on the Development of Christian Doctrine,* p. 300.

abort that can be exerted by fathers, family members, and friends. Finally, he notes the way in which a social and legal framework can channel a mother's decision toward abortion by presenting it as an acceptable option, indeed often the only acceptable option (*EV* 58-59). In *Evangelium Vitae*, moral agents are essentially social agents — their capacity to act well or badly is conditioned, although not determined, by the familial, institutional, and political contexts in which they live.

Second, John Paul II devotes a significant portion of the encyclical to social and cultural analysis. Building on Catholic social thought, he recognizes the responsibility to build a society that respects human life, especially in its weakest forms. He then proceeds to outline in some detail the component parts of a "culture of life," describing the contributions to be made by all segments of society from legislatures to family members (*EV* 90). His goal is nothing less than to mobilize not only Catholics, but all Christians in this effort. Social ethics, for John Paul II, is never a matter of natural law separated from the gospel. In fact, reflecting the renewed attention of the fathers of the council to the formative power of Scripture, *Evangelium Vitae* calls for renewed efforts at evangelization. "Like the yeast which leavens the whole measure of dough (cf. Mt 13:33), the Gospel is meant to permeate all cultures and give them life from within, so that they may express the full truth about the human person and about human life" (*EV* 95).

As my earlier discussion of *Veritatis Splendor* presaged, there is an area in which *Evangelium Vitae* exhibits more continuity than change: it assumes that there are intrinsically evil acts that ought never to be performed, no matter what the circumstances. These acts include not only euthanasia and abortion (intentionally killing innocent human life) but also contraception. He does not squarely face the hard objections that Catholics and others have raised to the claim that contraception is an intrinsically evil act, but dismisses them as "clearly unfounded" (*EV* 13). The widespread acceptance of contraception, in his view, is a mark of the pervasiveness of a "culture of death." Methodologically, this is far too quick a move; we should not simply label those who disagree with us morally benighted. Moreover, any natural law account has to consider relevant an emerging moral consensus on the morality of a particular act. Moreover, it cannot be ignored that contraception is accepted as a morally licit practice on at least some occasions, not only by post-Christian societies, but also by most Christians and most Jews. To argue that contraceptive practices are immoral because they have been abused is to prove too much (*"abusus non tollit usum"*). As the recent worldwide economic crisis shows, the practice of lending money at interest can also be abused, to great detriment. Yet the Vatican has shown no signs of reviving its former position that all lending money at interest is intrinsically evil (a position that continues to be held by many Muslims).[27]

What allows Pope John Paul II to be so confident — perhaps too confident — in his moral judgments about particular aspects of the moral law in the face of strong countervailing judgments? It is his faith in the capacity, and the right, of the Roman Catholic magisterium to speak definitively to questions of faith and morals. This right was reaffirmed by the Second Vatican Council, not only in *Lumen Gentium* (25), but also in *Dei Verbum* (10). Accordingly, we now turn to the second topic O'Malley identified as key to Vatican II, which pertains to the distribution of authority in the church.

## Center and Periphery

O'Malley describes the tension in the council between the minority and majority bishops over the proper relationship between papal primacy, on the one hand, and collegiality, among bishops, on the other. As he describes, "papal primacy 'developed' almost incrementally in a steady and almost continuous line up until the long nineteenth century, when it accelerated at (for the church) almost breathtaking speed."[28] Definitions of papal infallibility and the Marian dogmas combined with the growth of the Roman congregations to centralize power in the hands of the pope and the curia. Attempting to combat this centralization, the conciliar majority drew upon themes of *ressourcement* to argue for a more balanced relationship between the pope and the bishops. The majority drew upon earlier forms of this relationship in order to make room for more consultation and collaboration between the center and the periphery. O'Malley observes, "Collegiality was the supreme instance in the Council of the effort to moderate the centralizing tendencies of the ecclesiastical institution, of the effort to give those from the periphery a more authoritative voice not only back home but also in the center."[29]

27. For an account of how the church teaching developed on usury and other topics, see John T. Noonan, Jr., *A Church That Can and Cannot Change* (Notre Dame: University of Notre Dame Press, 2005).

28. O'Malley, *What Happened at Vatican II*, p. 302.

29. O'Malley, *What Happened at Vatican II*, p. 303.

*Evangelium Vitae* is, of course, a papal encyclical, and therefore an exercise of the papal authority whose legitimacy was reaffirmed by Vatican II. Quite strikingly, Pope John Paul II does not shy away from exercising the authority of his office. In fact, he writes:

> Therefore, by the authority which Christ conferred upon Peter and his Successors, and in communion with the Bishops of the Catholic Church, I confirm that the direct and voluntary killing of an innocent human being is always gravely immoral. This doctrine, based upon that unwritten law which man, in the light of reason, finds in his own heart (cf. Rom 2:14 15), is reaffirmed by Sacred Scripture, transmitted by the Tradition of the Church and taught by the ordinary and universal Magisterium. (*EV* 57)

Later in the encyclical, he makes similar formal declarations about the wrongfulness of abortion (*EV* 62) and euthanasia (*EV* 65).

What is striking about his declarations, however, is the collegial basis he explicitly asserts for them. In the introduction to the encyclical, he states that the Extraordinary Consistory of Cardinals in 1991 was devoted to threats to human life, and describes how the cardinals asked the pope to reaffirm "with the authority of the Successor of Peter the value of human life and its inviolability" (*EV* 5). In addition, he recounts how he wrote each of his brother bishops a personal letter asking for their cooperation in drawing up an appropriate document. In replying, according to the pope, "they bore witness to their unanimous desire to share in the doctrinal and pastoral mission of the church with regard to the Gospel of life" (*EV* 5).

One could, of course, question the degree to which the inquiries made by the pope were genuinely seeking an honest reply from each bishop whose opinion was sought. There is always a way to manipulate any process, as O'Malley's account of the political machinations at Vatican II reveals so clearly. Nonetheless, the fact that Pope John Paul II believed it important not only to consult before exercising his authority, but also to describe his process of consultation in some detail, is not insignificant.

## Rhetoric and Style

The third lens through which O'Malley invites us to view Vatican II is that of its rhetoric. As he notes, "The style of the documents of Vatican II is what at first glance as well as most profoundly sets it apart from all other Councils."[30] O'Malley argues that the style is that of the epideictic or panegyric genre, rather than the legalistic language characteristic of earlier councils. "Vatican II as a self-proclaimed pastoral Council was for that reason also a teaching Council."[31]

A style, of course, cannot be clinically described; it must be evoked in order to be communicated, and O'Malley does a marvelous job of evoking that style throughout his book. For our purposes, however, we will need to limit ourselves to illustration. Attempting to capture the style of the council, O'Malley writes:

> In its general orientation, as articulated especially in its most characteristic vocabulary, the Council devised a profile of the ideal Christian. That ideal, drawn in greatest length in *Gaudium et Spes,* is more incarnational than eschatological, closer to Thomas Aquinas than to Karl Barth, more reminiscent of the fathers of the Eastern Church than of Augustine — more inclined to reconciliation with human culture than to alienation from it, more inclined to see goodness than sin, more inclined to speaking words of friendship and encouragement than of indictment. The style choice fostered a theological choice.
>
> The result was a message that was traditional while at the same time radical, prophetic while at the same time soft-spoken. In a world increasingly wracked with discord, hatred, war, and threats of war, the result was a message that was counter-cultural while at the same time responsive to the deepest human yearnings. Peace on earth. Good will to men.[32]

In my judgment, *Evangelium Vitae* stands in rhetorical continuity with Vatican II, although it is clearly marked by the unique flair for the dramatic demonstrated by John Paul II, a former actor, in many of his communicative endeavors. Nowhere is that dramatic flair more evident than in his prophetic contrast between "the culture of life" and the "culture of death." For Americans, it is difficult not to think of this contrast in angry, almost bellicose terms, influenced as we are by the "culture wars" mentality.[33] Nonetheless, a careful reading of the encyclical reveals a far

---

30. O'Malley, *What Happened at Vatican II,* p. 305.
31. O'Malley, *What Happened at Vatican II,* p. 307.
32. O'Malley, *What Happened at Vatican II,* pp. 310-11.
33. See, e.g., Peter Kreeft, *How to Win the Culture War: A Christian Battle Plan for a So-*

more interesting and complex approach to the situation. John Paul II does devote significant prophetic attention to the cruelties of the "culture of death" and the "enormous and dramatic clash between good and evil" (*EV* 28). Nonetheless, his rhetoric evokes the heartbreak of the Book of Lamentations more than it does the fiery indictments of the Book of Jeremiah.

Moreover, the encyclical makes it clear that the way to combat the culture of death is not by "war" but by love. John Paul II devotes chapter 4 of *Evangelium Vitae* to a positive account of the "culture of life": it is the Gospel of Life, it is the Good News. He writes:

> By virtue of our sharing in Christ's royal mission, our support and promotion of human life must be accomplished through the service of charity, which finds expression in personal witness, various forms of volunteer work, social activity and political commitment. This is a particularly pressing need at the present time, when the "culture of death" so forcefully opposes the "culture of life" and often seems to have the upper hand. But even before that it is a need which springs from "faith working through love" (Gal 5:6). As the Letter of James admonishes us: "What does it profit, my brethren, if a man says he has faith but has not works? Can his faith save him? If a brother or sister is ill-clad and in lack of daily food, and one of you says to them, 'Go in peace, be warmed and filled,' without giving them the things needed for the body, what does it profit? So faith by itself, if it has no works, is dead" (2:14-17). (*EV* 87)

What about fighting against unjust laws, laws that promote abortion and euthanasia? Even here, a careful reading of the encyclical demonstrates John Paul II's awareness that changing the legal landscape cannot be accomplished solely by railing against the prevailing legal regime. Indeed, transcending the polarization between the American pro-life and pro–social justice movements, he strongly suggests that a society will not be able to rectify permissive abortion laws without *simultaneously* enacting a strong social program offering positive assistance to the vulnerable.[34]

Furthermore, John Paul II's rhetoric is thoroughly pastoral, and theo-

---

*ciety in Crisis* (Downers Grove, IL: InterVarsity, 2002). The cover of the book features two knights, faces masked, engaged in a sword fight.

34. "Here it must be noted that it is not enough to remove unjust laws. The underlying causes of attacks on life have to be eliminated, especially by ensuring proper support for families and motherhood. A family policy must be the basis and driving force of all social policies" (*EV* 90).

logically hopeful. While unequivocal about the grave wrong of abortion, he is markedly compassionate in his words toward women who have had them. In the most moving passage in the entire encyclical, he encourages such women not to give in to despair. "You will come to understand that nothing is definitively lost and you will also be able to ask forgiveness from your child, who is now living in the Lord" (*EV* 99). No sentence in the encyclical embodies the "spirit of Vatican II" more than this one does.[35]

## Conclusion

John O'Malley suggests that the "spirit of Vatican II" is best understood in terms of the rhetoric of the council, the third of three themes he identifies as hermeneutical keys to its interpretation. In my view, it applies to all three themes, at least with regard to changes in the field of moral theology influenced by Vatican II.

Consequently, I believe that *Evangelium Vitae* is a model of magisterial moral theology done in the spirit of Vatican II. One need not agree with each and every element of its analysis to appreciate the manner in which it incorporates and reflects O'Malley's key themes. Like *Gaudium et Spes*, *Evangelium Vitae* is realistic about the new threats to human life and dignity it identifies in the contemporary world, particularly in the contemporary West. It also reflects the pastoral constitution's fundamentally positive approach, in its rhetorically appealing and remarkably detailed call to build a "culture of life" in which each and every human being is respected, protected, and even loved.

Unfortunately, the image of *Evangelium Vitae* in the United States has been distorted by its place in the "culture wars." The major distortions are two. First, far from being a clarion call to care for the vulnerable and marginalized, building a "culture of life" all too often is reduced to politi-

---

35. Perhaps reflecting the tensions between legal and pastoral forms of discourse, there are in fact two official English texts of this passage. This version is taken from: http://www.vati can.va/edocs/ENG0141/__P10.HTM. There is also a later version that reads, "To the same Father and his mercy you can with sure hope entrust your child," from http://www.vatican.va/holy_fa ther/john_paul_ii/encyclicals/documents/hf_jp-ii_enc_25031995_evangelium-vitae_en.html. Apparently, after the first set of vernacular editions were issued, the Latin edition toned down the pope's assurances to reflect the fact that the church does not teach with certainty that unbaptized babies go to heaven. The Vatican then issued a second official translation — without, however, withdrawing the first.

cal opposition to the "culture of death," to the preservation or imposition of legal strictures against abortion, euthanasia, cloning, stem cell research, and gay marriage. It has no positive content of its own.[36] Seemingly lost is John Paul II's clear recognition that effective legal protection for vulnerable human persons must include not only legal prohibitions against taking their lives, but also positive forms of support for them and their nearly equally vulnerable caregivers.

Second, in the American context, the struggle between the "culture of life" and the "culture of death" tends overwhelmingly to be described in terms of "war." This in turn leads to seeing political opponents as enemies who must be defeated at all costs, rather than as fellow citizens who must be persuaded and enlightened. In contrast to many American culture warriors, John Paul II is a teacher, not a soldier. In his hands, the culture of life is positive; it is also extremely attractive. Evangelization is a process of communicating good news, not least by modeling what a life transformed by good news would look like.

In my view, American Catholics would do well to reread *Evangelium Vitae* in light of John O'Malley's account of the Second Vatican Council, rather than interpreting it in the context of our national political controversies. Doing so would allow us to see clearly that like the fathers of the council, John Paul II is offering us a call to holiness — not a call to arms.

36. See, for example, the website of the "Culture of Life Foundation," http://www.culture-of-life.org/.

# Vatican II and the Postconciliar Magisterium on the Salvation of the Adherents of Other Religions

*Francis A. Sullivan, S.J.*

In John O'Malley's masterful work *What Happened at Vatican II*, of the three issues he proposed as a key to understanding the council, he gave first place to that of maintaining the church's identity while dealing with the inevitability of change. He noted that John Courtney Murray had "put his finger on this first issue" when he called development of doctrine "*the* issue under the issues" at Vatican II.[1] Murray was no doubt referring to development that resulted in a change in Catholic doctrine, such as on religious freedom. The question I am asking is whether, in the documents of Vatican II and of the postconciliar magisterium, one can recognize a development resulting in change in the doctrine of the Catholic Church concerning the salvation of the millions of people who can be expected to live and die as adherents of non-Christian religions other than Judaism and Islam.[2] Specifically, my questions are the following: (1) Has there been such a development on the question of the role that the Catholic Church plays in the salvation of those non-Christians whom it does not reach with its missionary activity? (2) Has there been such a development on the question whether their own religions play a role in their salvation? I shall begin by recalling the official doctrine of the Catholic Church on these questions during the century prior to the Second Vatican Council.

The first pope to teach that non-Christians can be saved without ever becoming Christians was Pius IX, who in 1863 declared that "those who la-

---

1. John O'Malley, S.J., *What Happened at Vatican II* (Cambridge, MA, and London: Belknap/Harvard University Press, 2008), pp. 8-9.

2. I shall not treat questions concerning the salvation of Jews, or of Muslims, whose faith is based in part on biblical revelation.

bor in invincible ignorance concerning our most holy religion and who, assiduously observing the natural law and its precepts which God has inscribed in the hearts of all, and being ready to obey God, live an honest and upright life can, through the working of divine light and grace, attain eternal life."[3] Seven years later, at the First Vatican Council, a draft of a Constitution on the Church was prepared that followed the doctrine of Pius IX on this issue. However, only the articles of this draft that dealt with the papacy became conciliar doctrine.

In 1943 Pope Pius XII issued an encyclical on the *Mystical Body of Christ* in which he insisted on a strict identity between the Mystical Body and the Catholic Church, with the result that only Catholics were really its members. Referring to those who were not its members, meaning both other Christians and non-Christians, he wrote:

> We urge each and every one of them to be prompt to follow the interior movements of grace, and to seek earnestly to rescue themselves from a state in which they cannot be sure of their own salvation. For even though, by a certain unconscious desire and wish, they may be related to the Mystical Body of the Redeemer, they remain deprived of so many and so powerful gifts and helps from Heaven, which can be enjoyed only within the Catholic Church.[4]

Here, most likely through the influence of Sebastian Tromp, S.J., his principal collaborator in the writing of this encyclical, Pius XII introduced the ideas proposed back in the sixteenth century by the Jesuits Bellarmine and Suárez, that those who are not actually members of the church can be saved by the desire of belonging to it, and that even an implicit desire of belonging can suffice. It is true that the pope did not actually say that non-Christians can be saved, but this is surely implied by his saying that they may be related to the Mystical Body "by a certain unconscious desire."

That this was the correct interpretation of the encyclical was confirmed six years later by a letter of the Holy Office addressed to Archbishop Richard Cushing of Boston, which rejected the rigid interpretation of "No salvation outside the church" that was being propagated by Leonard Feeney, S.J. Here the Holy Office said:

3. *Quanto conficiamur moerore*, in *Enchiridion Symbolorum Definitionum et Declarationum de rebus fidei et morum*, ed. Henricus Denzinger and Adolfus Schoenmetzer, S.J., 34th ed. (Freiburg: Herder, 1967), document 2866 (hereafter cited as D-S).

4. *Acta Apostolicae Sedis* 35 (1943): 242-43.

To gain eternal salvation it is not always required that a person be incor-porated in reality *(reapse)* as a member of the church, but it is required that he belong to it at least in desire and longing *(voto et desiderio)*. It is not always necessary that this desire be explicit, as it is with catechu-mens. When a man is invincibly ignorant, God also accepts an implicit desire, so called because it is contained in the good dispositions of soul by which a man wants his will to be conformed to God's will. This is clearly taught by the Sovereign Pontiff Pope Pius XII in his doctrinal let-ter on the mystical Body of Christ.[5]

To sum up: on the question of the role that the church plays in the sal-vation of non-Christians, the official Catholic doctrine prior to Vatican II was that membership in the Catholic Church is so necessary, that in order to gain eternal salvation, non-Christians must belong to this church at least by an implicit desire. On the other hand, the official documents of this period say nothing that could throw light on the question whether their own religions could play a positive role in their salvation.

## The Doctrine of Vatican II on the Salvation of Non-Christians: The Successive Drafts and Final Text of *Lumen Gentium*

The draft of the Dogmatic Constitution on the Church that was discussed by the council for one week in 1962 echoed the teaching of Pius XII and the further explanation given by the Holy Office in its letter to Archbishop Cushing, asserting that "no one can obtain salvation unless one is a mem-ber of the church, or is related to it by desire." It further explained:

It is not only catechumens, who, moved by the Holy Spirit, aspire to en-ter the church with a conscious and explicit intention, who are related to the church by desire; but others also who do not know that the Cath-olic Church is the only true Church of Christ, can, through the grace of God, obtain a similar effect through an implicit and unconscious de-sire. This is the case whether they sincerely wish what Christ himself wishes, or, not knowing Christ, they sincerely desire to fulfill the will of God their Creator. For the gifts of heavenly grace are by no means lack-

---

5. D-S 3870-71. English trans. in Josef Neuner and Jacques Dupuis, eds., *The Christian Faith in the Doctrinal Documents of the Catholic Church*, 7th ed. (Alba House, 2001), pp. 855-56.

ing to those who, with a sincere heart, wish and seek to be renewed by divine light.[6]

This first draft, which had been drawn up by the Preparatory Theological Commission, received such severe criticism that it was withdrawn at the end of the first period, and a substantially new draft was discussed during the month of October in 1963. This followed the previous one in teaching that those who are not members of the Catholic Church can be joined to it through an implicit desire to belong to it. The treatment of the question begins with catechumens.

> Catechumens who, moved by the Holy Spirit, knowingly and explicitly seek to be incorporated in the church, are joined with it by desire. These people Mother Church embraces with her love and care. In its own way the same is true of those who, not knowing that the Catholic Church is the one true church of Christ, sincerely, with the help of grace, seek to fulfill the will of Christ, or, if they lack specific knowledge of Christ, seek, with internal faith, hope and charity, to do the will of God the Creator, who wishes every one to be saved.[7]

It is obvious that the phrase "In its own way the same is true" means that, although they will not have an explicit desire as catechumens do, both non-Catholic Christians and non-Christians can be joined to the Catholic Church (and thus be saved) by a desire that will be expressed in their sincere effort to do the will of Christ or of God.

In the 1963 draft there is a new article with the title: "Concerning Non-Christians as People to Be Drawn to the Church." The main theme of this article is the obligation of the church to evangelize non-Christians. However, it includes a positive statement about those who "in shadows and images seek the unknown God." Of these people it affirms: "Whatever of good is found among them is valued by the church as preparation for the Gospel and as light given by God, who from the beginning of the world effectively intends the salvation of all people."[8] This is the first appearance, in the successive drafts of what became *Lumen Gentium*, of a positive state-

6. *Acta Synodalia Concilii Vaticani Secundi,* 25 vols. (Vatican City: Typis Polyglottis Vaticanus, 1970-96), IV/1, 18-19. The translation of passages from the drafts is my own. For the final texts I use *Decrees of the Ecumenical Councils,* ed. Norman P. Tanner, S.J. (Washington, DC: Georgetown University Press, 1990).

7. *Acta Synodalia* III/1, pp. 189-90.

8. *Acta Synodalia* II/1, p. 221.

ment about the good elements to be found among non-Christians. It is particularly noteworthy that these are described as "light given by God," which clearly means that they are seen as of divine origin, rather than as merely the fruit of human searching for God.

During the interval between the 1963 and 1964 periods of the council, the draft of the Constitution on the Church underwent a very considerable revision, which involved some important developments in the conciliar doctrine on the salvation of non-Christians. Among these developments is the striking fact that in the 1964 draft, and then in *Lumen Gentium,* the only persons who are described as being joined to the Catholic Church by a desire of belonging to it are catechumens. I have quoted above the brief paragraph of the 1963 draft, which first spoke of catechumens as being joined to the church by desire, and then said that "in its own way" this was true also of other Christians and non-Christians whose dispositions were such as to imply such a desire. The change made in the 1964 draft is that it retains only the sentence that refers to catechumens as being joined to the Catholic Church by desire. The rest of the paragraph, which spoke of non-Catholic Christians and non-Christians as being joined to the Catholic Church by an implicit desire, is simply omitted. The explanation for this omission, given by the doctrinal commission responsible for the revision, is as follows:

> The words of the previous text: *In its own way this is true . . .* are not retained by the Commission. That idea is better expressed in no. 15 (previously no. 9). Besides, non-Catholic Christians do not have a desire of baptism, but baptism itself. Hence they cannot be placed in the same line with the non-baptized. Many Fathers spoke in this sense.[9]

This explanation makes it clear that what the commission wished to correct was the idea that non-Catholic Christians are joined to the Catholic Church merely by a desire to belong to it. With their revision of no. 9 of the 1963 draft (now no. 15 of the 1964 text), the commission had more fully explained the many ways, such as by Christian faith and sacraments, in which non-Catholic Christians are joined to the Catholic Church. What the commission was concerned about was the fact that the previous drafts, and, indeed, *Mystici Corporis,* which they had followed on the doctrine of the *votum ecclesiae,* had failed to take into account the difference between

9. *Acta Synodalia* III/1, p. 203.

the baptized and the nonbaptized as far as their bond with the Catholic Church was concerned. On the other hand, this revision of the text also removed the reference to the idea that non-Christians can have a salvific bond with the church by an implicit desire of belonging to it. It is not clear that the commission actually intended to exclude this idea, but in fact there is no reference in *Lumen Gentium* or in any other document of Vatican II to the idea that the salvation of non-Christians depends on their having an implicit desire of belonging to the church.

While the 1964 draft of *Lumen Gentium* does not speak of non-Christians as being related or ordered to the church by implicit desire, it does speak of them as ordered to the church "in various ways." This is first expressed in the final paragraph of the new Article 13, which the commission added to the chapter on the People of God on the theme of its catholicity. This final paragraph reads: "Therefore to this catholic unity of the people of God, which prefigures and promotes universal peace, all are called, and they belong to it or are ordered to it in various ways, whether they be Catholic faithful or others who believe in Christ or finally all people everywhere who by the grace of God are called to salvation."[10]

Given the fact that baptism is the sacrament by which people are incorporated into the church, it would seem that "those who belong to it" are the baptized, both Catholics and non-Catholics, while all others, being called by God's grace to salvation, are "ordered to it in various ways." The commission further spelled out these "various ways" in its revision of the article that had treated non-Christians as "people to be drawn to the church." Leaving the missionary work of the church to be handled in Article 17, the commission prepared a new article (16) on non-Christians as "those who, not having yet accepted the Gospel, are ordered to the people of God in various ways."

Five groups of people are mentioned, distinguished from one another on the basis of the knowledge of God that is characteristic of each group. They are listed in a descending order, from those whose knowledge of God is based, at least in part, on biblical revelation, to those who have not yet arrived at an explicit knowledge of God. First are the Jewish people, followed by the Muslims, who "acknowledge the Creator . . . [and] along with us adore the one and merciful God." Then come "those who in shadows and images seek the unknown God." Presumably the council is here referring to those who belong to one of the major non-Christian religions such

---

10. *Acta Synodalia* III/1, p. 187.

as Hinduism or Buddhism. The next paragraph describes the rest of non-Christians as either having, with God's grace, arrived at some knowledge of God and his will as it is known to them through the dictates of conscience, or as not having arrived at an explicit knowledge of God, but as striving to live a good life.

It is not difficult to see how Jews and Muslims are related to the church by their knowledge of God, since we share belief in the one God on the basis of biblical revelation. However, it is not clear how other non-Christians are related to the church by the knowledge of God to which they have arrived. On the other hand, this paragraph insists, again and again, on something by which all these different categories of people can be said to be "ordered to the church," namely, that they are all included in God's plan of salvation, and that they all receive the divine grace by which they can be saved. The idea that non-Christians are ordered to the church by the universal offer of saving grace is not expressed in the text, but it is significant that in its *relatio* on this article the doctrinal commission said: "Christ has objectively redeemed all men, and he calls and directs them to the church. All grace has a certain communitarian quality, and looks toward the church."[11] This can be understood in the sense that the ultimate goal of every offer of grace is that the person might be numbered among all those who "from Abel, the just one, to the last of the elect, will be gathered together with the Father in the universal church" (*LG* 2). Grace whose goal is participation in the "universal church" of the eschatological kingdom of God will also be ordered toward the church in its earthly state.

I suggest that we have here an answer to the question whether there has been a development, in the successive drafts of *Lumen Gentium,* on the question of the role of the Catholic Church in the salvation of non-Christians. Rather than being related to the church by an implicit desire of belonging to it, they are now understood to be ordered to it by the saving grace which God offers to them. While they remain "ordered" to the church whether they respond positively to grace or not, one can also conclude that if they do respond in such a way as to be justified, they will be related to the church by a spiritual communion in the grace of Christ, even though they do not know him as its source.

The question remains as to whether *Lumen Gentium* throws any light on the question whether the church not only is the goal toward which non-Christians are ordered by the offer of saving grace, but also plays

11. *Acta Synodalia* III/1, p. 206.

74

some role in the offering of that grace. I suggest that we have a positive answer to this question in the council's description of the church as the "universal sacrament of salvation." Vatican II introduced the notion of the church as "sacrament" in the first article of *Lumen Gentium,* describing it as being "in Christ as a sacrament or instrumental sign of intimate union with God and of the unity of all humanity." This makes it clear that the council's intention is to explain the nature and purpose of the church by comparing it with the sacraments, which are understood to be signs that have an instrumental role in causing the grace they signify. This idea is spelled out in *LG* 9, where it says of the church that "it is taken up by Christ as the instrument of salvation for all, and sent as a mission to the whole world as the light of the world and as the salt of the earth." Later on, in *LG* 48, the universal role of the church in salvation is stressed in a description of the establishment of the church. "Christ, when he was lifted up from the earth, drew all people to himself; rising from the dead, he sent his life-giving Spirit down on his disciples, and through him he constituted his body which is the church as the universal sacrament of salvation."

We now have an answer to the question whether the church plays an active role in the salvation of non-Christians whom the church does not reach with its ministry. As "universal sacrament of salvation," it must serve in some way as efficacious sign of their salvation. Even though there are many non-Christians to whom the church is not visibly present, it is, nevertheless, the unique social and public sign of the saving work that the Holy Spirit is doing "in a manner known only to God." I suggest that the church's effective role in the offering of Christ's grace to those whom it does not otherwise reach may be understood as accomplished through its celebration of the Eucharist. The Council of Trent, in its teaching on the Mass, says:

> In this divine sacrifice which is performed in the Mass, the very same Christ is contained and offered in a bloodless manner who made a bloody sacrifice of himself once for all on the cross. . . . For the benefits of that bloody sacrifice are received in the fullest measure through the bloodless offering.[12]

Vatican II, in its Constitution on the Sacred Liturgy, says: "It is through the liturgy, especially in the divine sacrifice of the eucharist, that the act of our

---

12. D-S 1743.

redemption is being carried out" (*Sacrosanctum Concilium* 1). The universal efficacy of this sacrifice is expressed in the new eucharistic prayers as
well. In the third we pray: "Lord, may this sacrifice which has made our
peace with you, advance the peace and salvation of all the world," and in
the fourth: "We offer you his body and blood, the acceptable sacrifice
which brings salvation to the whole world." The fact that only the church
can offer this sacrifice justifies describing the church as efficacious sign of
the salvation of non-Christians even when it cannot play a more directly
instrumental role by preaching the gospel to them.

Having seen that in its teaching on the church as universal sacrament
of salvation Vatican II has offered a new answer to the question of the
church's role in the salvation of non-Christians whom it does not reach
with its ministry, we turn now to the question whether *Lumen Gentium*
has offered any new light on the question whether their own religions may
play a positive role in their salvation.

I have noted above that the article of the 1963 draft on "Non-
Christians to be drawn to the church" included the positive statement that
"whatever goodness is found among them is considered by the church as a
preparation for the Gospel and as light given by God." The revised Article
16 strengthens this by saying: "Whatever goodness *and truth* is found
among them. . . ." I believe one would search in vain for any statement of
the magisterium prior to Vatican II that affirmed that one could find elements of goodness and truth among non-Christians, or that such things
should be recognized as light given by God. This is a first suggestion that
there may be elements of divine revelation in what non-Christians believe
and practice.

The new Article 17, "On the missionary character of the church," also
introduced a positive statement about the good to be found among non-
Christians. "The result of the church's activity is that whatever good is
found to be sown in the people's hearts and minds, or in their particular
rites and customs, is not only saved from destruction, but is made whole,
raised up and brought to completion to the glory of God." Here the mention of rites can be seen as the first positive reference to non-Christian religions in the documents of Vatican II. The term "sown" *(seminatum)* implies a reference to St. Justin's notion "seeds of the Word," which, as we
shall see, was invoked by the council several times in later documents.

What we have found in the 1964 draft of the Constitution on the
Church concerning the salvation of non-Christians became official
conciliar doctrine when *Lumen Gentium,* having been approved by the

overwhelming majority of the council fathers, was promulgated by Pope Paul VI toward the end of the third period, on November 21, 1964. Since the other conciliar documents that we will consider were revised during the fourth period, those responsible for their final revision were able take account of what had been said in *Lumen Gentium.*

## *Nostra Aetate:* The Declaration on the Church's Relation to Non-Christian Religions

As we have seen above, in Article 16 of *Lumen Gentium* the description of the various categories of non-Christians began with the Jews, and continued in descending order, from those whose knowledge of God is based, at least in part, on biblical revelation to those who have not yet arrived at an explicit knowledge of God. *Nostra Aetate* follows the opposite order, beginning with people who have a "certain perception of that unseen force which is present in the course of things and in events in human life," going on to speak of the Muslims and ending with its more extended treatment of the Jews. (As is well known, this decree began as a "Declaration on the Jews," and during the course of the council was expanded to include a treatment of Islam and other non-Christian religions.) As I have done with regard to *Lumen Gentium,* I shall limit my comments on these documents to what is said in them about those other religions.

In the case of *Nostra Aetate,* this means considering only what it says in Article 2. With regard to those who have "a certain perception of that unseen force which is present in the course of things and in events in human life," it goes on to say that sometimes there is found among them "an acknowledgement of a supreme deity or even of a Father," which "permeates their lives with a deep religious sense." It then speaks in some detail of Hinduism and Buddhism, as "religions associated with the development of civilization, which strive to answer these questions with more refined ideas and more highly developed language." Finally, it speaks of other religions that "strive in various ways to relieve the anxiety of the human heart by suggesting 'ways,' that is, teachings and rules of life as well as sacred rites." Referring to all those religions, it declares: "The Catholic Church rejects nothing of those things which are true and holy in these religions. It regards with respect those ways of acting and living and those precepts and teachings which, though often at variance with what it holds and expounds, frequently reflect a ray of that truth which enlightens everyone."

In this final phrase one can hardly fail to recognize an echo of John 1:9: "the true light which enlightens everyone was coming into the world." This means recognizing that "the ways of acting and living, the precepts and teachings" of religions that are not based on biblical revelation frequently reflect the divine light which the Word of God brought into the world.

This suggests that elements of divinely revealed truth may be found in a religion that is not based on biblical revelation. If this is so, it would seem to follow that such revealed truth would provide the basis for a response of supernatural faith.

## *Ad Gentes:* The Decree on the Missionary Activity of the Church

This decree begins by describing the church as "sent by God to the nations to be the universal sacrament of salvation," thus appropriating the sacramental understanding of the nature and mission of the church that had become official Catholic doctrine by the promulgation of *Lumen Gentium.* Above I have drawn a conclusion from the notion "universal sacrament of salvation" with regard to the church's role in the salvation of those who are not reached by its missionary activity. Here, however, the focus is on that activity, so that the conclusion is rather that the church "strives to proclaim the Gospel to all humankind."

What is first said about non-Christian religions in Article 3 of this decree would suggest that they are purely human efforts to seek God, but the sentence goes on to recognize that those efforts may lead towards the true God. The text is worth quoting.

> This all-embracing plan of God for the salvation of the human race is accomplished not only as it were secretly in their souls, or through the efforts, including religious efforts, by which they seek God in many ways . . . for these efforts need to be guided and corrected, even though in the loving design of God's providence they can at times be regarded as leading towards the true God or as paving the way for the gospel message.

Furthermore, a later passage recognizes that people who have not heard the gospel can already be gifted with faith. "God, through ways known to himself, can lead people who through no fault of their own are ignorant of the Gospel, to that faith without which it is impossible to please him" (Article 7).

Article 9 recognizes the presence of elements of truth and grace among people still to be evangelized, and describes these as "a secret presence of God, so to speak," which the church's missionary activity "frees from evil infections and restores to Christ their source." Then it repeats the statement already made in *Lumen Gentium* 17 that "whatever good is found to be sown in the minds and hearts of people or in their particular rites and cultures not only does not perish but is healed, elevated and perfected, to the glory of God, the confusion of the devil and the happiness of humankind." As I have suggested above, the reference to good "sown" can well be seen as recalling the idea of "seeds of the Word." This is confirmed by what is said in Article 11, which encourages missionaries to become familiar with people's national and religious traditions, and "with joy and reverence discover the seeds of the Word which lie hidden in them."

Finally, Article 15 says that the Holy Spirit, "who calls all to Christ by means of the seed of the Word and the preaching of the Gospel, stirs up in their hearts the submission of faith." I think this can be understood to mean that the Holy Spirit first calls non-Christians to Christ by the "seeds of the Word" that lie hidden in their own traditions, and that in this way the Spirit may stir up in their hearts the submission of faith even before they hear the preaching of the gospel.

## *Gaudium et Spes:* Pastoral Constitution on the Church in the World of Today

This Constitution has an important statement about the salvation of non-Christians in its Article 22. It begins with what is true of Christians, and goes on to apply this to "all people of good will."

> Christians are certainly subject to the need and the duty to struggle against evil through many tribulations and to suffer death; but they share in the paschal mystery and are configured to the death of Christ, and so are strengthened in the hope of attaining to the resurrection. This applies not only to Christians but to all people of good will in whose hearts grace is secretly at work. Since Christ died for everyone, and since the ultimate calling of each of us comes from God and is therefore a universal one, we are obliged to hold that the Holy Spirit offers to everyone the possibility of sharing in this paschal mystery in a manner known to God.

When we think about people "in whose hearts grace is secretly at work," we should recall what was said in *Ad Gentes* 3: "The all-embracing plan of God for the salvation of the human race is accomplished not only as it were secretly in their souls. . . ." In other words, in his sacramental economy of salvation God also uses visible means to lead people to himself. This raises the question whether, in leading non-Christians to himself, God uses their own religions as such means. In Karl Rahner's opinion, this question was not answered in the documents of Vatican II. Here is one way he expressed this view.

> In more than a millennium of struggle theology has overcome Augustinian pessimism in regard to the salvation of the individual and reached the optimism of the Second Vatican Council, assuring supernatural salvation in the immediate possession of God to all those who do not freely reject it through their own personal fault; our question now must be whether theology can regard the non-Christian religions with the same optimism.[13]

It is obvious that when Rahner said "our question now," he meant "after Vatican II." We must now see what the postconciliar magisterium has said on his question.

## Documents of the Postconciliar Magisterium: Paul VI and *Evangelii Nuntiandi*

In his postsynodal apostolic exhortation *Evangelii Nuntiandi,* Pope Paul VI spoke of the non-Christian religions in very positive terms.

> The church respects and esteems these non-Christian religions because they are the living expression of the soul of vast groups of people. They carry within them the echo of thousands of years of searching for God, a quest which is incomplete but often made with great sincerity and righteousness of heart. They possess an impressive patrimony of deeply religious texts. They have taught generations of people to pray. They are all impregnated with innumerable "seeds of the Word" and can constitute a true "preparation for the Gospel," to quote a felicitous

13. "On the Importance of the Non-Christian Religions for Salvation," in *Theological Investigations,* vol. 18 (New York: Crossroad, 1983), pp. 288-95, at 291.

term used by the Second Vatican Council and borrowed from Eusebius of Caesarea.[14]

However, in the next paragraph, Paul VI dwelt on the contrast between those religions and the religion of Jesus Christ.

> Even in the face of natural religious expressions most worthy of esteem, the church finds support in the fact that the religion of Jesus, which she proclaims through evangelization, objectively places man in relation with the plan of God, with his living presence and with his action; she thus causes an encounter with the mystery of divine paternity that bends over towards humanity. In other words, our religion effectively establishes with God an authentic and living relationship which the other religions do not succeed in doing, even though they have, as it were, their arms stretched towards heaven.

It is not clear to me how Paul VI reconciled those two aspects of this thought. If non-Christian religions are "all impregnated with innumerable seeds of the Word," how can they be merely natural expressions of religious striving toward God?

## John Paul II: *Redemptor Hominis*

In this, his first encyclical, Pope John Paul II already expressed that aspect of his thought about non-Christians that would become the key element of his teaching in their regard. This is respect for the presence and activity of the Holy Spirit in them and in their religions — a presence and activity that can be seen in their practice of virtue, their spirituality, and their prayer. We see this in the following passages of the encyclical.

> What we have just said must be applied     although in another way and with the due difference — to activity for coming closer together with the representatives of the non-Christian religions, an activity expressed through dialogue, contacts, prayer in common, investigation of the treasures of human spirituality, in which, as we know well, the members of those religions are also not lacking.[15]

14. *Evangelii Nuntiandi* 53.
15. *Redemptor Hominis* 6.

The missionary attitude always begins with a feeling of deep esteem for "what is in man," for what man has himself worked out in the depths of his spirit concerning the most profound and important problems. It is a question of respecting everything that has been brought about in him by the Spirit, which "blows where it wills."[16]

## John Paul II: *Dominum et Vivificantem*

In this encyclical Pope John Paul II further developed his theme of the universal activity of the Holy Spirit.

> We cannot limit ourselves to the 2,000 years which have passed since the birth of Christ. We need to go further back, to embrace the whole of the action of the Holy Spirit even before Christ — from the beginning, throughout the world and especially in the economy of the old covenant. For this action has been exercised in every place and at every time, indeed, in every individual, according to the eternal plan of salvation whereby this action was to be closely linked with the mystery of the incarnation and redemption, which in its turn exercised its influence on those who believed in the future coming of Christ. . . . But we need to look further and go further afield, knowing that "the wind blows where it wills," according to the image used by Jesus in his conversation with Nicodemus. The council, centered primarily on the theme of the church, reminds us of the Holy Spirit's activity also "outside the visible body of the church." The council speaks precisely of "all people of good will in whose hearts grace works in an unseen way. For, since Christ died for all, and since the ultimate vocation of man is in fact one, and divine, we ought to believe that the Holy Spirit in a manner known only to God offers to every man the possibility of being associated with this paschal mystery."[17]

## John Paul II: *Redemptoris Missio*

In his encyclical "On the Permanent Validity of the Church's Missionary Mandate," Pope John Paul II offered the following explanation of the way

16. *Redemptor Hominis* 12.
17. *Dominum et Vivificantem* 53.

in which God makes salvation accessible for people who are brought up in other religions.

> The universality of salvation means that it is granted not only to those who explicitly believe in Christ and have entered the church. Since salvation is offered to all, it must be made concretely available to all. But it is clear that today, as in the past, many people do not have the opportunity to come to know or accept the Gospel revelation or to enter the church. The social and cultural conditions in which they live do not permit this, and frequently they have been brought up in other religious traditions. For such people salvation in Christ is accessible by virtue of a grace which, while having a mysterious relationship to the church, does not make them formally part of the church but enlightens them in a way which is accommodated to their spiritual and material situation. This grace comes from Christ; it is the result of his Sacrifice and is communicated by the Holy Spirit. It enables each person to attain salvation through his or her free cooperation.[18]

Later on in this encyclical, Pope John Paul II has more to say about that "mysterious relationship" between the church and the salvation of those "outside her visible boundaries." In this passage, the pope is arguing against those whose understanding of the kingdom of God "ends up either leaving very little room for the church or undervaluing the church in reaction to a presumed 'ecclesiocentrism' of the past, and because they consider the church herself only a sign, for that matter a sign not without ambiguity."[19] John Paul II insists that the church as sacrament is a sign that effects what it signifies. Furthermore, the opponents' notion of the kingdom of God tends to detach it from Christ and from the church. The pope replied:

> If the Kingdom is separated from Jesus, it is no longer the Kingdom of God which he revealed. . . . Likewise one may not separate the Kingdom from the church. It is true that the church is not an end unto herself, since she is ordered towards the Kingdom of God of which she is the seed, sign and instrument. Yet, while remaining distinct from Christ and the Kingdom, the church is indissolubly united to both. Christ endowed the church, his Body, with the fullness of the benefits and means of sal-

18. *Redemptoris Missio* 10.
19. *Redemptoris Missio* 17.

vation. The Holy Spirit dwells in her, enlivens her with his gifts and charisms, sanctifies, guides and constantly renews her. The result is a unique and special relationship which, while not excluding the action of Christ and the Spirit outside the church's visible boundaries, confers on her a specific and necessary role, hence the church's special connection with the Kingdom of God and of Christ, which she has "the mission of announcing and inaugurating among all peoples."[20]

The "unique and special relationship" that is spoken of here is no doubt the same as the "mysterious relationship" between the church and the grace that is accessible to people who are brought up in other religious traditions, of which the pope spoke in Article 5 of this encyclical. Now the pope goes further, declaring that the church has a "specific and necessary role" in the saving work that Christ and the Spirit are doing outside the church's visible boundaries. It is true that he does not explain in what that "specific and necessary role" consists, but this is not surprising, since it is conferred on the church by a unique and special relationship that he has also called "mysterious."

Later on in this encyclical, John Paul II returns to the theme that is most distinctive of his treatment of the salvation of non-Christians, that is, the universal presence and activity of the Holy Spirit. What is notable in the following passage is his insistence that the Spirit is active not only in non-Christians, but also in their cultures and religions.

> The Spirit, therefore, is at the very source of man's existential and religious questioning, a questioning which is occasioned not only by contingent situations but by the very structure of his being. The Spirit's presence and activity affect not only individuals but also society and history, peoples, cultures and religions. . . . Again, it is the Spirit who sows the "seeds of the Word" present in various customs and cultures, preparing them for full maturity in Christ. . . . Excluding any mistaken interpretation, the inter-religious meeting held in Assisi was meant to confirm my conviction that "every authentic prayer is prompted by the Holy Spirit, who is mysteriously present in every human heart. . . ." Whatever the Spirit brings about in human hearts and in the history of peoples, cultures and religions serves as a preparation for the Gospel, and can only be understood in reference to Christ.[21]

20. *Redemptoris Missio* 18.
21. *Redemptoris Missio* 28.

## John Paul II: *Ecclesia in Asia*

In his postsynodal exhortation *Ecclesia in Asia,* Pope John Paul II further developed this theme, to which he says the Synod Fathers also drew attention.

> Following the lead of the Second Vatican Council, the Synod Fathers drew attention to the multiple and diversified action of the Holy Spirit who continually sows the seeds of truth among all peoples, their religions, cultures and philosophies. This means that these religions, cultures and philosophies are capable of helping people, individually and collectively, to work against evil and to serve life and everything that is good.[22]

If one recognizes that non-Christian religions, in virtue of the "seeds of truth" which the Holy Spirit has sown in them, are "capable of helping people to work against evil and to serve everything that is good," could one not also recognize that those religions are capable of helping people respond positively to the grace of Christ which the Spirit is offering to them? The pope does not draw this conclusion, but it does seem to follow from what he has said about the work of the Spirit in those religions.

I conclude my treatment of the writings of Pope John Paul II by observing that he has shed significant light on both of the questions I am asking. With regard to the role of the church in the salvation of non-Christians, he insists that the grace which makes salvation accessible to them has a mysterious relationship to the church — a unique and special relationship that confers on her a specific and necessary role in their salvation. With regard to the role their own religions can play in this, I would point to what I have just quoted from *Ecclesia in Asia,* and the conclusion that I believe can reasonably be drawn from it.

I shall conclude my discussion of the postconciliar papal documents with a quotation from the address that John Paul II gave in 1987 to the plenary session of the Secretariat for Non-Christians. (He later changed its name to Pontifical Council for Interreligious Dialogue.)

> There remain many questions which we have to develop and articulate more clearly. How does God work in the lives of people of different religions? How does the saving activity of Jesus Christ effectively extend to

22. *Ecclesia in Asia* 15.

those who have not professed faith in him? In the coming years, these questions and related ones will become more and more important for the church in a pluralistic world, and pastors, with the collaboration of experienced theologians, must direct their studious attention to them.[23]

Among the experienced theologians who have directed their studious attention to these questions have been the members of the International Theological Commission, which in 1997 published the fruit of its study of these questions in its document: *Christianity and the World Religions.*[24] (Documents of the ITC do not have magisterial authority, but they cannot be published without the approval of the Prefect of the Congregation for the Doctrine of the Faith who presides over it.) First I will quote what the ITC has said about the role of the church in the salvation of non-Christians. It treats this in its section on the church as "universal sacrament of salvation."

> When it was presupposed that all would enter into contact with the church, the necessity of the church for salvation was understood above all as the necessity of belonging to it. Since the church has been made aware of her condition as a minority . . . the necessity of the universal salvific function of the church has become a matter of prime importance. This universal mission and this sacramental efficacy in the order of salvation have found their theological expression in calling the church the universal sacrament of salvation. . . . Thus the church is not only a sign, but also an instrument of the kingdom of God, which breaks out with force. The church carries out her mission as the universal sacrament of salvation in *martyria, leitourgia and diakonia.*[25]

Above I have suggested that one way the church may be understood to exercise its role as universal sacrament of salvation is through its celebration of the Eucharist. Here is how the ITC explains the way in which the church carries out her mission as universal sacrament of salvation in *leitourgia.*

> In the *leitourgia,* the celebration of the paschal mystery, the church fulfills her mission of priestly service in representing all humankind. In a

---

23. *Acta Apostolicae Sedis* 79 (1987): 1319-20.
24. This was published in *Origins* 27, no. 10 (14 August 1997): 149-66.
25. *Christianity and the World Religions,* pp. 74-75.

way that, in accord with God's will, it is efficacious for all men, it makes present the representation of Christ who "was made sin" for us (2 Cor. 5:21) and who in our place "was hanged on the tree" (Gal. 3:13) in order to free us from sin.[26]

After discussing the universal role of the church in salvation, the ITC turns to the question of the role that the non-Christian religions may be understood to play in the salvation of their adherents. It first recalls the teaching of Pope John Paul II on the presence and activity of the Holy Spirit not only in individual non-Christians, but also in their cultures and religions. It goes on to say:

> Given this explicit recognition of the presence of the Spirit of Christ in the religions, one cannot exclude the possibility that they exercise as such a certain salvific function, that is, despite their ambiguity, they help men achieve their ultimate end. In the religions is explicitly thematized the relationship of man with the Absolute, his transcendental dimension. It would be difficult to think that what the Holy Spirit works in the hearts of men taken as individuals would have salvific value and not think that what the Holy Spirit works in the religions and cultures would not have such value. The recent magisterium does not seem to authorize such a drastic distinction.[27]

> Salvation is obtained through the gift of God in Christ, but not without human response and acceptance. The religions can also help the human response, insofar as they impel man to seek God, to act in accord with his conscience, to live a good life. . . . The search for the good is in its ultimate sense a religious attitude (cf. *Veritatis Splendor* 9, 12). It is the human response to the divine invitation, which is always received through Christ. . . . The religions can therefore be, in the terms indicated, means helping the salvation of their followers, but they cannot be compared to the function that the church realizes for the salvation of Christians and those who are not.[28]

While the International Theological Commission has closely followed the teaching of Vatican II and of John Paul II on the salvation of non-Christians, it has clearly drawn conclusions from this teaching that go be-

26. *Christianity and the World Religions,* p. 77.
27. *Christianity and the World Religions,* p. 84.
28. *Christianity and the World Religions,* p. 86.

yond what either the council or the pope drew from it. We shall now see that the same is true of a document issued by a dicastery of the Roman Curia, which does enjoy a delegated magisterial authority in matters that fall within its competence. Its doctrinal statements must also receive the approval of the CDF.

## Pontifical Council for Interreligious Dialogue:
*Dialogue and Proclamation*

The preparation of this document was initiated by the Pontifical Council for Interreligious Dialogue, but because it was also to treat "proclamation," which falls under the competence of the Congregation for the Evangelization of Peoples, its further development was the result of collaboration between the two dicasteries.[29] While it does not throw new light on the question of the role of the church in the salvation of those who are not reached by its missionary activity, it does make significant statements about the role of non-Christian religions in the salvation of their adherents.

As one would expect, it begins its discussion of the modern Catholic evaluation of other religions by quoting some of the statements made by the Second Vatican Council on this issue. It concludes:

> These few references suffice to show that the council has openly acknowledged the presence of positive values not only in the religious life of individual believers of other religious traditions, but also in the religious traditions to which they belong. It attributed these values to the active presence of God through his Word, pointing also to the universal action of the Spirit. . . . From this it can be seen that these elements, as a preparation for the Gospel, have played and do still play a providential role in the divine economy of salvation.[30]

It then recalls the teaching of Pope John Paul II, stressing his reflections on the "mystery of unity" which was manifested at Assisi, "in spite of the differences between religious professions." The Pontifical Council goes on to say:

29. This document was published in *Bulletin of the Pontifical Council on Inter-Religious Dialogue* 26, no. 2 (1991): 210-50.
30. *Dialogue and Proclamation* 17.

From this mystery of unity it follows that all men and women who are saved share, though differently, in the same mystery of salvation in Jesus Christ through his Spirit. Christians know this through their faith, while others remain unaware that Jesus Christ is the source of their salvation. The mystery of salvation reaches out to them, in a way known to God, through the invisible action of the Spirit of Christ. Concretely, it will be in the sincere practice of what is good in their own religious traditions and by following the dictates of their conscience that the members of other religions respond positively to God's invitation and receive salvation in Jesus Christ, even while they do not recognize or acknowledge him as their savior.[31]

Here the Pontifical Council, with the concurrence of the Congregation for the Evangelization of Peoples, made a more positive statement than had previously come from the Roman Magisterium about the role that non-Christian religions can play in the salvation of their adherents. However, the document went on immediately to say that it is difficult to identify in those traditions "elements of grace capable of sustaining the positive response of their members to God's invitation. It requires a discernment for which criteria have to be established. Sincere individuals marked by the Spirit of God have certainly put their imprint on the elaboration and the development of their respective religious traditions. It does not follow, however, that everything in them is good."[32]

One cannot simply say, therefore, that according to the Pontifical Council for Interreligious Dialogue, the sincere practice of their own religion is the way of salvation for non-Christians. Whether it can help them to respond to the grace of Christ depends on the presence in their religion of good elements that would dispose them to love their neighbor and to follow their conscience. For those who consistently choose to practice such good elements, it would seem to me that the presence in their religion of contrary elements would not exclude its recognition as a means that God has made available to help them attain salvation in Christ.

31. *Dialogue and Proclamation* 29.
32. *Dialogue and Proclamation* 30.

## Congregation for the Doctrine of the Faith: *Dominus Iesus: On the Unicity and Salvific Universality of Jesus Christ and the Church*

Here we are dealing with a document which, having been expressly approved by the pope, participates in his ordinary magisterium.[33] It does not, however, share his infallibility. In what follows, I shall first discuss what the CDF has said in this document about the universal role of the church in the salvation of humanity, and then about the role that the non-Christian religions can play in the salvation of their adherents.[34]

In the Introduction, the CDF says that as a consequence of certain relativistic theories by which the church's missionary proclamation is endangered today, a number of truths are held to have been superseded. One of these truths is "the universal salvific mediation of the church."[35] It is obvious that the CDF insists that each of these truths must be maintained. There can be no doubt that the term "universal salvific mediation" means that the church plays a mediating role also in the salvation of those whom it does not reach with its missionary activity. We shall see what further light this document provides on that mediating role.

In section 6, under the heading: "The Church and the Other Religions in Relation to Salvation," in explaining how the church is "universal sacrament of salvation" the CDF invokes the teaching of Pope John Paul II in *Redemptoris Missio* that for non-Christians, salvation in Christ is accessible by virtue of a grace that has a mysterious relationship to the church.[36] In the same place, the CDF says, "The church . . . has, in God's plan, an indispensable relationship with the salvation of every human being." This reflects, while it does not actually quote, the statement in *Redemptoris Missio*: "The result is a unique and special relationship which, while not excluding the action of Christ and the Spirit outside the church's visible boundaries, confers upon her a specific and necessary role."[37]

The "indispensable relationship which the church has with the salvation of every human being" is further specified by the CDF when it says:

33. Its teaching authority was thus explained by the CDF in its *Instruction on the Ecclesial Vocation of the Theologian*, no. 18.

34. *Dominus Iesus* was published in *Origins* 30, no. 14 (14 September 2000): 209-19. It is also available in *Sic et Non: Encountering Dominus Iesus*, ed. Stephen J. Pope and Charles Hefling (Maryknoll, NY: Orbis Books, 2002), pp. 3-23.

35. *Dominus Iesus*, in *Sic et Non*, p. 4.

36. *Dominus Iesus*, in *Sic et Non*, p. 20. Cf. *Redemptoris Missio* 10.

37. *Redemptoris Missio* 18.

"With the coming of the Savior Jesus Christ, God has willed that the church founded by him be the instrument for the salvation of *all* humanity." This is then described as a "truth of faith."[38] The church clearly has an instrumental role in the salvation of those to whom it preaches the gospel and offers the sacraments. But "all humanity" includes the great many people whom the church does not reach with its missionary activity. The church does not have the same kind of instrumental role in the salvation of people to whom it has not been able to preach the gospel. Perhaps this "truth of faith" can be understood in the sense that the church has a role of universal salvific mediation. As we have seen above, the International Theological Commission suggested that the church exercises this role of mediation for the salvation of people to whom it has not been able to preach the gospel, by its celebration of *leitourgia,* in which it offers "the acceptable sacrifice which brings salvation to the whole world."[39]

Now we must see what the CDF has said in *Dominus Iesus* that refers to the question whether non-Christian religions may play a role in the salvation of their adherents. As one would expect, the CDF has followed the lead of Vatican II and Pope John Paul II in recognizing the presence in those religions of "precepts and teachings" that "often reflect a ray of that truth which enlightens all men."[40] In treating the "sacred writings of the other religions," while denying that they should be called "inspired," the CDF says: "Certainly it must be recognized that there are some elements in these texts which may be de facto instruments by which countless people throughout the centuries have been and are able today to nourish and maintain their life-relationship with God." It goes on to say, "The sacred books of other religions, which in actual fact direct and nourish the existence of their followers, receive from the mystery of Christ the elements of goodness and grace which they contain."[41]

Another positive statement in *Dominus Iesus* about the elements contained in non-Christian religious traditions is the following:

> Certainly the various religious traditions contain and offer religious elements which come from God[42] and which are part of what "the Spirit

38. *Dominus Iesus* 22.
39. Fourth Eucharistic Prayer.
40. *Dominus Iesus* 2; *Nostra Aetate* 2.
41. *Dominus Iesus* 8.
42. The footnote reads: "These are the seeds of the divine Word *(semina verbi)* which the church recognizes with joy and respect."

brings about in human hearts and in the history of peoples, in cultures and in religions."[43] Indeed, some prayers and rituals of the other religions may assume a role of preparation for the Gospel, in that they are occasions or pedagogical helps in which the human heart is prompted to be open to the action of God. One cannot attribute to these, however, the divine origin or the *ex opere operato* efficacy which is proper to the Christian sacraments.[44]

Since it is certain that God provides to everyone the grace sufficient for their salvation, it is equally certain that God must also make it possible for everyone to arrive at the faith without which no one is justified. Such faith has to be a response to supernatural divine revelation. A question that arises here is whether those who are "invincibly ignorant of our most holy religion" can find in their own religions any divinely revealed truth to which they can respond with faith. There is a passage in *Dominus Iesus* which seems to deny this.

> The distinction between *theological faith* and *belief* in the other religions must be *firmly held.* If faith is acceptance in grace of revealed truth . . . then belief, in the other religions, is that sum of experience and thought that constitutes the human treasury of wisdom and religious aspiration which man in his search for truth has conceived and acted upon in his relationship to God and the Absolute. This distinction is not always borne in mind in current theological reflection. Thus theological faith (the acceptance of the truth revealed by the one and triune God) is often identified with belief in other religions, which is religious experience still in search of the absolute truth and still lacking assent to God who reveals himself. This is one of the reasons why the differences between Christianity and the other religions tend to be reduced at times to the point of disappearance.[45]

The first comment I would make on this passage is that it makes it clear that in *Dominus Iesus* the term "the other religions" is not meant to include Judaism or Islam, since their followers can have a faith that is

43. *Redemptoris Missio* 29.

44. *Dominus Iesus* 21. I have corrected the Vatican translation of the final sentence, which has "a divine origin or an *ex opere operato* efficacy," whereas the Italian has the definite article, and the Latin has "tribui nequit divina origo neve efficaccia illa quae christianorum sacramentorum est propria."

45. *Dominus Iesus* 7.

based, at least in part, on biblical revelation. A clear statement to that effect at the beginning of the document would have eliminated the misunderstanding that has led to some negative responses to it.[46]

My second comment is that it is not clear how the followers of those other religions can arrive at the faith that is necessary for their justification, if all they can find in their religions is "belief," understood as "religious experience still in search of the absolute truth and lacking assent to God who reveals himself." On the other hand, as we have seen above, in *Dominus Iesus* the CDF does recognize in those religions the presence of "precepts and teachings" that "often reflect a ray of that truth which enlightens all men." Are we to understand that the followers of those religions can arrive at supernatural faith by adhering to those precepts and teachings? The CDF does not answer this question in *Dominus Iesus,* but its more recently published *Notification* does suggest an answer to it.

## Congregation for the Doctrine of the Faith: *Dominus Iesus: Notification* on Toward a Christian Theology of Religious Pluralism by Father Jacques Dupuis, S.J.[47]

The reason the CDF gave for issuing this *Notification* concerning Jacques Dupuis is that the members of the congregation "found that his book contained notable ambiguities and difficulties on important points which could lead a reader to erroneous or harmful opinions." In order to "safeguard the doctrine of the Catholic faith from such harmful interpretations,"[48] the CDF composed this *Notification* as a series of ten propositions, setting forth the doctrines that Catholics "must firmly believe" or are "consistent with Catholic doctrine," and those that are "erroneous" or "have no foundation in Catholic theology." Several of these propositions deal with the role that non-Christian religions may play in the salvation of their adherents. Among these is the following:

> 4. It is consistent with Catholic doctrine to hold that the seeds of truth and goodness that exist in other religions are a certain participation in truths contained in the revelation of or in Jesus Christ. However, it is erroneous

46. For example, see the contributions by Ruth Langer and Qamar-ul Huda to the volume *Sic et Non,* ed. Pope and Hefling.

47. This *Notification* was published in *Origins* 30, no. 38 (8 March 2001): 605-7.

48. *Notification,* Preface.

to hold that such elements of truth and goodness, or some of them, do not derive ultimately from the source-mediation of Jesus Christ.

Here the intention of the CDF is to insist that since Jesus Christ is "the mediator, the fulfillment and the completeness of revelation,"[49] any divine revelation must be ultimately derived from him. But, provided that this is recognized, one may hold that the seeds of truth that exist in other religions are a certain participation in the revelation of Jesus Christ. I take this to mean that the CDF now agrees that the precepts and teachings of other religions that "reflect a ray of that truth which enlightens all men" are instances of divinely revealed truth to which, with the help of grace, the followers of other religions can respond with faith.

Another proposition, recognizing that non-Christian religions play a positive role in the salvation of their adherents, is found in the first part of no. 8:

> In accordance with Catholic doctrine, it must be held that "whatever the Spirit brings about in human hearts and in the history of peoples, cultures and religions, serves as a preparation for the gospel (cf. *Lumen Gentium* 16)."[50] It is therefore legitimate to maintain that the Holy Spirit accomplishes salvation in non-Christians also through those elements of truth and goodness present in the various religions.

Here we have a proposition that closely resembles the one made jointly by the Pontifical Council for Interreligious Dialogue and the Congregation for the Evangelization: "Concretely it will be in the sincere practice of what is good in their own religious traditions and by following the dictates of their conscience that the members of other religions respond positively to God's invitation and receive salvation in Jesus Christ, even while they do not recognize or acknowledge him as their savior."[51]

## Conclusion

In these official statements by organs of the Holy See we can recognize the striking development that has taken place in Catholic thinking about the

49. *Notification,* 3.
50. *Redemptoris Missio* 29.
51. *Dialogue and Proclamation* 29.

salvation of those who are "invincibly ignorant of our most holy religion." According to Pius IX, such people could be saved by the working of divine light and grace provided they observed the natural law. But there was no hint that Pius IX thought their own religions might provide elements of divinely revealed truth to which they could respond with faith, or elements of goodness that would dispose them to love their neighbor and respond positively to the saving grace that the Holy Spirit offered to them. This new way of thinking about the non-Christian religions is the fruit of a development that can have profound consequences for the peace of our religiously pluralistic world. It is, I submit, an instance of the kind of development that John Courtney Murray called "*the* issue under the issues at Vatican II," and to which John O'Malley gave first place among the three issues he proposed as a key to understanding what happened at Vatican II.

# The Catholic Church and Mission to the Jews

*John Connelly*

## Introduction

In recent years, nothing has vexed Catholic-Jewish relations more than the question of mission — the supposed duty of Christians to bring the gospel "to all nations" (Matthew 28). Some Catholics wonder why Jews should be excluded. Yet for Jews, converts from Judaism to Christianity are considered spiritually dead, "destroyed" *(meshumadim)* — manifestations in single human lives of age-old attempts to eradicate the Jewish people. When Benedict XVI announced a Good Friday Prayer in the spring of 2007 for the Jews "that God our Lord should illuminate their hearts, so that they will recognize Jesus Christ, the Savior of all men," the American Rabbi Michael Lerner was reminded of a history of forced conversions, expulsions, torture, and murder. For him the prayer was a "first step on a slippery slope toward the restoration of antisemitism in the Church as well as the restoration of authoritarian and feudal ways of thinking." Lerner had believed the Church put this past behind it at Vatican II, when it rejected the "call for conversion of the Jews."[1]

In fact the statement on the Jews in chapter 4 of the Vatican II declaration *Nostra Aetate* says nothing about converting Jews, and limits its vision

---

1. "After meeting with my teacher at the Jewish Theological Seminary, Abraham Joshua Heschel," Lerner explained, "Pope John XXIII was convinced that the call for conversion of the Jews was a central element in the process of demeaning Judaism, and so he sought to eliminate that teaching from the life of the Church, and instead to introduce the notion that Judaism should be thought of as a sister religion, not one that must be overcome and obliterated." Press release of 9 July 2007 at http://www.commonwealmagazine.org/blog/?p=1104 (10 May 2010).

to words taken from the minor prophet Zephaniah: "In company with the Prophets and the same Apostle [Paul], the Church awaits that day, known to God alone, on which all peoples will address the Lord in a single voice and 'serve him shoulder to shoulder' (Zeph. 3:9)." The statement neither includes nor excludes Jews, nor does it make clear whether final unity will occur within or beyond historical time. Yet it is true that the issue of converting Jews to Christianity was raised at the council, and indeed troubled the authors of *Nostra Aetate* more than any other issue, almost frustrating the production of a statement.

This is a lost story worth recovering, because the theologians at Vatican II rehearsed many of the points that have been debated in recent years. In what follows I try to recapture the contours of those forgotten debates about mission, then show how the issue has become muddled since the council's closing in 1965. Because the Vatican II heritage has been lost, the question of mission keeps returning to haunt Christian-Jewish relations.

Beyond instruction, this history also offers a couple of surprises. First, for all the talk these days of mission to the Jews, the Catholic Church of the modern period has devoted little to no resources to converting Jews. Its efforts at baptizing Jews appear as a tiny footnote in Christian missions to Jews, dwarfed by numerous well-funded Protestant enterprises extending into our own day. Second, those few Catholics who actively sought to convert Jews evolved into the Church's foremost opponents of anti-Semitism, and one of their number, Father John M. Oesterreicher, as a *peritus* at the Secretariat for Promoting Christian Unity, was the very person who contributed the compromise formula from Zephaniah cited above.

The Catholic Church did not fail to establish missions to the Jews out of tolerance. Before Vatican II the Church viewed itself as the "New Israel," having supplanted old Israel, which (following St. Augustine) had been maintained through postbiblical history in order to give unintended witness to the truth of Christianity. One day Jews would turn to Christ, yet the Church as a whole did not "target" Jews for conversion. In a book of 1978 Rabbi David Max Eichhorn explained why. "The Roman Catholic Church," he wrote, "makes no distinction between Jews and other non-Catholics. Therefore, as a denomination, it has operated no missions either in the United States or Canada specifically meant to convert Jews."[2] Internationally, one Catholic society existed focusing on Jews, the Notre Dame de

---

2. *Evangelizing the American Jew* (Middle Village, NY: Jonathan David Publishers, 1978), p. 158.

Sion order of priests and nuns, founded in 1852 by the convert brothers and priests, Marie-Théodore Ratisbonne and Marie-Alphonse Ratisbonne.[3] They established convents all over the world, yet those in North America confined their efforts to praying for the Jews' conversion.

## The Mission to the Jews of John M. Oesterreicher

Beyond this, Eichhorn mentions an Association of Prayer for the Conversion of Israel founded in Paris in 1903 — raised to an Archconfraternity by Pius X four years later — as well as an office of the Archdiocese of Vienna that existed between 1934 and 1938 with the aim of converting Jews, the *Opus Sancti Pauli*, directed by the Moravian convert priest John Oesterreicher — known before his emigration to the United States as Johannes.

Soon after German troops occupied Austria in March 1938, Oesterreicher made his way to Switzerland and then to Paris, where he spent time in libraries assembling arguments against racism and anti-Semitism for a book that appeared in early 1940 — only to be promptly pulped when the Gestapo entered that city.[4] By that point Oesterreicher was slipping out of Europe on an underground route that led to New York via Marseilles, the Pyrenees, and Portugal. His new domicile appeared to coincide well with his hope to reach more Jews.[5]

Yet he had enough experience with mission to tread lightly. In Vienna he had learned to avoid using that word at all costs because the Jews shrank back from it in horror. And though Oesterreicher believed that more Jews than ever were thinking of Jesus with "reverence and love," he also knew that Christ's followers often made baptism anything but inviting. "The persecutions of the past centuries have created a barrier that for many Jews is simply unbreakable," he confided to his friend the German theologian Karl Thieme in September 1945. "Please do not forget that many Jews first hear the name Christ in the form of the insult 'Christ murderer!' or in the accusation: 'You Jews nailed Christ to the cross!'"[6] Even in Vienna much of

---

3. They had first established a congregation of nuns in 1843.

4. It was reissued as John M. Oesterreicher, *Racisme — antisémitisme, antichristianisme* (New York: Éditions de la Maison Française, 1943).

5. Oesterreicher to Thieme, *Thieme Papers*, Institut für Zeitgeschichte (Munich) [hereafter: IfZG], ED 163/59, 10 May 1938.

6. September 1945 (undated), *Oesterreicher Papers*, Seton Hall University Library [hereafter: SHUL].

his ministry to the Jews was devoted to refuting arguments of Christian anti-Semites.

By 1946 Oesterreicher was corresponding with the Notre Dame de Sion leadership in France, hoping to bring their mission to northern America. Oesterreicher's correspondent, Father André Leroux, was not optimistic:

> About plans and methods of our founders concerning the mission for the Jews, I am afraid there is very little definite to be found. In their time, conversions were still rare exceptions. Fr. Theodore [Ratisbonne] thought that he had to provide only for the future, and so he did by founding the Sisters of Sion devoted to prayer and sacrifice. In fact, it was left to our generation to make out plans and look for methods. We tried [the] direct approach to the Jews: letters addressed to them. It proved a failure. In England for 25 years the Guild of Israel preached to them in open air. Scarcely any result. Except, that a certain amount of prejudices were dispelled. Finally, we came to the conclusion that besides prayer it was by preaching to Catholics, first, by fighting against antisemitism, by showing kindness to individual Jews and broad comprehension of the Jewish problems that we should best pave the way to reconciliation and eventually conversions.[7]

Oesterreicher confided in Father Leroux his own sense of the challenges awaiting apostles to the Jews. "The number of Jewish converts to the Church is very small in comparison with those to Protestantism," he wrote. "And there are numerous, almost countless Protestant missionary centers to evangelize the Jews, whereas the Catholic effort is very perfunctory." While there was "no sign of any movement . . . towards the Church among the Jews" there was "a great deal of bitterness." Jews wondered why the U.S. bishops had not stopped Father Coughlin, "whose attacks [against the Jews] were all the more dangerous because veiled."[8] Jews were antagonized by the "very common idea that antisemitism is caused by what is called the 'legend of the Jewish crucifixion'" and by Catholic "exclusivism," that is, a refusal to water down claims to the truth. "Liberal Protestantism" flattered Jews while keeping them "from understanding the true position of the Church." Protestants not only made better missionaries, they tended to infect Jews with their own anti-Catholicism.[9]

7. Leroux to Oesterreicher, *Oesterreicher Papers*, SHUL, 9 March 1948.

8. Oesterreicher to Leroux, *Oesterreicher Papers*, SHUL, 12 February 1946.

9. Jews were "influenced by the Protestant tradition in this country, and this tradition

Oesterreicher tried to adapt. He called a 1948 mass-produced brochure for Catholic teaching not "mission" but *Apostolate to the Jews.*[10] The war, he wrote, had made things more difficult, creating "a new barrier" for the Church, but "to an apostle, an obstacle can only be a challenge. When the horrors of the gas chambers became known they sent many Jews into anxiety and despair on the one hand, and on the other, drove them into irrational and feverish activities. More than ever they crave security, immuring themselves within a psychological ghetto."[11] The secularization of modern life supposedly caused "religious disintegration" and therefore "we might venture to say that a great many modern Jews have only some vague belief in God." In particular, Orthodox Jews encountered "extreme difficulty . . . among the complexities of the modern world."[12] Jews "held by many ties to the Jewish past, but greatly attracted to what gives itself out as 'progress,'" faced a "crisis." Rabbis themselves were saying they must send "Jewish missionaries to the Jews."[13] Yet for all its disintegrative powers, modernity could not destroy the Jewish people. "The Jews of all generations are held together by a bond not of their own making," Oesterreicher concluded, "not so much by their blood but by the will of God. They are preserved whether they know it or not, to give witness to Christ."[14]

By the early 1950s Oesterreicher's mission was failing even by his modest expectations. He offered courses in Catholicism to adults at St. Peter's Church (16 Barclay St.) in New York City, but, as he wrote to his Monsignor, the results were "rather disappointing." The "overwhelming majority of the people were Catholics and there were altogether only two converts who might not have come into the Church if it were not for these courses."[15] He hoped that St. Peter's might become a "center of my apostolate to the Jews, a point of radiation," yet he craved higher visibility, not a soap box or parish chapel from which he might catch the ear of un-

has always been hostile to the Catholic Church." Oesterreicher to Leroux, *Oesterreicher Papers,* SHUL, 12 February 1946.

10. He also spoke of "approach" rather than mission; see Oesterreicher, *The Apostolate to the Jews: A Study of the Church's Apostolate to the Jews, Its Theology, History, Methods and Present Needs* (New York: America Press, 1948), p. 6.

11. Oesterreicher, *The Apostolate,* p. 67.

12. Oesterreicher, *The Apostolate,* pp. 69-70.

13. Oesterreicher, *The Apostolate,* p. 71.

14. Oesterreicher, *The Apostolate,* pp. 70-71.

15. Oesterreicher to Msgr. Joseph Moore, undated (late 1952, early 1953). He had also lamented in a letter of 23 June 1951 (after his second course was concluding) that "there has not been a single convert I could call a fruit of the second course."

suspecting Jews on the streets of New York. He therefore went out to speak to audiences that wanted to hear him: American Catholics. In 1952 he was addressing Catholics in Indianapolis, Cincinnati, and points beyond.[16]

Hoping to intensify his "special work," in 1953 Oesterreicher opened an Institute for Judeo-Christian studies at Seton Hall University, where he published a quasi-scholarly journal on Jewish matters, *The Bridge*, with some pieces refuting anti-Semitic stereotypes, while others quarreled with Jewish authors about their faithfulness to Judaism.[17] During the 1950s no Jews wrote for him, and if there was interest at Seton Hall in Jewish thought, it was mainly to suggest openings to Christianity, as in Oesterreicher's major work of these years, *The Walls Are Crumbling: Seven Jewish Philosophers Discover Christ.*[18] At the outset the Judeo-Christian Institute was thus mission in another guise: Jews continued to exist, possessing legitimacy in terms of what they had done to prepare the world for Christ, and kept alive in order to become Christians.

Yet *The Bridge* also advanced neglected Catholic teaching, including the view that there could be salvation outside the Church. This was a point Oesterreicher's collaborator Father Edward Flannery underscored in a piece on the Finaly affair in which two baptized French Jewish boys who survived the Holocaust were returned to their family in Israel over much resistance. Flannery asked: "Must we despair at the salvation of the Finaly boys?" His answer was no: God wills that "all men be saved and brought to the knowledge of the truth." This was a view, here expressed by Charles Journet, upon which "all the theologians who treated the Finaly problem ended in one way or another."[19] Rebutting the common Christian view

---

16. He had half a dozen speaking engagements east of the Mississippi in late 1952, and he wrote his Monsignor that "many more retreats and lecture engagements . . . have been of fered to me." Oesterreicher to Msgr. Joseph Moore, *Oesterreicher Papers*, SHUL, 26 August 1952.

17. Oesterreicher to Msgr. Joseph Moore, *Oesterreicher Papers*, SHUL, 2 February 1951. Oesterreicher published the important piece by Pierre Charles, S.J., "The Learned Elders of Zion" (*The Bridge* 1 [1955]: 159-90), still cited in the history of uncovering the infamous hoax. He also published a work debating the loyalty of Jews to their own traditions.

18. (New York: Devin-Adair, 1952), with chapters on Marc Chagall, Edith Stein, Simone Weil, and Edmund Husserl. See Oesterreicher's letter to Thieme at the Feast of the Ascension 1954 (*Oesterreicher Papers*, SHUL): the point of *The Bridge* was to show how Jews were growing closer to Christians.

19. The French state and the French Catholic hierarchy decided in favor of the boys' extended family — and against their Christian temporary guardian. Edward H. Flannery, "The Finaly Case," *The Bridge* 1 (1955): 312. Flannery became the first Director of Catholic-Jewish

that Jews were dammed as Jews, Oesterreicher said that Jews were no more or less saved than anyone outside the Church. These were also the years in which Karl Rahner was developing his teaching on the pervasiveness of grace in the world after the coming of Christ, and its evident ("ordinary") availability to all human beings.[20] Such insights helped erode the edifice of mission.

In April 1961 John Oesterreicher received a letter from David W. Connor, a seminarian in New York who claimed to be "intensely interested in the work of converting our Jewish brethren." He had written a term paper on the Church's "organized efforts" in this regard, and "didn't dream that our efforts were so limited," especially compared to what the Protestants were doing. Had Oesterreicher realized his ambition for creating an "Institute of St. Peter," as described in the 1948 brochure *Apostolate to the Jews*?[21] Oesterreicher responded that there was no organization of this sort, nor was any diocese "assigning and training priests for the work of reconciliation between Church and Synagogue."[22] He thought there was no "hope of establishing a center like the one I outlined in 'The Apostolate to the Jews.'" The Institute of Judeo-Christian Studies at Seton Hall "differs from the proposed Institute of St. Peter mainly in these respects. It is an academic institution, its emphasis is on study and literary output, and its spirit is ecumenical rather than missionary." There was a parallel trend in the work of the sisters and fathers of Notre Dame de Sion.[23]

Why did Catholics not use "methods similar to those of Protestant missionary societies"? In part that was because "[s]ome of these methods are truly distasteful." Yet there was also "a great deal of inertia or lack of interest among Catholics. Not being as familiar with Holy Scripture as good Protestants are, they pay little attention to the role the Jewish people play in the economy of salvation." Oesterreicher also blamed trends in current

---

Relations for the Bishops' Committee for Ecumenical and Interreligious Affairs, serving from 1967 to 1976. In these years *The Bridge* also featured sympathetic portrayals of other non-Christians, including Simone Weil and Franz Werfel.

20. Wendell S. Dietrich, "*Nostra Aetate*: A Typology of Theological Tendencies," in *Unanswered Questions: Theological Views of Jewish-Catholic Relations,* ed. Roger Brooks (Notre Dame: University of Notre Dame Press, 1988).

21. Letter of 12 April 1961, *Oesterreicher Papers,* SHUL.

22. Letter to David Connor, *Oesterreicher Papers,* SHUL, 1 May 1961.

23. See for example the remarks of Joseph Lichten in 1971 about his work with the "Sisters of Zion and several other Catholic communities of men and women interested in education about Jews and Judaism." Doris Revere Peters, "Views 25 Years of Catholic-Jewish Relations," *Catholic Messenger* 26 (August 1971).

American society: "One of the reasons why so little is being done seems to be the lack of initiative among the Catholic faithful as well as priests. Like most Americans, perhaps even more so, we follow the trend or become overwhelmed by our daily routine." He continued:

> I shall not go on to describe this particular danger of American Catholic life, but the fact is that in the course of the years I have corresponded with and met many seminarians, diocesan and religious, who had a keen interest in the work of reconciliation between Church and Synagogue and a deep desire to do something. But when they left the seminary and got their various assignments, they became so preoccupied by their daily tasks that the desire has been lying dormant ever since or perhaps even died.[24]

At some point Connor shed his own interest in mission to the Jews. In the late 1960s he became a popular and politically active chaplain at Cornell University, a friend of the peace priests Philip and Daniel Berrigan, willing to take stands on issues of the day and practice active opposition. He became involved in interfaith work, and eventually left the priesthood and the Catholic Church, though he continued to work as pastor.[25]

## The Question of Mission at the Second Vatican Council

At the Second Vatican Council Oesterreicher got a chance to help formulate a new Catholic view of the Jewish people. From 1961 he served as advisor at the secretariat for Promoting Christian Unity, and helped draft the declaration *Nostra Aetate* (1965) on the Church's relations to non-Christian religions.[26] John O'Malley writes that the council's third session in the fall of 1964 was decisive in formulating a new vision of the Jewish people for the Catholic Church. The bishops broke into full debate during this session, reflecting the fault-line of O'Malley's narrative: those speaking most passionately for a strong condemnation of anti-Semitism tended to come from Transalpine countries and the United States, while oppo-

---

24. Letter to David Connor, *Oesterreicher Papers*, SHUL, 1 May 1961.

25. Connor was ordained in 1964 and served for a quarter century in Ithaca, NY, in part as Catholic chaplain at Cornell University (at Cornell's United Religious Work).

26. His position until 1963 was "consultor," and thereafter he was appointed *peritus*, or theological expert.

nents were from Mediterranean countries. At the center of their dispute were two issues: whether Jews could be considered responsible for killing Christ ("deicides"), and whether the Church should work for the conversion of Jews by any means whatsoever, including prayer.

Work on the statement on the Jews had begun in 1960 when John XXIII assigned the German Cardinal Augustin Bea to take up the question of the Jews among his tasks as President of the Secretariat for Promoting Christian Unity. No question proved more vexing for the council, and by the time of the bishops' great debate, opponents and supporters of a strong statement on the Jews had been gathering arguments and influence for over three years. Matters now came to a head because forces hostile to the statement succeeded in "doctoring" (in the words of Archbishop John Heenan of Westminster, Vice President of the Secretariat for Promoting Christian Unity) and thus weakening drafts of *Nostra Aetate* in the spring of 1964. Historians attribute the changes to authoritative members of the Roman Curia, operating with approval of Pope Paul VI, who was more ambivalent than his predecessor, and without the knowledge of Bea's Secretariat.[27] In the summer of 1964, the altered drafts were leaked to the public, and concern quickly focused on lines that raised the specter of Catholic mission to the Jews. The contested formulation read as follows: "It is also worth remembering that the union of the Jewish people with the Church is part of the Christian hope. Therefore, following the teaching of the Apostle (cf. Rom. 25) the Church waits with unshaken faith and deep longing for the entry of that people into the fullness of the people of God established by Christ."[28]

Knowledge of the changes stirred Rabbi Abraham Heschel to declare that he was "ready to go to Auschwitz any time if faced with the alternative of conversion or death."[29] The situation appeared so critical that the

27. They used concerns about Christian communities in the East as an excuse to forestall change. Studying remarks made on the texts, Miccoli traces the amendments undertaken in late June and early July 1964 to Paul VI and his immediate staff, including Luigi Ciappi, Master of the Sacred Palace. Miccoli concludes: "These reflections attest clearly to the deep hostility of authoritative members of the Curia to the direction taken in the declaration and to the basic reasons for it." Giovanni Miccoli, "Two Sensitive Issues: Religious Freedom and the Jews," in *History of Vatican II*, ed. Giuseppe Alberigo and Joseph A. Komonchak, vol. 4 (Leuven: Peeters, 2002), p. 150.

28. "Second Declaration on the Jews and Non-Christians," 28-29 September 1964, in *The Catholic Church and the Jewish People: Recent Reflections from Rome*, ed. Philip Cunningham, Norbert Hofmann, Joseph Sievers (New York: Fordham University Press, 2007), p. 195.

29. *Time*, 11 September 1964. The new draft was well known outside the Church. In a

American Jewish Committee arranged an audience for Heschel with the pope, after which the Rabbi left a lengthy theological memorandum for Bea's Secretariat.[30] Heschel had known Bea for several years, and through private meetings and memoranda (on behalf of the American Jewish Committee) urged a strong statement, with special concern for repudiation of deicide, recognition of the Jews' "permanent preciousness" before God, and a relinquishing of efforts at conversion.[31]

On 25 September 1964 Cardinal Bea presented the new draft to the 88th general congregation of the council, hoping to build consensus for revising it.[32] As a result of the bishops' discussion and debate, Archbishop Heenan announced in a speech four days later that "however good the intentions" of the redrafters, "the fact is that it has been taken badly by the Jews. For me that is sufficient reason for removing the quotation from the declaration."[33] Indeed, the offending paragraph was dropped when the *periti* began crafting a new draft based on the bishops' input, and, at Oesterreicher's suggestion within the Subcommittee for Jewish Affairs (of the Secretariat for Unity), replaced the offending text with the lines from Zephaniah quoted at the outset: "The Church awaits that day, known to God alone, on which all

---

statement of 3 September 1964 Heschel issued the following statement: "Jews throughout the world will be dismayed by a call from the Vatican to abandon their faith in a generation which witnessed the massacre of six million Jews and the destruction of thousands of synagogues on a continent where the dominant religion was not Islam, Buddhism, or Shintoism." Marc H. Tanenbaum, "Heschel and Vatican II — Jewish Christian Relations," paper presented at the Jewish Theological Seminary, 23 February 1983, p. 16, cited in Eva Fleischner, "Heschel's Significance for Jewish/Christian Relations," in *Abraham Joshua Heschel: Exploring His Life and Thought*, ed. John C. Merkle (New York: Macmillan, 1985), pp. 142-64.

30. Fleischner, "Heschel's Significance."

31. In a memorandum of May 1962 he had written, "In view of past historical events which brought great sacrifice and suffering to Jews on account of their faith as Jews and their race, and particularly in view of the fact that antisemitism has in our time resulted in the greatest crime committed in the history of mankind, we consider it a matter of extreme importance that a strong declaration be issued by the Council stressing the grave nature of the sin of antisemitism." Fleischner, "Heschel's Significance."

32. In July 1964 the bishops received copies of the new version from Cardinal Bea with a cover letter. Stransky Collection, folder 2, Archives of the Paulist Fathers, Washington, DC [hereafter A-CSP]. According to Robert C. Doty, Bea "delivered his introduction to the draft in terms that appeared to observers here to be an invitation to the more than 2,500 church dignitaries to amend it." "Council Gets Text on Jews with Hint of Amending It," *New York Times*, 26 September 1964.

33. Floyd Anderson, ed., *Council Daybook, Vatican II, Session 3* (Washington, DC: National Catholic Welfare Conference, 1965), p. 82.

peoples will address the Lord in a single voice and serve Him with one accord."[34] The erstwhile missionary to the Jews thus took a role in closing the idea of Catholic mission to the Jews. The effect was historical. Rabbi Heschel later wrote that "The Schema on the Jews is the first statement of the Church in history — the first Christian discourse dealing with Judaism — which is devoid of any expression of hope for conversion. . . . And let me remind you that there were two versions."[35]

Oesterreicher took his inspiration for the new formulation from the Old Testament, but the problem with the previous one was not so much the New Testament as its falsification: in particular of Paul's letter to the Romans. Ernst Ludwig Ehrlich, the European director of B'nai B'rith, made this point to Oesterreicher in letters written about a week before Bea addressed the bishops. In the first he wrote that as far as the "problem of conversion" was concerned he himself found "the relevant passage completely fine in a Catholic document. It does not speak of conversion but rather of eschatological addition of the Jews to the communion with Christ, thus a legitimate Christian hope." Still, for those Jews who were not "theologically educated" he did ask whether the text might be "modified."[36]

Yet five days later he wrote to say that he had changed his mind: in the meantime he "had time to concern myself intensively with the text and unfortunately have reached the same conclusion as Heschel." The issue for him was the miserable interpretation of the original Pauline texts. "Please do yourself and me a favor, and hurry to the Secretariat," Ehrlich implored Oesterreicher, and "show the people there that the text is simply wrong, and that a well-founded New Testament reading must be found . . . otherwise they will be making themselves laughing stocks before the entire world, that is, in front of everyone who can read the New Testament."[37] If "they had really stuck closely to the New Testament, there would be much less protest from the Jewish side." The doctored draft (the "Second Declaration"), which claimed to be inspired by Romans 11:25, actually "distorted" it: there was no mention by Paul of "entry" of the Jewish people

---

34. The council had reached an "impasse on how to do justice to Jewish objections as well as the Church's hope. When I proffered the present wording . . . the suggestion was enthusiastically accepted by the Fathers and Jewish officials present in Rome." Oesterreicher, *The New Encounter Between Christians and Jews* (New York: Philosophical Library, 1986), pp. 230-31.

35. "From Mission to Dialogue," *Conservative Judaism* 21, no. 3 (Spring 1967): 10ff.

36. Letter of 10 September 1964, *Oesterreicher Papers*, SHUL.

37. Oesterreicher, *The New Encounter*, p. 230.

into "the fullness of the people of God established by Christ"; rather, Paul had written (RSV): "a hardening has come upon part of Israel until the full number of Gentiles has come in, and so all Israel will be saved." It was the Gentiles and not the Jews who would come in. "Paul is speaking in a clearly eschatological sense," wrote Ehrlich, "because *'plenitudo gentium'* is clearly the apocalyptic full number of the Gentiles . . . any notion of conversion is excluded entirely. . . . I really cannot understand how they could claim to be making reference to Paul." He seemed sure of Oesterreicher's support because the two of them had already agreed "in Zurich" that Paul's vision was an "eschatological hope and not proselytism."[38]

Here a non-Christian was seeing in Christian revelation what Christians — here the "coordinating commission" of the council — had missed. Ehrlich confessed to being exasperated. "I am really puzzled how anyone could compose such an absurd text," he complained to Oesterreicher, "which is as un-Pauline as anything imaginable." Yet this was not so much a case of whether a Jew or Christian was interpreting the New Testament, but of how a theologian should read it. Ehrlich had a rigorous academic training in Germany (under Leo Baeck and others) and Cardinal Bea sought Ehrlich's advice several times during the council.[39]

Ehrlich portrayed himself as mediator between Jews who could not understand that *Decretum de Judaeis* had to be a Christian statement, and Christians themselves, unable to produce a Christian statement. "The Council is not a Jewish world congress," Ehrlich explained, "but one can only say about the Jews what the New Testament itself says, and which Christians believe is divine revelation. Paul knew exactly why he treated precisely Romans 11:25 as mystery." Thieme had asked Oesterreicher to represent the Jewish point of view; now Ehrlich asked him to "fight with all his energy to make sure that this really becomes a 'Catholic' document, and not some silly unbiblical nonsense."[40] He revealed remarkable faith in the power of the New Testament to foster understanding between Christians and Jews:

38. Letter of 15 September 1964, *Oesterreicher Papers*, SHUL.

39. Ehrlich wrote to Oesterreicher that he planned to be in Rome in October 1964 (letter of 10 September 1964, *Oesterreicher Papers*, SHUL), and he recalls meeting repeatedly at the council with Bea after a first meeting on Yom Kippur 1961. Bea, "a man of great warmth and intelligence, at first understood very little about Judaism. In the course of time he began to sense that there was a rich post-biblical Judaism." Rolf Vogel, ed., *Ernst Ludwig Ehrlich und der christlich-jüdische Dialog* (Frankfurt am Main: Josef Knecht, 1984), p. 23.

40. Letter of 15 September 1964, *Oesterreicher Papers*, SHUL.

In dealing with it over the years I have learned that the New Testament itself — when the text is properly interpreted — is the only chance, the only means of promoting understanding between Christians and Jews. It is a historic paradox that the Council, of all things, has departed from this basis in the New Testament and wants to correct the text of the New Testament with its own silly words.[41]

Ehrlich had come to recognize the vision of Paul as revelation: for Christians as well as Jews. Paul's eschatological hope was a point of intersection for the two faiths.[42]

Decades later Oesterreicher disputed the influence of American Jews in bringing about the new formulation. He claimed in private correspondence that Cardinal Bea never referred to Rabbi Heschel or the memoranda he produced for the AJC during the sessions of the Secretariat.[43] In part, Oesterreicher was responding to allegations of Christian anti-Semites that a "Jewish lobby" had somehow manufactured the text: there were many interest groups in Rome; why should Jews not have attempted to represent their interests?[44] Still, given the excellent rapport between Heschel and Bea, and his own evident long-lasting good relations with Ehrlich, and the fact that the Secretariat indeed dropped the offending paragraph directly after Heschel's and Ehrlich's interventions (and the bishops' great debate), it seems unlikely that the Jewish scholars' intervention was without effect. Bea's successor, Cardinal Johannes Willebrands, later wrote that he "vividly remembers the contribution which [Heschel] made to a specific point of the document *Nostra Aetate*."[45] Paul VI made explicit Heschel's influence in a general audience that took place shortly

---

41. Letter of 15 September 1964, *Oesterreicher Papers,* SHUL.

42. Letter of 15 September 1964, *Oesterreicher Papers,* SHUL.

43. Letter to Eva Fleischner, 28 April 1983, *Oesterreicher Papers,* SHUL.

44. Gregory Baum likewise contested the Jewish role as presented in a popular article in *Look* of 25 January 1966 ("How the Jews Changed Catholic Thinking"): "The contacts which the Jewish persons mentioned in the [*Look*] article had with the Secretariat of Christian Unity were altogether marginal in the whole story of the Council." In Vincent Yzermans, ed., *American Participation in the Second Vatican Council* (New York: Sheed & Ward, 1967), p. 59.

45. Heschel had learned of the plan of the secretariat to express "the hope for the conversion of the Jewish people to Christ at the end of time. . . . [H]e told the Pope that any inclusion of the theme of conversion would produce exceedingly negative reactions in the Jewish communities, and would nullify the many good things that the document contained. Indeed, all such thoughts were subsequently abandoned." Letter of Willebrands to Eva Fleischner (23 April 1983) cited in Fleischner, "Heschel's Significance."

after Heschel's death: "Even before we have moved in search of God, God has come in search of us."[46] The files of the Subcommittee for Jewish Affairs, contained in the papers of Father Thomas Stransky, theologian on the staff of Cardinal Bea, are full of letters from Jewish officials, including Joseph Lichten, Marc Tanenbaum, Arthur Gilbert, Zachariah Shuster, and Philip Hiat.[47]

In his own history of *Nostra Aetate* Oesterreicher admitted that his compromise formulation had succeeded in part because it found the acceptance of "Jewish officials in Rome."[48] Yet Christians and Jews still differed on how the "age to come" would look. Oesterreicher later wrote:

> The Council had no intention of ignoring the difference, yet it wished to bridge this gap. Traditional Judaism expects a time when all the nations of the world will join the people of Israel and accept the Torah as the law of life. The Christian hope, however, is that when the end of the ages comes, the righteous of the world will turn to Christ. [The Council repeats] the prophetic vision of all peoples addressing the Lord "in a single voice and serving Him shoulder to shoulder [that is, with one accord]" (Zeph. 3:9, see Is. 66:23, Ps. 65:4; Rom. 11:11-12). . . .[49]

Oesterreicher could have added that Jews and Christians also differ on what constitutes their differences. Rabbi Arthur Gilbert had written that Judaism does not require Gentiles to become Jews. And if one reads Isaiah near the line cited by Oesterreicher one has:

> 22: For, as the new heavens and the new earth which I am making shall endure in my sight, says the Lord, so shall your name and your race en-

46. The statement was made on 31 January 1973. The pope subsequently made clear that Heschel's writings were the source of that thought. See also *America*, 10 March 1973, p. 202. Cited in Fleischner, "Heschel's Significance."

47. Stransky's materials from 1964 contain a summary by Lichten (of the ADL) of the University of California study on the widespread belief of U.S. Catholics in the deicide charge, and generally the correlation between "negative religious ideas" about the Jews and "secular stereotypes" about the Jews. See "Beschuldigung des Gottesmordes und anti-jüdisches Vorurteil unter Katholiken," Box 10, folder 1, Stransky Collection, A-CSP. Tanenbaum (American Jewish Committee) prepared a statement ("The Jewish Decree") containing an interpretation of New Testament revelation on the Jews (esp. Romans 10–11) at the request of Cardinal Cushing, dated 29 September 1964. Box 10, folder 5, Stransky Collection, A-CSP.

48. Oesterreicher, *The New Encounter*, p. 231.

49. Oesterreicher, *The New Encounter*, p. 231.

dure . . . 23: and month by month at the new moon, week by week on the Sabbath, all mankind shall come to bow down before me, says the Lord.

The effects of chapter 4 of *Nostra Aetate* went beyond wording and extended to the symbolism of the statement; referring to the atmosphere of Christian-Jewish encounters in the United States before the decree was promulgated, Arthur Gilbert wrote that "Vatican II seemed already to have worked its magic."[50] Rabbi A. James Rudin has compared *Nostra Aetate* to the *Magna Carta* or the U.S. Constitution because it "broke new ground and provided the mandate for constructive change."[51] Rabbi Gilbert S. Rosenthal wrote that the "main points of the statement represent a Copernican revolution in Catholic thinking about the Jewish religion and people."[52] Geoffrey Wigoder, editor-in-chief of the *Encyclopaedia Judaica*, credits John XXIII with initiating a "revolution in the attitude of the Church as a whole," indeed "inaugurated a new era in the history of the church."[53] The "long-term impact of the Declaration was not so much perhaps in what it actually said as in the new attitudes it initiated."[54] Its "very tone constitutes a breakthrough. For example, its stress on the spiritual bond between the Church and the Jewish people and the statement that the Church 'received the Old Testament through the people with whom God concluded the Ancient Covenant' were unprecedented. The acknowledgement of the Judaic roots of Christianity, starting with the Judaic roots of Jesus himself, opened up vistas not previously possible."[55]

Because of attempts to appease critics in the Church, the statement fell short of some expectations. It diverged from the original draft by "deplor-

---

50. Rabbi Gilbert was director of Interreligious Cooperation for the Anti-Defamation League of B'nai B'rith. See his description of the "historic theological encounter" that took place at St. Vincent's Archabbey in Latrobe, Pennsylvania, in January 1965. Gilbert, *The Vatican Council and the Jews* (Cleveland and New York: World Publishing Co., 1968), pp. 168-69.

51. Cited in Michael A. Hayes, "From *Nostra Aetate* to 'We Remember': A Reflection on the Shoah," in *Christian-Jewish Relations through the Centuries*, ed. Stanley E. Porter and Brook W. R. Pearson (Sheffield, UK: Sheffield Academic Press, 2000), p. 429.

52. Rosenthal is executive director of the National Council of Synagogues. Gary Spruch, *Wide Horizons: Abraham Joshua Heschel, AJC, and the Spirit of* Nostra Aetate (New York: American Jewish Committee, 2008), p. 16.

53. Geoffrey Wigoder, *Jewish-Christian Relations Since the Second World War* (Manchester and New York: Manchester University Press, 1988), pp. 77-79.

54. Wigoder, *Jewish-Christian Relations*, p. 80.

55. Wigoder, *Jewish-Christian Relations*, pp. 77-79. Ehrlich also called it a breakthrough. See Vogel, ed., *Ernst Ludwig Ehrlich*, p. 24.

ing" rather than "condemning" anti-Semitism. Yet this meant that no longer could anyone portray hostility to Jews as compatible with Catholic doctrine.[56] *Nostra Aetate* did not use the word "deicide," yet because it cautioned against charging "what happened" in Christ's passion "against all the Jews," the statement is remembered as having refuted the deicide charge.[57] The Declaration might have done more to satisfy Abraham Heschel's request for reference to "the permanent preciousness" of Jews as Jews — something a number of council fathers had come close to expressing in other formulations.[58] Instead, in the words of Arthur Gilbert, parts of the Declaration left the impression that "the purpose of Jewish history or the meaning of Jewish scripture" was "preparation," such that Christians may deny the Jews' claim "still to have a divine mission to be a witness to God and a blessing for mankind."[59] "There was no reference," Geoffrey Wigoder has written, "to the nature of God's covenant with the Jewish people after Jesus; [*Nostra Aetate*] did not refer to the continuing role of the Jewish people after New Testament times."[60] It spoke of Israel as "the root of that well-cultivated olive tree onto which have been grafted the wild shoots, the Gentiles."

Yet even in 1968 Gilbert recognized that "Jews will not be without allies in defending their position on these issues." Such allies, within the Church, could base themselves on other words from the Declaration: "God holds the Jews most dear for the sake of their Fathers; He does not repent of the gifts He makes or of the calls He issues." These words define the basic terms for post–Vatican II debates: no Catholic could deny a continuing and vital Jewish role in postbiblical history. This understanding reflected the Pauline teaching suffusing the new Catholic vision, something also visible in the

56. Gilbert notes that the 1928 papal statement on the Jews had "condemned" anti-Semitism. *The Vatican Council*, p. 255, n. 13.

57. This was the conclusion drawn by the correspondent for the *New York Times* (Rachel Donadio) after the controversies of early 2009: "In his remarks on Thursday, Benedict reaffirmed the church's commitment to '*Nostra Aetate*,' the Vatican II document absolving Jews of deicide." *New York Times*, 13 February 2009, A8. John Pawlikowski has, however, noted that *Nostra Aetate* did not "absolve," Jews; rather, "it argued that there was no basis for the charge in the first place." "Reflections on Covenant and Mission Forty Years after *Nostra Aetate*," *Cross Currents* (Winter 2007): 71.

58. Karl Plank, "The Eclipse of Difference: Merton's Encounter with Judaism," in *Merton and Judaism: Holiness in Words — Recognition, Repentance, and Renewal*, ed. Beatrice Bruteau (Louisville: Fons Vitae, 2003), p. 70.

59. *The Vatican Council*, p. 205.

60. Wigoder, *Jewish-Christian Relations*, p. 78.

statements of bishops on the council floors.[61] In other words: this was a statement to be seen not simply on the background of the 1960s or the post-war era; it was a matter not of years or decades but of centuries. *Nostra Aetate* was an epochal break with teachings that had caused much pain.

## Mission to the Jews after the Council?

What about the question of mission? As noted, the declaration on the Jews of *Nostra Aetate* expressed a wish for unity of all humankind with God, and not of Jews with the Church. The word "mission" was not used either positively or negatively, nor was anything specific said about the nature of evangelization, to Jews or anyone else. Other Vatican II documents soft-ened the traditional insistence that there could be no salvation outside the church, while maintaining a call for evangelization. Paul's letter to the Romans makes clear reference to the persistence of "Israel" — understood by the Church to mean the Jewish people ("the stock of Abraham") — to the end of time. Prior to the council Catholic theologians had taught that Israel in the present had an exclusively spiritual connotation, with the Church constituting the "New Israel."

Oesterreicher's "solution," involving a displacement of questions on the unity of Christians and Jews to the vision of a minor prophet, did not end questions about how Jews fit into Christian visions of salvation, and the disputes since 1965 have their origins in this uncertainty. Ernst Ludwig Ehrlich may have been sure that Paul's vision was an "eschatological hope," but Christian theologians have wanted to take the question further. In-deed, some have argued that "eschatological time" began with the first coming of Christ.[62] If as Paul writes in Romans 11, "all Israel will be saved," how precisely will this happen? If "Israel" meant the Jewish people as an ethnic, cultural, and religious entity, and all humans are saved through Christ, do Jews need to turn explicitly to Christ?

Scripture scholars of the post–Vatican II era have fallen into two camps in their responses. One group (the "theological") holds that the en-tire section (from 10:17 to 11:36) remarkably fails to mention Christ; Paul writes that "all Israel will be saved" with no mention of a role held by Christ. This group projects the salvation of the Jews occurring apart from

61. Ernst Ludwig Ehrlich, "Die Juden und das Konzil," in *Judenhass: Schuld der Chris-ten?!* ed. Willehad Paul Eckert and Ernst Ludwig Ehrlich (Essen: Hans Driewer, 1964), p. 402.
62. Erik Peterson, *Die Kirche aus Juden und Heiden* (Salzburg: Pustet, 1934), p. 71.

Christ.[63] An opposing group argues that this fragment cannot be seen in separation from the overall thrust of Paul's teaching of justification by grace through faith. The Jesuit scholar Joseph A. Fitzmyer writes: "Paul is scarcely envisaging two different kinds of salvation — one achieved by God for Jews and one by Christ for Gentiles; that would be to go against his entire thesis about justification by grace through faith."[64]

Theologians also continue to debate what Paul meant by "a hardening has come upon part of Israel, until the full number of the Gentiles come in" (11:25). What is the full number? Is this all Gentiles, or as Erik Peterson has written, only "the full number of Gentiles as determined by God"?[65] If so, that left a huge task to complete before Catholics could think of the Jews. Furthermore: If Paul wrote that the Jews *will* be saved, why worry about them? In retrospect one must wonder at the passion for converting Jews of Christians like John Oesterreicher (a careful reader of Erik Peterson and his inspiration Leon Bloy), who had been inspired by Paul's letter to the Romans. Paul also wrote that he hoped to make Jews "jealous" because he was evidently pleasing to God.[66] Before Jews could enter the Messianic kingdom, Christians had to become Christian.

Following Abraham Heschel, Jewish commentators celebrated the Church's ability to talk about Catholic-Jewish relations without mentioning Jewish conversion, and until the papacy of Benedict XVI, the question of converting Jews had largely disappeared from mainstream concern. Statements from central Church offices on the Jewish people issued in the decades following Vatican II stressed growing respect for the Jewish tradition, the common heritage of Christians and Jews, the need to understand the other in the other's terms, and the challenges of combating Christian beliefs that have fed anti-Semitism.[67]

---

63. They argue that the "Deliverer" mentioned in 11:26 cannot be Christ because reference is made to a fragment of Isaiah. They note that the verb *sothēsetai* [σωθήσεται] is theological passive, i.e., "will be saved." For a summary view (major figures: Krister Stendahl, Mary Ann Getty) see John P. Gager, *Reinventing Paul* (Oxford: Oxford University Press, 2000), p. 141; Joseph Fitzmyer, S.J., "The Letter to the Romans," in *The New Jerome Biblical Commentary* (Englewood Cliffs, NJ: Prentice Hall, 1990), p. 861.

64. Reference to the "covenant" in 11:27 is taken here to mean Jeremiah 31:33 at its "definitive stage," i.e., as fulfilled in Christ (as in 1 Cor. 11:25; 2 Cor. 3:6). Fitzmyer, "The Letter to the Romans," p. 862.

65. Peterson, *Kirche aus Juden*, p. 63.

66. Karl Thieme, *Kirche und Synagoge. Die ersten biblischen Zeugnisse ihres Gegensätze im Offenbarungsverständnis* (Olten: Verlag Otto Walter AG, 1945), p. 211.

67. "Catholic reflections describe the growing respect for the Jewish tradition that has

On the twenty-fifth anniversary of *Nostra Aetate* in 1991, the Pontifical Council for Inter-Religious Dialogue released a statement titled *Dialogue and Proclamation,* which called Jesus Christ "the only mediator between God and man" and stated that "God's reign and the church are distinguishable but not separable." The Church's evangelizing mission included several elements, one of which, titled "proclamation," involved "an invitation to a commitment of faith in Jesus Christ and to entry through baptism into the community of believers."[68] A footnote informed readers that the statement did not pertain to relations between Catholics and Jews: because the "spiritual patrimony" between them was so great it had special requirements, stated in documents released in 1974 and 1985.[69]

The first of these, the "Guidelines and Suggestions for Implementing the Conciliar Declaration *Nostra Aetate*" (released by the newly created Commission for Religious Relations with the Jews), said nothing about avoiding attempts to convert or baptize, presumably because that would have seemed absurd in an emerging dialogue aimed at overcoming centuries of misunderstandings. The Guidelines meant to "encourage and foster religious relations between Jews and Catholics."[70] "After two thousand years, too often marked by mutual ignorance and frequent confrontation," wrote the authors of the Guidelines, "the Declaration *Nostra Aetate* provides an opportunity to open or to continue a dialogue with a view to better mutual understanding."[71] They desired a "new relationship between

unfolded since the Second Vatican Council." Cardinal Edward Idris Cassidy, excerpted from his book, *Ecumenism and Interreligious Dialogue* (New York and Mahwah, NJ: Paulist, 2005), pp. 252-56.

68. The full title is *Dialogue and Proclamation: Reflection and Orientations on Interreligious Dialogue and the Proclamation of the Gospel of Jesus Christ,* at http://www.vatican.va/roman_curia/pontifical_councils/interelg/documents/rc_pc_interelg_doc_19051991_dialogue-and-proclamatio_en.html (retrieved 25 May 2010).

69. Footnote 8. For a full treatment, cf. Commission for Religious Relations with Jews, *Guidelines on Religious Relations with Jews,* 1 December 1974 (in Austin P. Flannery, O.P., ed., *Documents of Vatican II,* rev. ed. [Grand Rapids: Eerdmans, 1984], pp. 743-49); "Notes for a Correct Presentation of Jews and Judaism in Catholic Preaching and Catechesis," 24 June 1985, in *Origins* 15, no. 2 (4 July 1985): 102-7.

70. The Commission was created by Paul VI on 22 October 1974 and joined to the Secretariat for Promoting Christian Unity. The statement was released 1 December, and is available at http://www.vatican.va/roman_curia/pontifical_councils/chrstuni/relations-jews-docs/rc_pc_chrstuni_doc_19741201_nostra-aetate_en.html (retrieved 6 May 2010).

71. "To tell the truth, such relations as there have been between Jew and Christian have scarcely ever risen above the level of monologue. From now on, real dialogue must be established."

Jews and Christians," and therefore a "better mutual understanding and renewed mutual esteem. On the practical level in particular, Christians must therefore strive to acquire a better knowledge of the basic components of the religious tradition of Judaism; they must strive to learn by what essential traits the Jews define themselves in the light of their own religious experience." Sensitive to the tradition of supersessionism, the Guidelines admitted that Christians as well as Jews awaited the "perfect" fulfillment of God's promises at some point in the future, but they failed to be more precise, simply repeating the compromise formulation found by John Oesterreicher in 1964 without further commentary.[72]

The Commission for Religious Relations with the Jews also produced the second document from 1985 titled "Notes on the correct way to present the Jews and Judaism in preaching and catechesis in the Roman Catholic Church."[73] While affirming Christian universalism the drafters reaffirmed the light touch of *Nostra Aetate*. Christ's promise involved all people, there was "one flock and one shepherd," and the Church "must witness to Christ as the Redeemer for all," but no project was envisioned to baptize the Jews or any other people. In line with earlier statements, the drafters looked forward to an unspecified time when the Church, "realized already in Christ, yet awaits its definitive perfecting as the Body of Christ." Christ would save all, but the Church did not specify when or how.

During his papacy John Paul II often signaled the continuing validity of the promises made to Israel, for example in a 1980 speech to Jewish leaders at Mainz, when he spoke of Jews as "the people of God of the Old Covenant never revoked by God," or in 1987 in Miami, when he called the Jewish people "partners in a covenant of eternal love which was never revoked."[74] Citing yet another such statement the authors of "Notes" reflected upon the "the permanence of Israel (while so many ancient peoples have disappeared without trace)" as "a historic fact and a sign to be interpreted within God's design." Israel remained a "chosen people, 'the pure olive on which were grafted the branches of the wild olive which are the

72. "With the prophets and the apostle Paul, the Church awaits the day, known to God alone, on which all peoples will address the Lord in a single voice and 'serve him with one accord' (Zeph 3:9)" (*Nostra Aetate*, Art. 4).

73. By the Commission for Religious Relations with the Jews, 24 June 1985, at http://www.vatican.va/roman_curia/pontifical_councils/chrstuni/relations-jews-docs/rc_pc_chrstuni_doc_19820306_jews-judaism_en.html (retrieved 25 May 2010).

74. Cited in Mary C. Boys, "Does the Catholic Church Have a Mission 'with' or 'to' Jews?" *Studies in Christian-Jewish Relations* 3, no. 1 (2008): 5.

gentiles,'" and its permanence was "accompanied by a continuous spiritual fecundity, in the rabbinical period, in the Middle Ages, and in modern times, taking its start from a patrimony that we long shared," so much so that "the faith and religious life of the Jewish people as they are professed and practiced still today can greatly help us to understand better certain aspects of the life of the Church."[75]

During these years American theologians and bishops worked at greater precision in formulation, precisely in the knotty issue of mission. In 1985 the Secretariat for Catholic-Jewish Relations of the Bishops' Committee for Ecumenical and Interreligious Affairs at the National Conference of Catholic Bishops issued "Guidelines for Catholic-Jewish Relations," explicitly rejecting "proselytism," which, it claimed, did "not respect human freedom."[76] Yet here they opened room for misinterpretation, because proselytism in common parlance means the simple act of trying to make converts.[77] Among experts, however, this word had assumed a purely negative meaning. In 1998 Cardinal Edward Cassidy, President of the Pontifical Council for Promoting Christian Unity, and President, Commission for Religious Relations with the Jews, defined "proselytism" as "the use of unworthy means to attract members of other churches or even unchurched persons to their fold. Misrepresentation of the other, or of one's own community, is a common source of tension."[78]

In August 2002 the Ecumenical and Interreligious Affairs Committee of the United States Conference of Catholic Bishops and the National Council of Synagogues USA issued *Reflections on Covenant and Mission*, representing the culmination of discussions between Jewish and Catholic leaders who had been meeting for two decades.[79] Drafted by the theolo-

---

75. John Paul II, 6 March 1982.

76. Under Point 6 of the general principles: "Proselytism, which *does* not respect human freedom, is carefully to be avoided. While the Christian, through the faith life of word and deed, will always witness to Jesus as the risen Christ, the dialogue is concerned with the permanent vocation of the Jews as God's people, the enduring values that Judaism shares with Christianity and that, together, the Church and the Jewish people are called upon to witness to the whole world." http://www.usccb.org/prayer-and-worship/liturgical-resources/lent/guidelines-for-catholic-jewish-relations.cfm (retrieved 25 May 2010).

77. According to the *Oxford English Dictionary*, to proselytize is "to make, or seek to make, proselytes or converts."

78. Cited in Lawrence Uzzell, "Don't Call It Proselytism," *First Things*, October 2004, p. 14.

79. http://www.bc.edu/research/cjl/meta-elements/texts/cjrelations/resources/documents/interreligious/ncs_usccb120802.htm (retrieved 25 May 2010).

gians Mary C. Boys, Philip A. Cunningham, and John T. Pawlikowski, the document was not meant as a definitive formulation, but as a spur to further study and discussion.

Building on earlier texts, *Reflections* called the Church's relation to the Jewish people "unique." The authors drew upon formulations of German Cardinal Walter Kasper, successor to Cassidy as President of the Pontifical Commission for the Religious Relations with the Jews, who had written that Catholics believed "God's infinite grace is surely available to believers of other faiths," but it was "only about Israel's covenant that the Church can speak with the certainty of the biblical witness." This is because Israel's scriptures form part of our own biblical canon and they have a "perpetual value . . . that has not been canceled by the later interpretation of the New Testament." According to Kasper, Jews dwelt "in a saving covenant with God," and therefore the Church had a very special relation to them, excluding "mission":

> The term mission, in its proper sense, refers to conversion from false gods and idols to the true and one God, who revealed himself in the salvation history with His elected people. Thus mission, in this strict sense, cannot be used with regard to Jews, who believe in the true and one God. Therefore, and this is characteristic, there exists dialogue but there does not exist any Catholic missionary organization for Jews.[80]

Then perhaps stretching what could fruitfully be said about matters enveloped in mystery, the authors of *Reflections* pondered whether Christians "ought to invite Jews to baptism." On one hand, they wrote, "the Catholic Church must always evangelize and will always witness to its faith" and thus welcomes and accepts "sincere individual converts from any tradition or people, including the Jewish people." Yet, on the other, "the Jews' witness to the kingdom, which did not originate with the Church's experience of Christ crucified and raised, must not be curtailed by seeking the conversion of the Jewish people to Christianity. The distinctive Jewish witness must be sustained."

In retrospect, this seems a question *mal posée*, asking the Church to take responsibility for more than it could bear: Had the Jewish witness ever required the Catholic Church to sustain it? And, had not some (if few)

---

80. Cited in the text of *Reflections on Covenant and Mission* from a formal statement made by Kasper at the seventeenth meeting of the International Catholic-Jewish Liaison Committee in May 2001, and repeated later that year in Jerusalem.

Jews continually felt drawn to Christianity in the modern age, with or without explicit invitations from Church authorities? Why attempt to touch such a question with words? Obviously no Catholic would tell anyone not to become Catholic. Conversion is a personal decision. Furthermore: What could it mean to seek the "conversion of the Jewish people"? Is this not an otherworldly, fantastic goal? Why then pronounce an intention not to do it? The light touch of *Nostra Aetate* seemed lost.

To some, the authors of *Reflections* were saying that the Catholic Church was not interested in accepting Jewish converts. Cardinal Avery Dulles forcefully criticized the statement in an article that appeared in the Jesuit magazine *America* in October 2002. First, he demanded that the Church not relent on evangelization. Citing popes Paul VI and John Paul II, Dulles wrote that "there is no true evangelization if the name, the teaching, the life, the promises, the Kingdom, and the mystery of Jesus of Nazareth, the Son of God, are not proclaimed." The Church had no choice but to be "a clear and unequivocal proclamation of the person of Jesus Christ." Then he argued that Jews could never be excluded from the Church's mission:

> Even if, with Cardinal Kasper, one were to limit "mission" to the apostolate to the Gentiles, the church would not be absolved of her God-given responsibility to proclaim Christ to all the world. Peter on Pentecost Sunday declared that the whole house of Israel should know for certain that Jesus is Lord and Messiah and that every one of his hearers should be baptized in Jesus' name (Acts 2:38).

Finally, Dulles wrote that the Jewish covenant did not continue; promises to Jews were still valid, but fulfilled through Christianity. He cited the "most formal statement on the status of the Sinai covenant" from the Letter to the Hebrews: the first covenant is "obsolete" and "ready to vanish away" (Heb. 8:13). Christ, wrote Dulles, "abolishes the first [covenant] in order to establish the second" (Heb. 10:9).[81]

One evident problem with Dulles's article was that John Paul, whom he cited as an unwavering proponent of evangelizing Jews, had, as noted,

---

81. Dulles continued: "These passages from Hebrews do not overturn Paul's insistence in Romans that the promises of God to Israel remain valid. The Hebrew Scriptures, containing God's promises, have enduring value, but are to be interpreted in the light of Christ to whom they point forward. The elect have obtained what was promised, though the rest were hardened (Rom. 11:7)." "Covenant and Mission," *America* 187, no. 12 (21 October 2002): 9.

repeatedly affirmed that the Sinai covenant remained in force. In a rebuttal printed in the same issue of *America,* Boys, Cunningham, and Pawlikowski pointed to the deeper flaw: Dulles was reading the Letter to the Hebrews without regard for Catholic tradition. According to a finding of the Pontifical Biblical Commission from 1993, Catholic teaching had "'gone its own way' and 'set aside' the opinion of the author of Hebrews about Israel's covenant."[82] The article continued:

> The magisterium can explicitly contradict an idea of an individual New Testament author, because the Catholic tradition is one of commentary, not *sola scriptura.* The author of Hebrews, convinced that he was living in the final stages of human history, could argue that the Old Covenant had yielded to the New. Two millennia later, however, in a church whose pope has prayed for God's forgiveness for the sins of Christians against Jews, such an assertion is unacceptable.[83]

In other writings, Father Pawlikowski has noted that the bishops at Vatican II entirely neglected the Letter to the Hebrews — the preferred source of Cardinal Dulles — in their new vision of the Jewish people.

In making their argument for a total reversal in Catholic thinking on Jews and Judaism,[84] the bishops of the Council bypassed almost all the teachings about Jews and Judaism in Christian thought prior to Vatican II and returned to chapters 9-11 of Paul's Letter to the Romans

---

82. Therefore, they continue, "Pope John Paul II has on many occasions declared that Jews are 'the people of God of the Old Covenant, never revoked by God,' 'the present-day people of the covenant concluded with Moses,' and 'partners in a covenant of eternal love which was never revoked.'" "Theology's 'Sacred Obligation': A Reply to Cardinal Dulles," *America* 187, no. 12 (21 October 2002): 11-16.

83. "Theology's 'Sacred Obligation.'"

84. His summary of this reversal: "Since at least the second century of the common era the prevalent position in Christian thought was that Jews had been replaced in the covenantal relationship with God by the newly emergent Christian community, the 'true Israel,' because of Jewish failure to acknowledge Jesus as the expected Messiah and Jewish responsibility for his eventual death on the cross. In contrast, *Nostra Aetate* affirmed the continuity of the Jewish people in the covenantal relationship, underscored the constructive influence of the Jewish tradition on Jesus and the early Church, and said that there never was a basis in fact for the historical deicide accusation against the Jews that over the centuries was the source of their persecution and at times even death." John Pawlikowski and Hayim Goren Perelmuter, *Reinterpreting Revelation and Tradition: Jews and Christians in Conversation* (Franklin, WI: Sheed & Ward, 2000), p. 25.

where the Apostle reaffirms the continued inclusion of the Jews in the covenant after the coming of Christ even though this remains for him a "mystery" that defies complete theological explanation. In one sense, the bishops in *Nostra Aetate* were picking up where St. Paul left off in the first century.[85]

With Boys and Cunningham, Pawlikowski further argued that the Church had built upon this understanding in subsequent years, expanding upon and even correcting Scripture. Paul, unable to imagine the fecund Judaism that we have witnessed since the time of Christ, had referred to Israel as broken off, dead branches. The 1985 "notes" had spoken of "the permanence of Israel" as "accompanied by a continuous spiritual fecundity" over the ages. "So interpreting Romans 11 today," the authors continue, "entails respecting the ongoing spiritual life of Judaism. Far from being dead branches, Jews still draw nourishment from the good olive tree."[86] Yet perhaps this counterargument went too far, in effect taking Paul's dead branches and regrafting them — something the Apostle had reserved for an unspecified time in the future. The notion of dead branches coming to life suggests a miraculous, mysterious event, perhaps not amenable to the language of theological scholarship.

Through the controversies of recent years one bishop, Cardinal Walter Kasper, successor to Bea and Willebrands, has presided over the Pontifical Council for Promoting Christian Unity. Thus the man who told audiences in 2001 that mission was inappropriate for the Jews because they already believed in the One True God had to explain to the world seven years later why Pope Benedict XVI was praying for the Jews on Good Friday. Yet Kasper already had experience in mediating mixed messages from the upper hierarchy, having told concerned Jews in 2000 that the declaration *Dominus Iesus* — according to which those outside the Church were in a "gravely deficient situation" — did "not enter into Jewish-Catholic dialogue."[87]

---

85. Pawlikowski, *Reinterpreting Revelation*, p. 25. Pawlikowski specified in a 2005 talk what had been ignored: the Church fathers, papal pronouncements, citations from earlier conciliar texts, and other books of Scripture, especially the Letter to the Hebrews. See Markus Himmelbauer, "Ein neuer Geist in Kirche und Gesellschaft," http://www.jcrelations.net/de/?item=2588 (retrieved 26 January 2008), recording a meeting on *Nostra Aetate* that occurred in Vienna in 2005.

86. http://www.vatican.va/roman_curia/pontifical_councils/chrstuni/relations-jews-docs/rc_pc_chrstuni_doc_19820306_jews-judaism_en.html (retrieved 25 May 2010).

87. According to Prof. David Berger, Jews had also worried about the declaration's un-

Kasper could not deny that the Good Friday Prayer released by Benedict XVI in February 2008 was targeted at Jews, however. "Let us also pray for the Jews," it read, "that God our Lord should illuminate their hearts, so that they will recognize Jesus Christ, the savior of men."[88] Such words seemed disconnected from the spirit of Vatican II, reflected for example in the 1970 edition of the Roman missal, which had stated:

> Let us pray for the Jewish people, the first to hear the word of God, that they may continue to grow in the love of his name and in faithfulness to his covenant. . . . Almighty and eternal God, long ago you gave your promise to Abraham and his posterity. Listen to your Church as we pray that the people you first made your own may arrive at the fullness of redemption. We ask this through Christ our Lord, Amen.

How could a Good Friday prayer that Jews turn to Christ be released decades after *Nostra Aetate,* which almost failed over precisely the question of Jews turning to Christ? We do not know for sure, but it seems the pope acted on his own authority, perhaps trying to balance formulations of those engaged in interreligious dialogue with concerns of traditionalists within the Church. Benedict's prayer contained a second part more in keeping with the tradition of Vatican II: "Almighty and eternal God, who want that all men be saved and come to the recognition of the truth, propitiously grant that even as the fullness of the peoples enters Thy Church, all Israel be saved." In other words, as German bishop Heinrich Mussinghof has suggested, was the pope perhaps suggesting that "the full number of Gentile peoples (Goyim) must first enter the Church by baptism, while the salvation of all Israel is left to the mysterious workings of God"?[89] *Nostra*

---

derstanding of "interreligious dialogue" as constituting "part of the Church's evangelizing mission." Edward Idris Cardinal Cassidy, *Ecumenism and Interreligious Dialogue: Unitatis Redintegratio, Nostra Aetate* (New York: Paulist Press, 2005), p. 217. The declaration was released by the Vatican Congregation for the Doctrine of the Faith, headed by Cardinal Joseph Ratzinger, and had the following to say about "mission": "The Church's universal mission is born from the command of Jesus Christ and is fulfilled in the course of the centuries in the proclamation of the mystery of God, Father, Son, and Holy Spirit, and the mystery of the incarnation of the Son, as saving event for all humanity." http://www.vatican.va/roman_curia/congregations/cfaith/documents/rc_con_cfaith_doc_20000806_dominus-iesus_en.html (retrieved 11 May 2010).

88. These replaced a formulation in the prayer for the Jews in the 1962 edition of the Roman missal.

89. Mussinghof is the chairman of the subcommission on "Questions of Jewry" of the

*Aetate* struck a compromise between those inside and outside the church, but this prayer may have signaled an attempt to appease competing voices within the Church.

Given his liberal views, Cardinal Kasper was caught in a difficult position. Within a day of the prayer's release, he was attempting damage control. Kasper explained to the German Catholic Press Agency:

> If the Pope speaks of the conversion of the Jews, then one must understand him correctly. He quotes literally from the eleventh chapter of Paul's letter to the Romans. There the Apostle says that we Christians hope that when the full number of the Gentiles have entered the Church, then all of Israel will be converted. That is an eschatological hope for the end of times and does not mean that we have the intention of conducting a mission to the Jews, in the way that we have a mission to the Gentiles.[90]

A week later Kasper wrote the Chairman of the International Jewish Committee on Interreligious Consultations, Rabbi David Rosen, as follows:

> The text is a prayer inspired by Saint Paul's letter to the Romans, chapter 11, which is the very text that speaks also of the unbroken covenant. It takes up Paul's eschatological hope that in the end of time all Israel will be saved. As a prayer the text lays all in the hands of God and not in ours. It says nothing about the how and the when. Therefore there is nothing about missionary activities by which we may take Israel's salvation in our hands.

The Cardinal's words are remarkable for two reasons: first, they make no reference to the pope's prayer calling for illumination of the Jews. But second, the new prayer has no connection to Romans 11, instead modifying an earlier prayer inspired by 2 Corinthians 3:14 ["Let us pray for the Jews that almighty God remove the veil from their hearts"].[91] If one reads Romans 11, one finds no talk of all Israel being "converted," of illumina-

---

Ecumenical Conference of the German Bishops' Conference. Speech at the International Council of Christians and Jews yearly meeting, Berlin, 7 July 2009, at http://www.iccj.org/de/?item=473#21 (retrieved 23 May 2010).

90. http://www.kath.net/detail.php?id=18969 (retrieved 7 February 2008).

91. 2 Corinthians 3:14: "But their minds were hardened; for to this day, when they read the old covenant, that same veil remains unlifted, because only through Christ is it taken away."

tion, of Jews "entering the Church," or even of Christ. Rather, one finds the images and ideas that inspired the drafters of *Nostra Aetate:* "Has God rejected his people, by no means!" "Have they stumbled . . . by no means!" "If you do boast, remember it is not you that supports the root, but the root that supports you!" "The gifts and the call of God are irrevocable."[92] But Kasper is correct that Romans contains the inscrutable theological vision about the end of times alluded to in *Nostra Aetate:* "Lest you be wise in your own conceits I want you to understand this mystery, brethren: a hardening has come upon part of Israel, until the full number of Gentiles come in, and all Israel will be saved."

The wording "will be saved" *sothēsetai* [σωθήσεται] is future passive.[93] Does it require active conversion efforts of Jews by Christians? This was the question *mal posée* addressed by the U.S. Council of Bishops in its June 2009 *Notes on Ambiguities,* which sought to correct shortcomings of the 2002 *Reflections* statement, often falsely thought to have carried the council's approval.

On the one hand, the bishops chided drafters of *Reflections* for going too far, having rendered "even the possibility of individual conversion doubtful" by implying that it was "generally not good for Jews to convert, nor for Catholics to do anything that might lead Jews to conversion because it threatens to eliminate 'the distinctive Jewish witness.'" "Some caution should be introduced here," the bishops wrote, "since this line of reasoning could lead some to conclude mistakenly that Jews have an obligation not to become Christian and that the Church has a corresponding obligation not to baptize Jews."

On the other hand the bishops ventured further into mission territory than any statement on the Jews released by a major Catholic teaching office since Vatican II. *Reflections* had affirmed that "the Church respects religious freedom as well as freedom of conscience and that, while the Church does not have a policy that singles out the Jews as a people for conversion, she will always welcome 'sincere individual converts from any tradition or people, including the Jewish people.'" Yet this formulation struck the American bishops as too weak:

92. Though of course, as scholars note, one cannot imagine that Paul thought the salvation of Jews happened separately from Christ; still, he did not write this. He wrote: "If their rejection means the reconciliation of the world, what will their acceptance mean but life from the dead?" (Rom. 11:15).

93. For discussion see Fitzmyer, "The Letter to the Romans," pp. 861-62.

This focus on the individual fails to account for St. Paul's complete teaching about the inclusion of the Jewish people as a whole in Christ's salvation. In Romans 11:25-26, he explained that when "the full number of the Gentiles comes in . . . all Israel will be saved." He did not specify when that would take place or how it would come about. This is a mystery that awaits its fulfillment. Nevertheless, St. Paul told us to look forward to the inclusion of the whole people of Israel, which will be a great blessing for the world (Rom 11:12).

It seems the bishops were operating in ignorance of the Vatican II documents forged in the shadow of the Holocaust. They said explicitly what the drafters of *Nostra Aetate* had learned not to say at all: that the Church looks forward to the day when the Jewish people turn to Christ, that is, when Jews convert to Christianity. They failed to appreciate that for Jews, ethnic (or what the Jewish thinker Erich Kahler called "tribal") and religious identity are inseparable. To say that the Jewish people will become Christian in historical time is to say that they will cease to exist as a people. The word that grew out of the experience of the Shoah to describe such an event is genocide. Historically, conversions of entire peoples have happened by force. The lesson seems to be this: unless Paul's vision of "all Israel" being "saved" is maintained as a strictly eschatological hope, it must seem a threat to Jews. That is why Rabbi Heschel reacted so strongly in 1964.

Catholics involved in dialogue with Jews felt blindsided by this statement, which seemed to justify the gravest fears of Jews: that for Christians, dialogue was mission in disguise.[94] A letter from Jewish organizations decried the bishops' assertion that "the fulfillment of the covenants, indeed, of all God's promises to Israel, is found only in Jesus Christ." According to such a view, "the Mosaic covenant is obsolete and Judaism no longer has a reason to exist."[95] Jews listened not only to the words released by offices of the Catholic Church, but to their implications.

---

94. See for example John Borelli, "Troubled Waters: Catholic-Jewish Relations in the United States Have Grown Strained," *America* 202, no. 5 (22 February 2010): 20-23.

95. The organizations included the American Jewish Committee, the Anti-Defamation League, the National Council of Synagogues, the Orthodox Union, and the Rabbinical Council of America. Jerry Filteau, "Jewish Groups Question Dialogue with Catholics," *National Catholic Reporter*, August 28, 2009.

## Conclusion: *Nostra Aetate* 2.1

A glance into the history of *Nostra Aetate* suggests that the controversies of recent years in Catholic-Jewish relations have been counterproductive and probably unnecessary. The essential thing that has been forgotten is that Catholic teaching does not obligate Christians to imagine Jews as Christians. We see replicated in recent debates the discussions from the early 1960s. Then as now Jews say: it means nothing when Christians proclaim they will not force us to become Christian. That, after all, is no longer possible. The real question is: Does your faith cause you to want to see us disappear? To imagine a world bare of Jewish culture, Jewish ritual, Jewish faithfulness? A world with no one to keep kosher or say Kaddish? If so, then let us forget about dialogue because it is a farce, a preliminary stage to Jews' supposed "illumination," that is, conversion to Christianity. Such were the views of Martin Buber and Abraham Heschel as told to the theologian Karl Thieme or to Cardinal Bea.

Jews do not object to Christians who understand their mission as "witnessing Christ."[96] Yet in Jewish eyes Christianity becomes less Christian precisely when it puts on a mask of mission. As noted above, Benedict's Good Friday prayer immediately reminded Rabbi Lerner of mission in its full history, including the Inquisition. Just after World War II, Max Eisen described the mission to the Jews as "largely unethical and unchristian in its methods"; therefore

> all segments of organized Jewry have always opposed missionary activity among Jews. They consider it to be a deterrent and destroyer of good and friendly relations between Jews and Christians; it is a perpetual irritant and at best a form of "higher anti-Semitism." The offering of social services, food and clothing parcels and other inducements to converts and prospective converts is on a level with commercial bribery and such missionary activities are, therefore, analogous to corrupt practice. Missionaries have done much harm in attempting to destroy the faith of a people esteemed for its firm loyalty, and to separate children from their parents and from domestic tradition. Of great annoyance too is the attitude on the part of Christian missionaries to the Jews that an act of infi-

---

96. Celia Deutsch describes mission as follows: "Christians bear witness to Jesus through a life in service of others, that is, in a life which bears the pattern of Jesus' own." In Leon Klenicki and Geoffrey Wigoder, eds., *A Dictionary of the Jewish-Christian Dialogue* (New York: Paulist, 1995), p. 143.

delity is considered praiseworthy, and poor attendance at the Synagogue a cause for jubilation.[97]

Yet the American bishops have said precisely this: that the moment when Jews cease to practice their religion is a moment Catholics should "look forward to." Such is the implication of erroneously teaching that Paul proclaimed the "Church" must include the "Jewish people."

Writing under the shadow of the destruction of Europe's Jews, the Catholic theologian Karl Thieme pondered how Christians should continue their vocation of proclaiming the gospel to the entire world. In 1944 he still felt that Catholics must actively convert Jews. Yet by 1950, in debates with Protestant mission societies, he wrote that evangelization by word should continue, but far more important "now" — that is, in the post-Holocaust world — was "evangelization by deed." Therefore, relations with Jews had to become ecumenical, and mission shift to Christians: to make them truly Christian.[98]

John Oesterreicher's life journey remains instructive for those interested in mission to the Jews because perhaps no Catholic in modern history was more determined to convert Jews. In 1960, he sacrificed his friendship to Karl Thieme over this question, also alienating the *Freiburger Rundbrief* circle, the most serious advocates of Christian-Jewish understanding in Europe, who considered him a closed-minded advocate of converting all Jews. Yet after the council he arrived at the same position they did. In a 1970 retrospective of *Nostra Aetate*, Oesterreicher summarized what he took to be the Church's attitude:

> A major obstacle to constructive dialogue between Christians and Jews is the suspicion of some Jews that the [Vatican II] Statement [on the Jews] is but a screen for missionary efforts and the dialogue but a new device to win converts. A few Jews, by no means unfriendly, may even say that the Church cannot help it: She is missionary by her very nature. . . .
>
> To come to the contemporary scene, there is in the Church today no

---

97. Max Eisen, "Christian Missions to the Jews in North America and Great Britain," *Jewish Social Studies* 10, no. 1 (January 1948): 64 and 66.

98. Karl Thieme, "Die Christen, Die Juden und das Heil," *Frankfurter Hefte* 4, no. 2 (February 1949): 119; letter of Karl Thieme to Conrad Hoffmann, Committee on the Christian Approach to the Jews, International Missionary Council, London, 19 December 1950. NL Thieme, ED 163/39, IfZG.

drive, no organized effort to proselytize Jews, and none is contemplated for tomorrow. Though the Church will always profess Jesus as the Savior of all humanity; though she will never abandon her vision of a humanity united in the living God; though she will continue to welcome wholeheartedly to her ranks Jews who have been led to believe in Jesus as the Christ — they are, after all, essential to her make-up as the Church of Jews and gentiles — she cannot treat the worshippers of the Holy One, blessed be He, as if they dwelt 'in the land of death's dark shadow' (Mt 4:16 NEB; Is. 9:1).[99]

Oesterreicher asked whether Christianity and Judaism were not "two ways of righteousness that have complementary functions." Christianity and Judaism should coexist, both actively serving the cause of God's justice, their "polarity" meant to "be an agent that makes both communities, and the world with them, run toward the final consummation of which the prophets dreamed." "Do not both communities," he asked, "each in its own way, serve the will of God, and though seemingly apart, push together toward the ultimate goal: God's perfect reign and man's delivery from all and every evil?"[100] This was very close to the vision enunciated by Karl Thieme in 1958, approximating a position we now call two-covenant theology — something Pope Benedict has explicitly rejected.[101]

In his talk, Oesterreicher quoted from a paper in which the Sisters of Sion "resolutely eliminated every attempt at proselytism as contrary to the Church." They rejected "proselytism" because it sought to "make conversion an end without taking into account God's mysterious conduct. He alone knows what is best for the soul." In other words, foremost advocates of Jewish conversion had drawn similar conclusions to his.[102] Likewise, the

---

99. John M. Oesterreicher, *The Rediscovery of Judaism: A Re-examination of the Conciliar Statement on the Jews* (South Orange, NJ: Institute of Judaeo-Christian Studies, 1971), p. 39.

100. Originally in "Brothers in Hope," vol. 5 of *The Bridge*, ed. Oesterreicher (New York: Herder & Herder, 1970), pp. 27-30; reprinted in *The Rediscovery of Judaism*, p. 56. The passage begins as follows: "I have no doubt that at the end of the ages, the chasm will be closed, even though I do not know exactly by what wonder of grace unity will come. Is it necessary, indeed, possible that in the present eon . . . we do away with the opposing vision of Christians and Jews? Is their polarity . . ." (etc.).

101. Oesterreicher, *The Rediscovery of Judaism*, p. 57.

102. In September 1962, just as the council in Rome was getting under way, the Congregation's General Council suggested that the sisters shift their efforts to countering anti-Semitism. The sisters of Sion had spent their days teaching and doing charitable work, as

Sion fathers discovered they first had to combat stereotypes about Jews among Christians if they were to make "really existing" Christianity attractive to Jews. In March 1953 Father Paul Démann of the Sion fathers began publishing the *Cahiers de Sion* with the aim of strengthening "the links between the church and Israel, to explain their common spiritual patrimony, to define and promote a truly Christian attitude to Jews and Judaism, to work thus for an authentic rapprochement, having in mind the fullness of the People of God," that is, both Christians and Jews.[103] With fellow converts Geza Vermes and Renée Bloch, Démann led a campaign from the Paris offices of *Cahiers* against the anti-Semitism of French Catholic textbooks.[104]

John Oesterreicher thus made at least two conversions in his life: one from Jew to Catholic, another from Catholic missionary to Israel to advocate among Catholics for Israel — including the State of Israel. How to account for the change? As suggested, the issue was partly a practical one. In prewar Vienna Oesterreicher began to realize that mission was self-defeating if Christians remained anti-Semites: that is, when they behaved as "poorly baptized Gentiles." In the late 1950s Oesterreicher was arguing that Christians could not preach Christ to the world if they did not give an example through their lives. Or, to use a word dear to present-day advocates of mission: one could not "proclaim" Christianity if one did not live Christianity.

Then he entered the cauldron of the Vatican Council's theological debate and reflection, out of which emerged an appreciation for Paul's promise that "all Israel will be saved." For Oesterreicher, this experience meant increasingly intimate exchanges with Jewish scholars. Ernst Ludwig Ehrlich has been mentioned, but there was also Joseph Lichten, a "pioneer" in interfaith relations, for many years director of the intercultural affairs

---

well as praying for the conversion of Israel. Mary C. Boys, "The Sisters of Sion: From a Conversionist Stance to a Dialogical Way of Life," *Journal of Ecumenical Studies* 31, nos. 1-2 (Winter-Spring 1994): 36.

103. Cited in Boys, "The Sisters of Sion," pp. 37-38, n. 26.

104. Among their publications was *La Catéchèse chrétienne et le peuple de la Bible* (Paris: Cahiers sioniens, 1952). See the discussion in Geza Vermes, *Providential Accidents: An Autobiography* (Lanham, MD: Rowman & Littlefield, 1999), pp. 100-103. See also the interview of Vermes on Austrian Radio National, 28 August 1999, at http://www.abc.net.au/rn/relig/spirit/stories/s47729.htm (retrieved 18 April 2005). Bloch died tragically in 1955, and Vermes left the Church and Démann the congregation. Olivier Rota, "Dépasser les cadres du philosémitisme. La vision œcuménique de Paul Démann," *Archives Juives* 40, no. 1 (2007): 117-30.

department, Anti-defamation League of B'nai B'rith. As representative of the ADL at the Second Vatican Council, Lichten is well known for having brought concrete information on the role of the deicide charge in fomenting anti-Semitism among American Catholics.[105] Lichten's relations with Oesterreicher dated from 1961 and lasted until the former's death in 1987, in the course of which the Monsignor spent happy social hours in the company of Lichten and his wife Carol in Italy as well as the U.S.,[106] and on occasion pumped the ADL representative for information about what was going on in the Vatican.

A second key friendship began inauspiciously for Oesterreicher. In February 1957 he received a letter from Rabbi Jacob Petuchowski of Hebrew Union College rebuking him for taking bits of a review written for *Commentary,* and using them to advertise for subscriptions to *The Bridge.*[107] In fact, Petuchowski had disputed the scholarly character of articles that poorly disguised the assumption that Jews must become Christians. Yet in the end, the Rabbi wrote, one could hardly expect Christians to have any other belief. Dialogue meant that both sides were strengthened in their respective faiths. From 1964 until the Rabbi's death in 1991 the two maintained a vigorous correspondence, advising each other on all manner of issues, and becoming personally close, with Oesterreicher going out of his way to visit Petuchowski in Cincinnati (and sharing dinner with the Rabbi, his wife, and children).[108] Oesterreicher was eager for the Rabbi's commentaries on his writings, and Petuchowski came to respect Oester-

105. Daniel F. Polish, "A Very Small Lever Can Move the Entire World," in *Unanswered Questions: Theological Views of Jewish-Catholic Relations,* ed. Roger Brooks (Notre Dame: University of Notre Dame Press, 1988), pp. 87-88.

106. Oesterreicher addressed Lichten as "Joe"; Lichten addressed Oesterreicher as "Monsignor John." *Oesterreicher Papers,* SHUL.

107. He concluded his letter of 25 February 1957 to Oesterreicher, which begins "Dear sir": "In my future contacts with literature emanating from the Institute of Judaeo-Christian Studies I shall, of course, be guided and warned by the precedent which your circulation department has set." Oesterreicher roared back, criticizing Petuchowski for his treatment in the review of Raïssa Maritain, but also sending volume two of *The Bridge.* Petuchowski's review of *The Bridge,* vol. 1, appeared in *Commentary* May 1956. *Oesterreicher Papers,* SHUL.

108. After a visit to Notre Dame, Oesterreicher made a detour on his way home in Cincinnati. Petuchowski, delighted, writes (16 February 1966): "far more important than what we think of Maurice Eisendrath is the prospect of your coming to Cincinnati, and the substitution of some good viva voce talk for laborious correspondence.... [I]f you could be in Cincinnati on Sunday March 27, my wife and I would be delighted to have you join us for dinner, and we could spend the rest of the evening in my study, talking." This was their first personal meeting. *Oesterreicher Papers,* SHUL.

reicher's interpretations of Christian teachings about the Jews, regarding them as refreshingly enlightened.[109]

The two were frank about disagreements; Petuchowski, for example, strongly dissented from Oesterreicher's view that one could absolve the Church from fostering anti-Semitism over the ages. The Church had rarely employed its real institutional power to hold back anti-Semites among its own faithful, Petuchowski argued, all the while excommunicating "all kinds of 'erroneous' doctrines and teachings."[110]

The more Oesterreicher spoke to Jews the more his language changed. As a working group of German Catholic Christians and Jews has recently written: If there is dialogue, there is no mission; if there is mission, there is no dialogue.[111] Precisely when Christians engage Jews on a human level, and extend bonds of Christian charity, they discover that mission with its implicit supersessionism is impossible. Christians who grow to esteem and love Jewish persons will not hope for a destruction of their Jewish personality. Father John Pawlikowski, among the most active and productive Catholics involved in Christian-Jewish relations after Vatican II, has made the point compellingly. In a tribute to recently deceased Rabbi Michael Signer, Abrams Chair of Jewish Thought and Culture at Notre Dame, he wrote:

> I knew in my heart that I could never speak to Michael in the words and tone of *Dominus Iesus* because the depth of his spirituality forged within the Jewish tradition but also drawn from his encounter with Christianity demanded something more positive and personal. There is no way at

109. In his introduction to Oesterreicher's *The Rediscovery of Judaism,* he closed with the words: "Conceivably, there may be other less charitable and human 'interpretations' of the Conciliar statement than the one offered by Monsignor Oesterreicher; and great searchings of the heart will yet have to take place with the Church before the stereotypes and the rigidities of the past will finally be overcome. But, when the time comes, we hope and pray that the generous and humane 'interpretation' outlined in this booklet will be the one which — like Hillel's 'interpretation' in the rabbinic tradition — is accepted as decisive."

110. On 18 July 1965 Petuchowski wrote that one cannot simply separate Christianity from anti-Semitism. "After all the Roman church, of all religious institutions, has its discipline, and throughout history, it has seen fit to ban and to excommunicate all kinds of 'erroneous' doctrines and teachings. Yet, when it comes to antisemitism, the Church has been all too sparing in exercising that discipline."

111. *"Nein zur Judenmission, Ja zum Dialog zwischen Juden und Christen,"* statement of working group *"'Juden und Christen' beim Zentralkomitee der deutschen Katholiken,"* 9 March 2009, at http://www.zdk.de/data/erklaerungen/pdf/Nein_zur_Judenmission_2009 _03_09_(Broschuere)_1238657494.pdf (retrieved 24 May 2010).

the level of such personal encounter that I could say that my spirituality was superior to his despite my deep commitment to the gospel.[112]

Superficially, mission can take many different forms, from forced conversion to subtle proselytism. Yet common to all is an attitude of Christian superiority and therefore disrespect. To transcend mission one must therefore transcend this attitude. The authors of *Notes on Ambiguities* may have sought to protect the Church from accusations of opportunism. But the point about ecumenism replacing mission is not that mission is not (or is no longer) opportune; the point is that it was never opportune because it was never Christian. When Christians approach Jews as neighbors, they will seek to affirm rather than deny their dignity.

The language in part four of *Nostra Aetate (De Judeisis)* reflected an understanding that proclaiming the gospel, like any form of communication, involves listening as much as it involves speaking. The document's drafters had "heard" what the slightest hints of mission sounded like in Jewish ears, and their text therefore became a case in point of subtle elaboration, of humility in the face of ultimate questions. There seems a lesson as well here for those who would like to build upon *Nostra Aetate*, perhaps formulating a *Nostra Aetate* 2.1: that their audience includes Jews as well as Christians, and those who attempt to gain too tight a hold on elusive truths risk setbacks. John Borelli called the U.S. bishops' *Notes on Ambiguities* a "unilateral and premature attempt to be doctrinally precise, jeopardizing the relations with Jews necessary for dialogue."[113]

Yet there is also another lesson from the Church's experience with mission to the Jews. The audience includes Christians as well as Jews. Perhaps Catholics should not "invite" Jews to baptism, but neither can they close their doors. Without converts, especially converts from Judaism, there would be no Church to begin with. In more recent times, it is hard to imagine, without converts, breakthroughs in Christian-Jewish relations. Converts bring fresh sensitivities that the Church would otherwise not have. In a time when very few Christians knew or cared about relations to Jews (from the 1930s to 1950s), virtually every one of note involved in furthering dialogue was a convert. The final draft of *de Judeis* was prepared by three converts of Jewish origin: John Oesterreicher, Gregory Baum, and

---

112. http://www.ccjr.us/news/in-memoriam/michael-signer/tribute-to-michael -signer?start=50 (retrieved 24 May 2010).

113. Borelli, "Troubled Waters," p. 23.

Bruno Hussar.[114] But in the intellectual development stretching up to that point, virtually every person involved in arguing against anti-Semitism was a convert, starting with Leon Bloy, then his godchildren Jacques and Raïssa Maritain, Oesterreicher's allies Karl Thieme and Dietrich von Hildebrand, Waldemar Gurian (who with Oesterreicher and Thieme authored the first major Catholic statement on the Jewish question in 1937), the Swiss Rudolf Lämmel, the Czech Albert Fuchs, the Austrian Walter Berger, the Germans Eric Peterson and Annie Kraus, and the Hungarian Aurel Kolnai.

Major initiatives in the Church to combat anti-Semitism stemmed from converts. We have mentioned *Cahiers de Sion*, but there was also Oesterreicher's publication *Die Erfüllung* in Vienna of the 1930s, and Hildebrand's *Der Christliche Ständestaat*. At the First Vatican Council in 1870 the brothers Lémann — Jews who had become Catholics and priests — presented a draft declaration on relations between Church and Jews stating that Jews "are always very dear to God because of their fathers and because Christ has issued from them according to the flesh." This was an initiative without precedent.[115] A half century later, the Dutch nun and convert and former anarchist Maria Francesca Van Leer founded an initiative with two Dutch priests favoring greater understanding called "Amici Israel." It demanded an end to calling Jews "deicidal," to targeting Jews for "conversion" (they preferred speaking of "return"), and to speaking without respect for Jewish ritual. Instead, the group urged Catholics to underscore God's special love for the people of Israel, and the permanence of this love.[116]

As John Pawlikowski has argued, there is much work to be done beyond recapturing the legacy of *Nostra Aetate*'s chapter 4, which did away with the sources of anti-Semitism, but did not provide a new language, a new vision for Christian-Jewish relations, which figure as an awkward footnote (as noted above in the case of *Dialogue and Proclamation*) or not

114. Riccardo Burigana and Giovanni Turbanti, "Zwischen den Sitzungsperioden," in *Geschichte des Zweiten Vatikanischen Konzils*, ed. Giuseppe Alberigo and Günther Wassilowsky, vol. 4: *Die Kirche als Gemeinschaft* (Ostfildern: Grünewald, 2006), p. 643, n. 216.

115. As a petition it was signed by 508 of 1,087 bishops in attendance; the petition was withdrawn to prevent greater support of this than of the draft on papal infallibility, which had reached 510 signatures. René Laurentin, *L'église et les juifs à Vatican II* (Paris: Cerf, 1967), pp. 43-44.

116. This from their brochure *Pax super Israel.*

at all in general statements about the Church's relation to other faiths. In the case of *Dominus Iesus* no footnote appeared, and readers were left to speculate, to interpret through the lens of other statements and assume that its strong language did not apply to the Jews.[117] As Pawlikowski writes, the new language in statements about Christian-Jewish relations has not yet impinged upon Catholics in terms of their "theological identity."

There is something strange about the present situation, in which the Church strains relations with Jews over the future of a mission to the Jews that it never really had — while ignoring the lessons of those very few who practiced mission a generation or two earlier. Those lessons are vital, but don't result in simple answers. The challenge for Catholics remains not only to affirm, but to build upon the insight — affirmed many times by John Paul II and others — that Jews are embraced by the saving grace of the covenant made to them, while not denying that Christ's offer of redemption extends to all humankind. That challenge faced the drafters of *Nostra Aetate* as it faced Paul: Will theologians of the future improve upon the Apostle's eschatological vision? The Catholics and Jews who formulated last year's statement on mission to the Jews of the Central Committee of German Catholics thought not. "When, how and whether Jews and Christians will encounter each other on their way to the 'Kingdom of God' is a mystery of God hidden from us humans," they wrote. And they concluded with Paul's final words of chapter 11 in the letter to the Romans — the chapter in which Paul pondered the relation between his kinfolk and the emerging Church. "O depth of wealth, wisdom, and knowledge in God," he wrote. "How unsearchable his judgments, how untraceable his ways! Who knows the mind of the Lord? Who has been his counselor? Who has ever made a gift to him, to receive a gift in return? Source, Guide, and Goal of all that is — to him be glory forever! Amen."

117. For example, John Pawlikowski is left to extrapolate from Cardinal Kasper's own extrapolations from the writings of Cardinal Ratzinger. "Cardinal Walter Kasper," Pawlikowski writes, "in commenting on the question of Jews and *Dominus Iesus*, cites Ratzinger's statement that Jews are an altogether special case in terms of their relationship with the Church. Ratzinger describes Judaism as the foundation of Christian faith, a perspective that Kasper takes to mean *Dominus Iesus* is not applicable to the Jews. The question remains as in 1964 one of how the end of time is envisioned." "Reflections on Covenant and Mission Forty Years after *Nostra Aetate*," *Cross Currents* (Winter 2007): 86-87 Rabbi Michael Signer emphasized the fact that Jews were not explicitly mentioned in *Dominus Iesus*, writing, "We should not be worried by this document. It does not mention Jews and Judaism. There is no retrenchment of the position of the Vatican or the American bishops toward dialogue with Judaism." Michael A. Signer, "A Jewish Response to *Dominus Iesus: On the Unicity and Salvific Universality of Jesus Christ and the Church*," http://jcrelations.net/en/index.php?id=780 (retrieved 25 May 2010).

# A Soldier of the Great War: Henri de Lubac and the Patristic Sources for a Premodern Theology

*Robin Darling Young*

> *The Catholics of this country have fallen into mere custom in the practice of their religion, to the point where they don't bother themselves to know whether it is true or false, [or] whether they do, or do not, believe; and this kind of mechanical faith accompanies them unto death.*[1]

The French-born American writer Julien Green (d. 1998), author of *Each in His Own Darkness*, along with a river of novels and journals, wrote the above lines in a pseudonymous pamphlet, after he graduated from the University of Virginia and returned to the France for which he had fought in World War I. An exiled Southerner, nostalgic for the Confederacy and troubled by his homosexuality, Green had converted to Catholicism at sixteen, two years after his beloved mother's death. He longed keenly for an ancient social unity, and France had supplied both displaced son and nostalgic mother with an antiquity and a national defeat to cherish — analogous to the South's. Yet "unto death," Green realized, French Catholics failed to supply his needs. They were complacent, unmoved by the drama of faith — in short, bored.

Green may have recorded what he sensed of the secularization that had, in France and the rest of Europe, progressed from a political arrangement to a disease of the Christian soul. Did they believe in that savior, and

---

1. "Les catholiques de ce pays sont tombés dans l'habitude de leur religion, au point qu'ils ne s'inquiètent plus de savoir si elle est vraie ou fausse, s'ils y croient ou non; et cette espèce de foi machinale les accompagne jusqu'à la mort." Julien Green, *Pamphlet contre les catholiques de France* (Paris: Plon, 1963 [1924]).

his church, for whom Green had longed? Their "mechanical faith" may have satisfied some, but its putative causes troubled another thoughtful Catholic and veteran, too. Henri de Lubac's entire career as a theologian and scholar seemed directed beyond the apparent topics of his research in early Christian and medieval theology, toward the reanimation of Catholic society, and, in turn, his thought and writing were an animating genius of the Second Vatican Council, which took seriously — after a century of retreat and avoidance — the situation of the old church in a new, postrevolutionary world.

Like Green, de Lubac was troubled by the Church in France and in Europe generally, as it emerged from the terrible years of war: not only did its people display the disheartening symptoms of religious apathy, but the theology of the church — and, more importantly, the theology *about* the church, its ecclesiology — was stale, outdated, and inadequate. Like Green, de Lubac understood that contradiction and paradox marked the path of a human being, and of the church, in the world. This Pauline sense of the Christian's simultaneous desire and alienation he saw rooted in the gospel as well. It marked the church with mystery from its origins:

> De Lubac was a master of paradox. He envisioned the Church as both a paradox and a mystery. Of the latter dimension he said, "The Church is a mystery for all time out of man's grasp because, qualitatively, it is totally removed from all other objects of man's knowledge that might be mentioned. And yet, at the same time, it concerns us, touches us, acts in us, reveals us to ourselves."[2]

De Lubac published these lines in the afterglow of the Second Vatican Council, communicating his own appreciation of the patristic and medieval theology that, before the calcifying effects of scholastic thought *de ecclesia,* reflected further on that Gospel and Pauline sense of the Christian life — singly and corporately — as a pilgrimage and a soul-stirring mystery. Over the course of the next two decades, de Lubac would retain his sense — rooted in the early Christian doctrine of the preexistent, heavenly

---

2. See Dennis M. Doyle, "Henri de Lubac and the Roots of Communion Ecclesiology," *Theological Studies* 60 (1999): 209-27, with useful bibliography of studies to that point. Here he quotes, p. 212, from *The Church: Paradox and Mystery,* trans. James R. Dunne (New York: Alba House, 1969), p. 14. See also Brian E. Daley, "The *Nouvelle Théologie* and the Patristic Revival: Sources, Symbols and the Science of Theology," *International Journal of Theology* 7 (2005): 362-82.

Church — that at its core, or in its eschatological destination, the Church is among the mysteries belonging to God, full of light and goodness, destined to return to its heavenly origins at the end of the world's history. But what actually appeared on earth in the twentieth century, after the council's interpreters and engineers swiftly and with forcible unanimity reshaped the postconciliar rituals and customs of the church, appalled some and disappointed many, including de Lubac. He began to register his unease with the effects of the revolutionary theology he had launched.

This essay argues that de Lubac's evocation of patristic ecclesiology and its sense of the ecclesiastical mystery failed to live up to its promise in the confusion and sometimes-rancorous debates that have marked the forty-five years since the conclusion of the council. It did so, not because de Lubac misrepresented that tradition, but because his synthesis of early Christian thought, particularly in *Catholicism,* represented it only partially.[3]

De Lubac did not, and perhaps could not, investigate, recognize, and adequately represent the dark sea of conflict and disagreement in the first several centuries of Christianity *as a characteristic of the church itself* — a sea of conflict over which Origen, and even Augustine on his happier days, seem to sail confidently in their portrayals of Christianity as a pilgrim church. Absent from de Lubac's considerations — and therefore from his expectations — were the bitter polemics among early Christians about the Church itself and about its teaching, discipline, and habits — especially its habits of aggressive apologetics and rhetorical attack against "the gentiles" — the pagan majority. Absent, as well, was the early Christian warfare against the Jews that appeared already in the second century, and gained real velocity in the fifth; absent, too, was its growing depreciation of women and human sexual expression. In short, de Lubac appreciated a certain early Christian rhetorical evocation of the Church as mystery, without studiously attending to the drumbeat of strife beneath the mystic chords of ecclesiastical memory. Thus, I argue, the very nostalgic, romantic theology of the Church and its early theology — the *ressourcement* finally legitimized at the council — failed to prepare de Lubac, and many other hopeful reformers, for the rancorous conflict that followed. It was a premodern theology that has not, at least so far, contained and shaped the changes that it helped to inspire.

3. Henri de Lubac, *Catholicism,* trans. Lancelot C. Sheppard (New York: Mentor-Omega, 1964 [1947]).

\*     \*     \*

De Lubac's own younger confrere, John W. O'Malley, S.J., has chronicled exquisitely the preparations and course of the council and has demonstrated how the French Jesuit had an impact on that meeting. For one thing, de Lubac's role in the revival of patristic literature as a tradition and an "outlook" crucial for the renewed life of the church predated the council by more than forty years; and, for another, his presence as a formerly silenced, and now vindicated, theologian was interpreted as a signal that changes were in order.

O'Malley's book shows how the "adaptation of patristic outlook and language became widespread among younger theologians in Europe."[4] O'Malley relates how the cardinal-archbishop of Cologne, Josef Frings, urged another cardinal to free the conciliar documents from the wooden language of standard theological handbooks, and "speak instead the vital language of Scripture and the Church Fathers."[5] Frings's ghostwriter then was none other than the future Benedict XVI, the young theologian Josef Ratzinger.

Neither de Lubac nor Ratzinger foresaw the unintended results of the council. In the years following it, their Catholic cultivation of ancient patristic thought became, first, a means for various kinds of liberalization and more recently, an instrument of conservative reaction. Yet in seeking to revive an apparently lively, less problematic, even mythologically archaic form of language and liturgical life, the council fathers, inspired by the work of de Lubac and others, unwittingly set in motion an engine of nostalgia no less powerful than Green's evocations of the American South. Its measure may be taken both by recent appeals to patristic theology to justify the "theology of the body" (a corrupting thing generally mistrusted by the "fathers of the church") and by recourse to patristic exegesis as a weapon against historical-critical study of the scriptures.

It is ironic, then, that the theologian whose thought partially inspired and guided two of the great Constitutions of the Second Vatican Council is often taken to be a herald of the Roman Catholic Church's delayed engagement with the challenges of modernity.[6] Henri de Lubac, S.J., *peritus* at the

---

4. John O'Malley, S.J., *What Happened at Vatican II* (Cambridge, MA, and London: Belknap/Harvard University Press, 2008), p. 76.

5. O'Malley, *What Happened at Vatican II*, p. 76.

6. See, for example, R. R. Reno's extreme statement of this view in "Theology After the Revolution," *First Things* (May 2007), a review of Fergus Kerr's *Twentieth-Century Catholic*

council and contributor to its schemata, had already in two ways helped initiate this *ressourcement* of theology. First, he devoted some of his early writings to a critique of the Thomist construal of nature and grace. Second, he turned to the past to investigate and revive the theology — and particularly the scriptural exegesis — of early Christian authors to call forth a fuller sense of the mysteries of the church and of its sacred writings.

In what follows I will consider de Lubac's earliest book, *Catholicism*, as the first instance and overall example of de Lubac's efforts. After exploring the context of this first major work in the French Catholic community, I will undertake a close reading of it in order to lay out the origin of certain themes that were taken up nearly three decades later in the schemata for conciliar documents. I hope thus to contribute to discussion about the construction of the theology of the council as a way of illuminating that council's documents, clarifying their origins, and throwing light on de Lubac's postcouncil disillusionment.

The Second Vatican Council differed from previous ecumenical councils. It met not to address a heresy or a schism; it was convened to address the church itself. In announcing the council, Pope John XXIII affirmed "the need to reaffirm doctrine and discipline," and also affirmed two more aims: "the enlightenment, edification and joy of the entire Christian people," and the extension of "a renewed cordial invitation to the faithful of the separated communities to participate with us in this quest for unity and grace, for which so many souls long in all parts of the world."[7]

These aims suggest that in the minds of some ecclesiastical writers — and the pope himself — the church had in some way become a problem that had to be addressed; and indeed, the work of many Roman Catholic theologians in the decades before the council, while it extolled and de-

---

*Theology.* Reno writes, "Like Lonergan, de Lubac is characteristic of the Heroic Generation: He helped destroy the theological culture that, however inadequate, provided the context for a proper understanding of his generation's lasting achievements." Reno calls these theologians "the revolutionaries who did so much to shape the Catholic Church of the second half of the twentieth century" — not a compliment, in his view. Another example of a popular assessment — but a more positive one — can be found in Maureen Sullivan, O.P., *The Road to Vatican II: Key Changes in Theology* (New York: Paulist, 2007), pp. 21-22: "One of the central goals of de Lubac and the other ressourcement thinkers was to bring about a contact between Catholic theology and contemporary thought. . . . De Lubac's inquiries were grounded in an accurate exegesis of scripture and a serious study of the early church fathers. He also provided an openness to those outside the Roman Catholic faith with an approach to the supernatural that underlies all religions."

7. O'Malley, *What Happened at Vatican II*, p. 17.

fended the church, was clearly preoccupied with the question of how to make the church able to appeal to mid-twentieth-century humanity. De Lubac was only one of these theologians; but he is widely acknowledged to be one of the most influential in this project of apology and evangelization. The following essay is a tribute, then, to the grand work of historical investigation and illumination that John O'Malley has accomplished, and has given to his readers.

## The Context of de Lubac's Catholicism in Early Twentieth-Century France

Henri de Lubac's writings — particularly his early ones — do indeed sound the themes of modern personalism and even anticipate some of the views of its related philosophy, existentialism. Yet it would be mistaken, in my view, to interpret de Lubac's writings as a response to modernity that takes into account and acknowledges the vexed questions of the nineteenth century. The implications of Darwin's works for Catholic teachings and the subsequent controversies they stirred among Christians in general, and for Catholics in particular, leave de Lubac's writing untouched. The implications of evolution for either Thomist or early Christian conceptions of human nature and destiny have, in fact, never been squarely addressed.

Likewise, the historical studies of the late nineteenth and early twentieth centuries do not find a sustained and considered response in his works. Closer to his area of study than the theory of evolution were the works of the historians Ernest Renan (d. 1892), Alfred Loisy (d. 1940), and Louis Duchesne (d. 1922),[8] with their thoroughgoing challenges to the pious and received understanding of early Christianity as identical, minus heresy, to later Roman Catholicism. Yet their works seem not to have influenced de Lubac's. The condemnation of modernism in 1907, and the imposition of the anti-modernism oath in 1910 — with which seminarians and profes-

---

8. For a description of the career of Duchesne, who despite his approach to historiography never parted company with the church, see W. H. C. Frend, "Mgr Louis Duchesne (1843-1922): Critical Churchman and Historian," in *From Dogma to History: How Our Understanding of the Early Church Developed* (London: SCM Press, 2003), pp. 108-43. De Lubac was aware of the work of the critical historians, and particularly of Adolf von Harnack, but he rejected Harnack's sundering of Hellenism from biblical Christianity. See *Catholicism*, p. xx.

sors and some other clerics were taxed with an annual recitation[9] — probably to some extent contributed to his subsequent failure to engage these thinkers. Duchesne, for instance, finished his *Early History of the Christian Church* in 1905, but its emphasis upon the struggles among early Christian groups did not alter de Lubac's largely harmonized presentation of early Christian theological themes.[10]

De Lubac, a brilliant thinker whose reading was hardly confined to theological subjects, seems to have chosen another path. He was a scion of French aristocracy, essentially a son of the nineteenth century, and forced into the terrible war that crushed Europe's way of life, de Lubac seems to have been among those who sought a refuge elsewhere, before the corrosive modernity of the postwar twentieth century crushed the way of life of his social class. Like his humbler English coeval J. R. R. Tolkien, de Lubac turned to a reconstructed, dramatic, and heroic antiquity — already known to be an imaginary antiquity — for the literary sources of a true and noble way of life.[11] A kind of heroism can be drawn from the literature of the early church, whose combative asceticism seemed to inspire de Lubac's participation in the Resistance during World War II, when he understood as spiritual combat the opposition to Nazi racism and deportation of Jews.[12]

Thus it would be plausible to propose that de Lubac's approach extends, but in a different mode, the approach of Leo XIII, particularly in *Rerum Novarum* and *Providentissimus Deus*. In effect, de Lubac's approach rests upon a mythology of the "patristic age," in which the *catholica*, perhaps best understood as the divinely given bond uniting Christianity (the term comes from Irenaeus), is the mystery of God's presence through his incarnate son. By means of such an approach, the deflating results of

9. From 1910 to 1966. See Donald Cozzens, *Sacred Silence: Denial and Crisis in the Church* (Collegeville, MN: Liturgical Press, 2004), pp. 37, 43 — although some crossed their fingers behind their backs (personal confidence to the author by a seminarian in the 1960s at the Catholic University of America).

10. Louis Duchesne, *Early History of the Christian Church from Its Foundation to the End of the Fifth Century*, 4th ed. (New York: Longmans, 1925). See, e.g., chapter 11, "Gnosticism and Marcionism," in the same volume.

11. For an interesting discussion of the Catholic and theological aims of Tolkien in *The Lord of the Rings*, see Nicholas Boyle, *Sacred and Secular Scriptures: A Catholic Approach to Literature* (Notre Dame: University Press, 2005), pp. 253-60.

12. See, for example, "*Le combat spirituel*," pp. 282-95, in *Théologie dans l'histoire*, vol. 2: *Questions disputées et résistance au nazisme* (Paris: Desclée de Brouwer, 1989) (originally in *Citée nouvelle* [1943]: 769-83).

historical-critical biblical exegesis can be avoided entirely. In de Lubac's telling, the spiritual exegesis of its scriptures, old and new covenant both, communicates the symbols and truth of the Incarnation. Its theology communicates again — once it comes into view from behind neo-scholastic accretions — the joyful, and poignant, desire for God implanted into all human beings. De Lubac sounds this very note later in his work, when he writes of the Bible and its interpretation by (a limited range of) patristic exegetes: "There soon rings out everywhere the triumphal hymn, whose first notes we heard in St. Irenaeus, then in Clement and Origen, in Hilary and in Ambrose. Now-opened eyes saw the Gospel everywhere in the Law and the Church everywhere in Israel."[13]

Such a view of the energizing effects of patristic literature, first articulated in book form in *Catholicism,* may have had a broad appeal for many French Catholics in the uncertain and dire period between the wars. After all, the Oxford movement in the Anglican Communion had, in the previous century, brought about (in the view of its proponents) a partial restoration of a more coherent, traditional, and anti-secularist Christian faith and practice.[14]

Yet, although it had rejuvenated some parts of the Anglican Church with its *Library of the Fathers* (and propelled others toward Rome), this *ressourcement* had taken place seventy-five years previously and in a church unattached to the systematization of a theology based on Thomas Aquinas. Although de Lubac's "nouvelle théologie," as hostile neo-Thomists called it, did not gain its full audience until after World War II, it was already resulting in numerous publications aimed at restoring the patristic sources of theology to a wider audience — not to clerics alone but to all the French laity.[15]

---

13. Henri de Lubac, *Scripture in the Tradition* (New York: Crossroad, 1967), pp. 15-16. The troubling, even chilling, implications of such a supersessionist view did not become apparent to most Catholic thinkers until after World War II; indeed, in *Catholicism* de Lubac wrote (p. 36): "Judaism passed to Christianity its understanding of an essentially social salvation" (*"le judaisme donne au christianisme sa conception d'un salut essentiallement social"*), and he meant it as a tribute.

14. See Kenneth Leech and Rowan Williams, eds., *Essays Catholic and Radical: A Jubilee Group Symposium for the 150th Anniversary of the Beginning of the Oxford Movement, 1833-1983* (London: Bowerdean, 1983); and Edward R. Norman, *Church and Society in England 1770-1970: A Historical Study* (Oxford: Clarendon, 1976).

15. For an account of the rise of the scholarly and/or theological field of patristics in Europe, from the nineteenth to the mid-twentieth centuries, see Elizabeth A. Clark, "From Patristics to Early Christian Studies," in *The Oxford Handbook of Early Christian Studies,* ed. Susan Ashbrook Harvey and David G. Hunter (Oxford: Oxford University Press, 2008),

Many of de Lubac's works, were they to have actually been written in the first centuries of Mediterranean Christianity, could have been described as protreptic — that is, as hortatory rhetoric in the service of conversion. De Lubac's mild and hopeful tone is repeated in the two documents of Vatican II over which they seem to have had the most influence — *Lumen Gentium* and *Gaudium et Spes.*

Yet de Lubac's early works presuppose a *catholica* that was a *desideratum* but cannot be demonstrated ever to have existed. For all that his version of the *catholica* gained the benefits of a community free of the distinction between the natural and supernatural, de Lubac's evocation stifles the voices of the controversy that guided Origen's exegesis or Irenaeus's catalogue of heresies rebutted. Missing are the cultures of early Christianity that are neither Greek nor Latin, and unaccounted for is the mutual borrowing among pagan and Christian. Invisible are the outbursts of apocalyptic fervor or the burgeoning collections of canon laws. Absent are the aggravations and seemingly needful restrictions upon female Christians. Most hauntingly, there is no acknowledgment of the ongoing presence of the Jews as claimants to the Hebrew scriptures and their interpretation.[16] The latter is especially mysterious in light of de Lubac's theory of human unity, and, while under the Vichy government, his perilous criticism of anti-Semitism.

Even the personalist influence has not been thoroughly absorbed in his work. For all that de Lubac read and appreciated Dostoevsky, his version of patristic thought is most unlike the Russian's reproduction of polyphonic subjectivity in personal relationships and human communities. In theology, de Lubac seemed early on to prefer a synthesis and a monologue; his is a monosexual Christianity that, like Tolkien's fellowship, calls forth a nobility of thought and action for the purposes of inspiration. As Fergus Kerr has noted, "in a way de Lubac re-created a whole premodern Catholic sensibility which he wanted to inhabit."[17]

---

pp. 7-41. See also Charles Kannengiesser, "Fifty Years of Patristics," *Theological Studies* 50 (1989): 633-56, and "The Future of Patristics," *Theological Studies* 52 (1991): 128-39.

16. Again, in *Scripture in the Tradition,* de Lubac is drawn to say the following while praising the "spiritual understanding" of Scripture as developed from Irenaeus through Origen to Gregory the Great: "The ancient Jews, those at least who were faithful, did understand Scripture, to the extent that God then willed that they understand it; but those Jews who, by refusing to recognize Jesus Christ, refused to recognize the New Covenant lost their understanding of Scripture itself" (pp. 90-91), and, more straightforwardly, "without Jesus Christ the Old Testament is a cadaver."

17. Fergus Kerr, *Twentieth Century Catholic Theologians* (Oxford: Blackwell, 2007), p. 69.

To make that observation is not to diminish the grandeur, the "primeval forest" of de Lubac's work.[18] It is worth stating, though, that de Lubac's work failed to acknowledge the clash that has always accompanied Christian thought once it becomes published. Had it done so, the influence of his work might have been felt in a more realistic way when incorporated into the documents of an ecumenical council charged with *aggiornamento*.

De Lubac himself abjured a return to the past — even a more sympathetic past than the one to which Garrigou-Lagrange was attached. Yet his selective and harmonized reading of early Christian documents may have misled the young theologians who expected it to rejuvenate the present church, especially when accompanied by the liturgical renewal, a parallel *ressourcement* with which it was sympathetic. The promise of an organic, unified church, a world that could draw in the greater world as its lost relation, may have depended upon the wish for a restored organic unity that had been fractured in the sixteenth century, when the territorial churches replaced the loosely connected regions of the medieval church and the ever more centralizing remainder became the Roman Catholic Church, already exporting the Tridentine faith to the colonies of Catholic regimes.

Further in the past, the unitary world of the imagined patristic *catholica* had depended almost entirely upon the political and cultural unity brought by the later Roman empire, and spread by the church that empire made its own; 1918 brought the conclusive termination of its successors with the dismemberment of the Dual Monarchy and the brutal termination of the Russian imperial family. Yet without thoroughly absorbing the historicist view of Christianity, it was impossible to recognize that the original source of theological unity lay in the rhetoric of the empire.

The book *The Mystery of the Supernatural* contained de Lubac's overt criticism of neo-Thomism and its view of human nature.[19] Attempting to establish the correct reading of Aquinas's thought by means of discovering Suarez's errors in citing spurious works of Thomas, as well as by a rereading of Christology, de Lubac was facing down a settled opinion in Catholic theology that can easily be represented by Msgr. Joseph Pohle's article on

18. Hans Urs von Balthasar, *The Theology of Henri de Lubac* (San Francisco: Ignatius, 1991), p. 23.

19. Henri de Lubac, *The Mystery of the Supernatural*, trans. Rosemary Sheed (Southwark: Chapman, 1967). See John Milbank, *The Suspended Middle: Henri de Lubac and the Debate Concerning the Supernatural* (Grand Rapids: Eerdmans, 2005), for an account of the controversy. See also Noel O'Sullivan, "Henri de Lubac's *Surnaturel*: An Emerging Christology," *Irish Theological Quarterly* 72, no. 1 (2007): 3-31.

actual grace in the 1909 *Catholic Encyclopedia*. To the author of the following statement, though, de Lubac's aspirations and expressions would have seemed impermissibly vague. Pohle wrote:

> Actual grace is that unmerited interior assistance which God, in virtue of the merits of Christ, confers upon fallen man in order to strengthen, on the one hand, his infirmity resulting from sin and, on the other, to render him capable, by elevation to the supernatural order, of supernatural acts of the soul, so that he may attain justification, persevere in it to the end, and thus enter into everlasting life.[20]

For de Lubac, such a view represented a calcified, and even false, reading of St. Thomas on the subject of grace. Certainly it did not represent the thought of the fathers, no matter where any one of them stood on the matter. Because he struggled against, and for a time was hounded by, the defenders of the right-wing reading of St. Thomas, de Lubac has gained the aura of a knight of faith. The romanticism about him shared by his admirers corresponds in some way to the ardent romanticism with which he approached his own work, a work of retrieval of ancient greatness for a church ever more deserted by her children in the years between the two wars. De Lubac "exposed himself to the attacks of a tutiorist scholastic theology, armed with nothing but the historical and theological truth. Of the three martyrs for truth, he was the most tortured, far beyond the tortures endured by Blondel."[21]

Yet this hagiographical narrative overlooks the ways in which de Lubac and others turned from the pressing questions as specified above, and, in combating the reactionary forces in the church, ultimately engaged in a remythologizing without having truly considered the prior demythologization. But their project seemed therapeutic for the church in the difficult period between the two world wars.

## Catholic Intellectuals in Postwar France

In a France swinging politically between restored monarchy and republic, the lively voices of Catholic intellectuals in the late nineteenth and early

---

20. *The Catholic Encyclopedia*, vol. 1 (New York: Robert Appleton Company, 1909). Pohle was an original member of the faculty of the new Catholic University of America, and later published a *Dogmatic Theology* in twelve volumes.

21. Balthasar, *The Theology of Henri de Lubac*, p. 13.

twentieth century may have obscured the changes in Catholic practice that presaged, not an engagement with personalist Christianity, but a general disengagement from the Christian religion entirely. A good example can be found in the writings of Julien Green, who, as mentioned, made the terrible discovery of not a few converts — that the Catholic practice he had fervently adopted was among many of its native citizens "of a mechanical kind."

Of his fellow-convert to Roman Catholicism, Jacques Maritain later wrote that Green, like Leon Bloy, railed not without reason at "the religion of those who believe that they believe in God and live as if God didn't exist."[22] This young man of genteel Southern heritage, transplanted to France, became a Catholic in 1914. Ten years later, disillusioned and discouraged, he wrote the *Pamphlet contre les catholiques de France*, noting over thirty years later of his surname, "It said clearly that I loved God, but as to 'Delaporte [of the gate]' . . . What gate? I liked better not to know [the answer]. There was the gate of paradise and that of hell."[23]

Born only six years before Henri de Lubac, and like de Lubac a foot soldier in the French forces in World War I, Green shared the disquiet of many Catholic intellectuals of the period between the world wars. For the *Pamphlet*, he chose "contours pascaliens" to shock the reader's sensibilities with 249 sentences on faith and *ennui* — and, no doubt, to express the struggles with religious faith and keen sensuality that mark as well his journals and novels. Green's *pensées* attempt to give voice to the religious emotions elicited by the personalist movement as marks and occasions for the expression of the depth — and loneliness — of the human being in solitude, and for the bonds connecting the person with the entire community of humanity.

Green was neither philosopher nor theologian. Yet his impatience with the conventions of the French Catholic population makes him one of a large and variegated segment of thinkers to which de Lubac, immured in ecclesiastical institutions, belonged as well. They were anguished; they were earnest; they feared for the life of the Church in France; they bent their learning toward its rejuvenation.[24]

---

22. "La religion de ceux qui croient qu'ils croient en Dieu et vivent comme si Dieu n'existait pas." Jacques et Raïssa Maritain, "Préface au livre de Julien Green," in *Ouvres complètes*, vol. 12 (Fribourg: Éditions Universitaires; Paris: Éditions Saint-Paul, 1992), p. 1289.

23. "Disait clairement que j'aimais Dieu, [mais] quant à Delaporte . . . Quelle porte? J'aimais mieux ne pas le savoir. Il y avait la porte du paradise et celle de l'enfer." Green, *Pamphlet*, p. 5.

24. M. Eigeldinger, *Julien Green ou la Tentation de P'irréel* (Paris: Éditions des Portes de

For this group of thinkers — personalists inspired by Emmanuel Mounier such as Blondel, Claudel, Rousselot, even Peter Maurin — the challenges of eighteenth-century rationalism were less feared than passé. Like the Russian-exile personalists with whom they sometimes conversed in Paris — Sergei Bulgakov and Nicholas Berdyaev — they were confronting the damage inflicted upon human communities by the industrialization of certain regions of France and the various left-wing socialist movements of the nineteenth century. Since the late nineteenth century, Russian philosophers had been turning back to their ancient traditions in an attempt to regain a sense of the dignity and the destiny of humanity and to place it within the orbit of Christianity. Their personalism was a distinctly Christian attempt to refresh Russian culture with a religious culture that did not deal automatically with its members, but could conceive grandly of humanity before God — infusing, as it were, a grand sense of the human being through a liturgized literature. If Soloviev and Florensky brought forward Dostoevsky's keen sense of the human, and returned it explicitly to Christianity, they were not alone in thinking that a return to ancient Christian literature — the fathers of the church — could help the Russian community confront both rationalism and political mass movements, with the dehumanization implicit in both.

Their works stimulated the numerous books composed by Bulgakov and Berdyaev as they took up residence in the exiled Russian community of Paris — where those who still hoped for a revival of Russian Christianity gathered in the Institut Saint-Serge and acted, to the degree that they could, as the intellectual community that, from its distance, could not only keep the Russian church's existence alive, but infuse its (traditionalist, rigid) institutions with the urgent questions of the moment.

The setting of the Catholic population in France was vastly different from that of the Orthodox exiles there, and yet both contained groups that looked beyond mere political compromise and social security, toward a personal, but not unmediated, encounter between God and humanity. It was the still-living, but faint, voice of the ancient tradition that, for both groups, could awaken and overcome the fossilization and complacency of the recent past.

Yet as John O'Malley has written in chapter two of *What Happened at Vatican II*, the situation in the institutions — particularly in the seminar-

---

France, 1947); J. M. Dunaway, *The Metamorphoses of the Self: The Mystic, the Sensualist, and the Artist in the Works of Julien Green* (Lexington: University of Kentucky Press, 1978).

ies and schools — of the Roman Catholic Church, both in France and elsewhere in Europe, was significantly different. The double blows of the Enlightenment and the revolutions in Europe from the 1780s through the 1840s had precipitated a strong counter-reaction in Catholic culture and in the hierarchy. One of the effects of the First Vatican Council was to ratify in reaction to modernity the attachment to the neo-Thomist approach to theology, launched by Leo XIII and even more firmly asserted in the wake of the modernist controversy. So despite the work of Möhler, von Hügel, and Newman in his Catholic period, Catholic theology seemed firmly in the grip of the manualist approach — and firmly opposed to recent, controversial theories having to do with evolution, on the one hand, or critical biblical theory, on the other.

Thus paradoxically Catholic theology — at that time the business only of the clergy — was drawn toward an appropriation of ancient theology much more slowly than were the Orthodox theologians mentioned above. It was drawn toward an existentialist or personalist approach much more slowly than the nonclerical followers of Mounier.[25] The long-lasting ecclesiastical reaction against Loisy and Tyrell, and against Liberalism in general, had led to the crackdown on modernism and the emphasis upon the necessity of teaching theology in the footsteps of Thomas Aquinas. Thus right through the four periods of the council, there were theologians and bishops who viewed the new approaches in theology and in biblical studies with unease and distaste, and they resisted their influence.

Not all those who studied and taught the theology of Thomas Aquinas were supporters of the neoscholastic model or of the particular authorities in the church who regarded that model as indispensable. In the twenties and thirties, Jacques Maritain, for instance, was, in the French church, intent upon putting forward the vital philosophy of Thomas Aquinas in an-

---

25. As Ralph Gibson noted, however, already in French Catholicism of the nineteenth century there was a shift in emphasis: whereas the church of the postrevolutionary period had retained a Tridentine model, with an emphasis on the world and the body as sources of evil, and on sin and guilt — the *pastorale de la peur* — in the course of the nineteenth century "priests came increasingly to emphasize the love between God and man. . . . The whole direction of French spirituality changed, from one of asceticism and renunciation, toward that emphasis on the love of God that made the spirituality of Saint Theresa [*sic*] of Lisieux so immensely popular. . . . French Catholicism was in the process of evolving from a religion encouraging a sense of guilt and fear to one of encouraging a sense of God's forgiving love." Ralph Gibson, *A Social History of French Catholicism, 1789-1914* (London and New York: Routledge, 1989), pp. 272-73.

swer to needs, as he saw them, of modern society. Among the Dominicans, of course, Thomas was the central theological authority, and Congar and Chenu, while they contextualized Thomas and his theology, never abandoned him.

The Jesuit theologians of Lyons were the thinkers who really began the work of patristic *ressourcement,* and they began it immediately after the conclusion of the Great War. Two names are linked as the first to embark on the study of patristic sources as a way of redirecting, and reanimating, Catholic society. Although their approaches and their studies were very different, their work — particularly in the publication of the series *Sources chrétiennes* — overlapped and contributed to each other's (and both were later named cardinals). The younger of the two men, Jean Daniélou (1905-1964), entered the Society of Jesus in 1929 and, like de Lubac, studied in Jersey and then at Lyons, where he appears to have been turned toward his lifelong study of Gregory of Nyssa, Origen, and patristic exegesis. But Daniélou, willing as he was to join in the program of de Lubac, would not become a theologian; he remained a scholar of patristics and an ecclesiastic more directly involved in ministry. Although his scholarly and priestly reputation led him to be considered a candidate for the papacy, his influence upon a change of direction in Catholic theology *per se* was less than de Lubac's.[26]

De Lubac was the older man, and thus the teacher to Daniélou. Born in 1896, he entered the Society of Jesus in 1913. His first studies were in Jersey, but they were interrupted by his enlistment in the French forces in 1914, at the beginning of the war. De Lubac's life, it seems safe to say, was permanently affected by the war in a way that Daniélou's was not. Although the same cultural upheaval affected their society and their presuppositions, de Lubac served and was wounded in the head; he suffered peri-

---

26. Daniélou's background and life differed markedly from de Lubac's as well, as the child of a family riven by *odium religiosum.* He was the older brother (by two years) of the famous Hindologist Alain Daniélou, who himself engaged in a revival of ancient culture, though in his case the erotic religions of India. The younger brother reflected, in his autobiography, on the rigor and moral cruelty of the French Catholic bourgeoisie and in particular on his mother, wife of an anticlerical lawyer, who expelled him from the household and established a female religious order there. He wrote that although she had eventually showed him great tenderness at the end of her life, "my mother was a prisoner of the Church and its totalitarian ideology." However, he considered Jean a saint and a martyr to scandalous rumor at the time of his death. Alain Daniélou, *The Way to the Labyrinth: Memories of East and West* (New York: New Directions, 1987), pp. 20, 28-29.

odically from the effects of his wound. He surely suffered as greatly from the loss of several of his best friends in the war. He returned to his studies after his discharge, and was ordained in 1927. He began teaching theology in Lyons and gained pupils, among whom the most well known were Daniélou and Hans Urs von Balthasar. The latter wrote several explanations of his work that can supplement de Lubac's own, later, recollections.[27] Both men, not surprisingly, remember their early lives as scholars inside the institutions of the church — institutions that had been closed or suspended during the four years of the war, but whose continuity seemed assured once they reopened, and their custodians, the officials of religious orders, returned to guide them.

Yet the world into which de Lubac returned from the war was one that presented a starkly different picture from the one he had left behind in 1913 to become a priest and a scholar. Although his generation had suffered the restrictions imposed by the Third Republic in France, these anti-ecclesiastical measures were not unfamiliar after the strains of nineteenth-century French culture — split between an increasing sense of *laïcité* and the swelling devotions to newly found shrines such as Lourdes and La Sallette. Religious institutions took them in stride.

So did the strains of French society, and European society in general, after the war. The nineteenth century, as O'Malley makes clear, had generally been one of reaction in the European Catholic Church. But this was particularly true for France; if Bismarck had initiated one Kulturkampf, the reaction against the Catholic Church in France seemingly had led both to the outbursts of piety associated with Lourdes and La Sallette, and to the increasingly reactionary stance of the Catholic traditionalist group, which would culminate in the early twentieth century with *Action française* and the extension under Pius X of the *Sodalitum Pianum* to combat modernism in every diocese. A moment of respite in some ways, of course, from the Catholic point of view, had been the pontificate of Leo XIII, and indeed two of the best well-known themes of Leo's pontificate could be seen as being fulfilled in the work that de Lubac undertook for himself. The first was the response to modernism in *Providentissimus Deus*, and the second was the response to the labor union movement in

---

27. *The Theology of Henri de Lubac* is a collection of Balthasar's accounts of de Lubac. By de Lubac himself is *Mémoire sur l'occasion de mes écrits* (Paris: Cerf, 1989); and *At the Service of the Church: Henri de Lubac Reflects on the Circumstances That Occasioned His Writings* (San Francisco: Ignatius, 1993).

*Rerum Novarum.* In the second, the pope had responded favorably to those within the church who wished to move away from monarchism and the impulse to return to a premodern, medieval society on the model of guilds and fixed social stations. But in the first, the pope had responded to Loisy and Tyrell, who had themselves tried to take seriously the historical research of biblical scholars and the implications of social democratic movements.

To some degree, these were the very tensions within French Catholicism that formed de Lubac, even though they do not appear directly in his early writings. His response to the question of social democracy, and to Marxism and socialism, was the collectivism to be found in the fathers of the church — with its emphasis upon the social bonds that connected all mankind and made the latter the object of Jesus' saving work.

De Lubac's response, however, to the historical investigations of Duchesne — or, even worse, to the investigations of Protestant historians — was to update, in effect, the recommendations of *Providentissimus,* and to return to the investigation of the fathers of the church and to connect them with the biblical text in order to find the resources for the rejuvenation of the Catholic tradition. That this made him unpopular with the right wing in France, and particularly with the strict Thomists among the Jesuits or in Rome, as evidenced, ultimately, by the 1950 encyclical *Humani Generis,* does not diminish the conservatism of de Lubac's effort.

Indeed, this can be seen in the praise that Balthasar lavishes upon him in his memoir of de Lubac:

> Whoever stands before the forty or so volumes of Henri de Lubac's writings . . . feels as though he is at the entrance to a primeval forest. . . . To one who begins to penetrate and become familiar with these major works, this seeming jungle reveals the order of an organic whole . . . that unfolds an eminently successful attempt to present the spirit of Catholic Christianity to contemporary man in such a way that he appears credible in himself and his historical development as well as in dialogue with the major forms of other interpretations of the world — and even feels confident in proposing the unique complete ("catholic") solution to the riddle of existence.[28]

Yet the everyday world after 1913 was dramatically changed. The following description evokes the confusion of the period — a sense against which

28. Balthasar, *The Theology of Henri de Lubac,* p. 23.

the walls of the church could hardly protect their inmates. Its author, rendered stateless in the annexation of Bukovina by Romania, writes of the displacement and disorientation of his parents' generation — the very generation to which de Lubac belonged:

> On the surface, the world seemed unchanged, but it was all the more spooky for that. In the first installment of the worldwide war which had come only to a temporary halt in 1918 and broke out all the more fiercely two decades later, an order had been destroyed in which, up to then, everybody had put faith. Critical voices had not been lacking: the world before 1914 no longer considered itself the best of all possible ones. But it was a world in which culture still rated high. The meat grinders of Ypres and Tannenberg, the hellish barrages of Verdun and the Isonzo shattered all illusions. A species of men arose from that ghostly landscape of bomb craters and trenches whose bestiality was unconstrained. A free field was given to the Hitlers and Stalins to come.
>
> For the class to which my parents belonged, this meant a fall into chaos, into impotence and deprivation, hopelessness and squalor. What today is designated by the collective noun bourgeoisie lived with an imperturbable faith in what Robert Musil's Count Leinsdorf called "property and learning." All the trust in life that these two pillars had supported collapsed together with them. The resulting changes in reality were so sudden, unpredicted and incomprehensible that at first they seemed more like a monstrous nightmare. The desire to wake from the bad dream gave rise to the utopia of the 1920s, one of the worst byproducts of which was to be the Third Reich. But most people remained stunned and paralyzed: sleepwalkers in an alienated present.[29]

De Lubac was no sleepwalker — but from the time of the war, he seems to have devoted himself to recovering sources from the past that could answer to both the despair and the aspirations characteristic of European thinkers in those twenty years between the two wars. He was also no stranger to the problem of alienation, both in the church and in the wider European society to which the church should appeal. There is a kind of mourning tone that suffuses de Lubac's work, particularly *Catholicism*, a mourning perhaps alleviated during Vatican II but become more acute in the years after the council.

---

29. Gregor von Rezzori, *The Snows of Yesteryear: Portraits for an Autobiography*, trans. H. F. Broch de Rothermann (New York: Knopf, 1989), p. 64.

## Catholicism

As Joseph Komonchak has observed, from the time of de Lubac's earliest published work, the theologian made an effort to surmount a "separated theology" that reinforced the church's separation from the world: "a church closed in upon itself, alienated from the larger world, unable and even unwilling to undertake to redeem it."[30] As Komonchak notes, "de Lubac considered one of the causes of this cultural and political alienation to be a distinctly modern theory of the relationship between nature and grace."[31] Whether de Lubac was correct in thinking that a faulty theology was responsible for the problems of Catholic culture after the eighteenth century, it does seem clear that his work, from the very first, was meant both to call attention to an earlier, more confident stance of the church and to bridge the distance between the habits and attitudes of the church and those of the postwar world. De Lubac taught fundamental theology at Lyons and was not a trained historian. His turn *ad fontes* represented, four centuries later, something like the efforts of the Protestant reformers to uncover the original structure and attitude of the Christian community as it existed before the church became the papally dominated, unevangelical institution that they thought it had wrongly become. It was not, however. De Lubac wanted to refresh the church with forgotten fathers, not use their ideas as a criterion to measure the church's misdirection. Here de Lubac would have been in agreement with Congar's later work, *True and False Reform in the Church:* true reform returns to the principles of Catholicism.[32] De Lubac began:

> The philosophical problem itself no longer appears as a matter of pure science . . . many who would not have dreamt of disputing its historical claims or criticizing its metaphysical foundations are beginning to be doubtful of its permanent value. "How," they ask in particular, "can a religion which apparently is uninterested in our terrestrial future and in human fellowship offer an ideal which can still attract the men of today?"[33]

---

30. Joseph Komonchak, writing in a critical and incisive review of John Milbank's *The Suspended Middle,* in *Pro Ecclesia* 17, no. 4 (2008): 464-69.

31. Komonchak, review of *The Suspended Middle,* pp. 464-65.

32. See Yves Congar, *True and False Reform in the Church,* trans. Paul Philibert (Collegeville, MN: Liturgical Press, 2011).

33. De Lubac, *Catholicism,* p. ix.

"In answer to all this," de Lubac continues, "we may quote this simple assertion of a believer and a theologian: 'Fundamentally the Gospel is obsessed with the idea of the unity of human society.'"[34] De Lubac meant the work to be read by all believers, not merely by theologians-in-training; in that sense he wanted to reach beyond the world of conferences to novices, and to demonstrate the unity of witnesses in the common tradition, to what Catholicism really meant and toward what it was aimed.

The historian is inclined to read this book in at least two ways. First, of course, the book is a product of its own time and of the specific, religious problems that, as Lubac has stated, occasioned it. The production of the secular by the actions of the dominant religious body in Europe resulted, de Lubac believed, from a hitherto unnoticed theological error that had established the realm of "pure nature" supposedly not conceived by Aquinas. In other words, a theoretical mistake ultimately led to the destruction of the religious because of an attempt to describe a metaphysical zone in which the religious could operate. One might say that this was the problem of Jansenism in a different vein[35] — and that, conversely, it secured that the supernatural was available but was still extrinsic to the human being. De Lubac would later attack this problem in *The Mystery of the Supernatural*, the book for which he was punished by Rome and by his Jesuit superior.

In *Catholicism*, de Lubac was on a different track. This was his first book, and it was the result of his early reading and lecturing on various theological problems, upon which he had brought to bear a conviction that he had developed from combing through the volumes of *Patrologia Graeca* and *Latina* during his twenties and early thirties. Of de Lubac at this stage, Balthasar writes that he understood the development of atheism as "Western man's turning away from his Christian origins," out of resentment and disgust, so that anti-theism takes the place of religion.[36] This understanding led him to a certain sympathy even for Proudhon, with his

34. E. Masure, conference in *Semaine sociale de Nice* (1934), p. 229; in de Lubac, *Catholicism*, p. 15.

35. See Leszek Kolakowski, *God Owes Us Nothing: A Brief Remark on Pascal's Religion and on the Spirit of Jansenism* (Chicago: University of Chicago Press, 1996), for a study of the theology of Pascal and Port-Royal, and the resultant compromise on the part of ecclesiastical authorities; it marked French Catholicism deeply.

36. Henri de Lubac, *Le Drame de l'humanisme Athée* (Paris, 1963 [1944]), p. 5, in Balthasar, *The Theology of Henri de Lubac*, p. 29.

criticisms of the church as a source of opposition, the "anti-theology" of which the late nineteenth- and early twentieth-century theology was so full. De Lubac's response can already be found, according to Balthasar, in *Catholicism;* it "sets the style and orientation for all that will follow, reveals the fundamental decision as a decision for fullness, totality, and the widest possible horizon."[37] This requires de Lubac to identify rigidities in Catholic thought. In this early work, de Lubac identified "the abandoning of the concrete, salvation-historical thought of the Fathers and high scholasticism in favor of a rationalistic thought that has led to the separation in anthropology between (self-contained) natural finality and supernatural orientation."[38] Here Balthasar refers to *The Mystery of the Supernatural,* but it was true as well of *Catholicism.* Of the latter, he wrote:

> "He brought all newness in bringing himself." Irenaeus' dictum about Christ, often quoted by de Lubac, may stand as the title of the attempt to understand the three great personal achievements of our author in their mutual interdependence. *Catholicism* placed Christ's Church in a coordinate system: first, (vertical) transcendence of Christianity (as an individual historical form among others) to the totality of the world-redemption contained in it; then, (horizontal, temporal) transcendence of the time of promise to the time of fulfillment, of the Old Covenant to the New Covenant.[39]

The term "salvation-history," taken by Balthasar from biblical theology, asserts that the grand narrative of the Bible is the salvation of the people of God, and through them, the world — a Christian reading of the history of the covenant(s), but one meant by its Protestant originators to emphasize the great mission of the church to the world in place of their own scholastic orthodoxies.

Another interpretation of the book comes from a preface by then-Cardinal Joseph Ratzinger, published in a reissue of the English translation. Writing on the fiftieth anniversary of *Catholicism,* Ratzinger described his excitement at encountering the book in the early fifties, when it was apparently making its rounds among German Jesuits. On the eve of the new millennium, and with a jaundiced view of the direction of some Catholic theologies since that time, Ratzinger remarks, "It fascinated theo-

37. Balthasar, *The Theology of Henri de Lubac,* p. 28.
38. Balthasar, *The Theology of Henri de Lubac,* pp. 28-29.
39. Balthasar, *The Theology of Henri de Lubac,* p. 61.

logians in the fifties everywhere and his fundamental insights quickly became the common patrimony of theological reflection."[40]

Yet there were distortions in the intervening period, and a Catholic attitude that had been overly individualistic had been replaced by something even worse, Ratzinger implies: "The social dimension which de Lubac saw rooted in deepest mystery has often sunk to the merely sociological. . . . Instead of a leaven for the age, or its salt, we are often simply its echo."[41] Here Ratzinger refers to the uprooting and in his view destruction that accompanied the "spirit of the council," and for which he has proposed a "hermeneutic of continuity" as a corrective. Neither the theology nor the church of the years post 1965 is different from the previous nineteen and a half centuries (by his count). That is why Ratzinger emphasizes the institution that is, according to him, the point of *Catholicism:*

> He makes visible to us in a new way the fundamental institution of Christian Faith. . . . [H]e shows how the idea of community and universality, rooted in the Trinitarian concept of God, permeates and shapes all the individual elements of Faith's content. The idea of the Catholic, the all-embracing, the inner unity of I and Thou and We . . . is the key that opens the door to the proper understanding of the whole. . . . [De Lubac] lets the voice of the fathers of our Faith speak so that we hear the voice of the origin in all its freshness and astonishing relevance.[42]

One might want to object that de Lubac at least implicitly recognizes that the Faith has mothers as well, since he included in the appendix to *Catholicism* a quotation from Julian of Norwich's *Revelations of Divine Love*. Yet she is the exception that proves the rule; one of the characteristics of this and other representative works of the "patristic revival" is their studied avoidance of any mention of women, children, or other representatives of social difference in favor of a monosexual "mankind" to whom the appeal of the fathers is made, and from whom it allegedly sprang.

This point allows for a transition to a general observation about the work. Written during a period when second-wave feminism was being hotly debated in France — a consequence both of the high proportion of

---

40. Joseph Cardinal Ratzinger, "Foreword," in de Lubac, *Catholicism: Christ and the Common Destiny of Man* (San Francisco: Ignatius, 1988), p. 12.

41. Ratzinger, "Foreword," p. 12.

42. Ratzinger, "Foreword," p. 11.

single women due to loss of the generation of eligible bachelors in the war and of the consequent movement of women into the industrial and semi-professional workforce — *Catholicism* directs its call elsewhere. One thinks that the audience — originally members of male religious orders — was broadened primarily to lay male Catholics who might recognize in themselves the nobility of mankind as sketched by the fathers of the church. And for the most part, the appeal to the fathers of the church as a source of refreshment to their latter-day descendants has indeed been made mostly by male scholars and theologians — going so far as to propose that the "complementarity" upon which the theology of the body is founded actually springs from the fathers themselves. Here for convenience only Origen needs to be listed, who thought that sexual activity between husband and wife, even in a continent relationship, was polluting to such an extent that it required them to pray in a room other than their bedchamber.[43]

Although this matter may seem beside the point, it is actually not. *Catholicism* proposed a view of the church that was inclusive and unifying. As we have seen, it has been credited with stirring up enthusiasm for patristic theology not as mere archaeology but as a source of renewal. Further, it is generally regarded as containing *in nuce* the major themes of de Lubac's later works — which though not systematic in the theological sense, had a tremendous impact upon a younger generation and set the stage for at least three constitutions of the council. Therefore it is worth looking at *Catholicism* again, not only from the point of view of its immediate context and later impact, but as a construction placed upon the theological ideas of early Christianity. How does *Catholicism* represent patristic thought, and precisely what does it revive? Balthasar wrote:

> de Lubac [beyond the methods of Maritain, Gilson, Blondel] thought there was a thinking illumined by the light of Christian faith, a thinking as the Church Fathers practiced it and for which he thought he could find points of departure in Gabriel Marcel.[44]

43. Origen of Alexandria, "On Prayer 20," in *Origen: An Exhortation to Martyrdom, Prayer, and Selected Works*, ed. and trans. Rowan Greer (Mahwah, NJ: Paulist, 1979). It has taken the scholarly labors of an Orthodox nun, Sr. Nonna Verna Harrison, to show that implicit in the theology of Gregory of Nyssa is a conviction of the essential equality of the (temporarily) gendered members of the human race. See Verna E. F. Harrison, "Male and Female in Cappadocian Theology," *Journal of Theological Studies* 41 (1990): 441-71.

44. Balthasar, *The Theology of Henri de Lubac*, p. 16.

*Catholicism* has, it must be admitted, a certain maddening quality, which can be described as the rhetoricization of the dialectic. De Lubac knows what is wrong with Catholicism in the period in which he writes; he names particular tendencies without being very specific about where and in whom they are to be found. Thus he does not prove his assertions by means of evidence. Rather, he states them and backs away. He identifies misconceptions of Catholicism that are to be found in current French authors — its closed character, its concern for individual salvation from a corrupt world, its "detachment." But this serves to make a point that de Lubac will repeat in the following pages:

> This shows the full extent of the misunderstanding. We are accused of being individualists even in spite of ourselves, by the logic of our faith, whereas in reality Catholicism is essentially social. It is social in the deepest sense of the word: not merely in its applications in the field of natural institutions but first and foremost in itself, in the heart of its mystery, in the essence of its dogma. It is social in a sense which should have made the expression "social Catholicism" pleonastic.[45]

De Lubac goes on to say that such a misunderstanding can be laid at the door of Catholics themselves — and that his book is meant to correct it. The pages of *Catholicism,* he writes, "are addressed to believers who are concerned to have a better understanding of the faith by which they live."[46]

This gives de Lubac the opportunity to again back away from matters that he will not address: Christianity's part in social progress or a plan for social reform that it could inspire; the *catholica,* or "the rich resources of scripture and the great doctors on the subject of man's solidarity with the universe, or on our relations with the world of pure Spirits." No treatise on "the mystical body," "the Catholic principle of Tradition," or "Catholic Action."[47] In short, de Lubac steers clear of ethics or its consequences, and of history and its complications.

Rather, his object in the twelve chapters that make up the work is to demonstrate Catholicism's "social character." To that end, de Lubac attempts to take an old form of theological statement — from the fundamental theology that he himself taught at Lyons — and infuse it, by means

---

45. Balthasar, *The Theology of Henri de Lubac,* p. xi.

46. Balthasar, *The Theology of Henri de Lubac,* p. xi.

47. Balthasar, *The Theology of Henri de Lubac.* The quotations in this paragraph are from pp. xi-xii.

of his kind of dialectic of negation and evocative statement, with new content. Balthasar's concise summary of the work is helpful here: the first section (chapters one through four) "develops the idea of total solidarity in four steps. They are, first, that God intends to redeem mankind as a whole in Christ; second, that the church Christ founded "can be ordered only to this totality of redemption" by reunifying fragmented man. Third, the sacraments of baptism, confession, and Eucharist, the central sacraments of Christianity, promote this reunion by means of incorporation, reconciliation, and communion; as Balthasar states, "the Eucharist above all is the mystery of the deepest union with the brothers." Fourth, eternal life — "communion in the trinitarian God: the heavenly Jerusalem" is the goal of these sacraments.[48]

The second section of the book, Balthasar states, "unfolds the historical dimension in five steps." Here de Lubac already begins his approach to non-Christian religions that characterizes them as nonhistorical, offering only "an individualistic doctrine of evasion." The five chapters of the second section of the book thus concern themselves with the Incarnation as an entry into history; the division of "salvation-history" into the two periods of the Old and New Covenant; the way in which other religions contain portions of the truth that are fulfilled only in and by Catholic truth; the reason for the "late arrival" of Christ (the "preparation" of humanity by the Logos, the absorption and transformation of the world by the Church). Chapters ten through twelve are, according to Balthasar, "complementary."[49] As he notices, the tenth chapter could stand as the introduction to the entire work, and because that seems to be an accurate statement, it is well to scrutinize this chapter in particular.

De Lubac begins this chapter, "The Present Situation," with a quotation from Ernest Renan's *Marc-Aurèle*.[50] Renan believed that Christianity had, until the beginning of the third century, been simply a source of personal consolation for a few fortunate individuals. Renan's life and work was an understandable irritant for de Lubac, but in the course of the chapter he concedes that individualism had overtaken Western culture, and Catholicism with it, that it was a dangerous misinterpretation of Christianity; and that the approach of the fathers of the church, "the philosophy of his-

---

48. Balthasar, *The Theology of Henri de Lubac*. The quotations in this paragraph are from pp. 36-37.

49. Balthasar, *The Theology of Henri de Lubac*, p. 37.

50. Ernest Renan, *The Origins of Christianity*, vol. 6 (London: Mathiesen, 1881), p. 166.

tory . . . of humanity in time," had not remained the orientation of Christianity.[51] Then, however, de Lubac goes on to absolve theology: the rise of individualism had penetrated the life of the church from outside; unchecked, it had led to Marxism.

A second problem was the way in which the church had tended to teach against heresies, inadvertently defining its teaching against, and therefore in the terms of, its enemies:

> [The theologian] often accepts questions in the form in which the heretic propounds them, so that without sharing the error he may make implicit concessions to his opponent, which are the more serious the more explicit are his refutations. Can it be maintained that Catholic exegesis, in certain instances of narrow-mindedness, was never influenced in that way by the Protestant idea of the Bible? And nowadays, seeing the matter in its proper perspective, don't we realize that the "separated" philosophy of recent centuries has found its correlative in a "separated" theology? . . . But for about three centuries, faced by the naturalist trends of modern thought on the one hand and the confusions of a bastard Augustinianism on the other, many could see salvation only in a complete severance between the natural and the supernatural.[52]

In the introduction to the book, de Lubac alerts the reader to his purpose first by specifying what he has not accomplished. More than seventy years later, the historian is in a position to evaluate what he did accomplish, both consciously and unwittingly. Susan Wood summarizes well the conscious intention behind de Lubac's theological project, begun shortly after 1918 and worked out over the course of fifty years:

> The key to an understanding of the social unity of the human race . . . is the realization that for him anthropology is inseparable from Christology. . . . [W]hat it means to be human is inseparable from union with Christ in the whole Christ. Supposing that de Lubac's theology is at least in part motivated by its historical context, his emphasis on the social character of Catholicism and on the human person's supernatural destiny may find its proximate historical impetus in his response to the nineteenth-century atheist hermeneutic represented by Comte, Feuerbach and Nietzsche. De Lubac's emphasis on the social character of Ca-

---

51. Renan, *The Origins of Christianity*, p. 167.
52. Renan, *The Origins of Christianity*, p. 171.

tholicism not only represents a retrieval of a patristic theme consistent with the interests of the "new theology," but also responds to the neoscholastic interpretation of human finality as well as to the nineteenth-century atheist humanism which converted theology to anthropology. . . . By stressing the unity of the human race and then interpreting this unity by its reference to Christ, de Lubac in effect converts anthropology back into theology and responds to Comte's charge of individualism.[53]

Wood notes that the Appendix to *Catholicism* is an example of the "retrieval of the patristic theme" connecting Christ and the human community. It is useful, therefore, to conclude with a brief examination of this Appendix.

It is clear throughout *Catholicism* that de Lubac intended the entire book to be an antidote to the "evil" of individualism. A symptom of the evil is a disappointment "caused by the bitter fruits of individualism in all branches of theology. . . . A better but still too imperfect knowledge of the patristic period, as well as of the golden age of medieval theology, studied in conjunction with the former, is a considerable guarantee of success."[54]

It seems clear that de Lubac had identified a modern problem — unity versus individualism — for which he sought a premodern prescription. The subject matter of de Lubac's Appendix is, of course, the *catholica* — the unity of faith — as evidenced here in another collection of texts from antiquity to modernity and grouped by subtheme. A full analysis of this Appendix would be tiresome at this point, but two observations are useful. First, this Appendix is in de Lubac's work analogous to an ancient or medieval *florilegium.* Second, this *florilegium* is utterly decontextualized so that the differences among genre, intention, setting, and even vocabulary are erased in the interest not only in the larger theme of unity but in the interest of the unity among the extracted texts themselves. The collection includes ancient, medieval, and modern European authors; it spans the Greek East and Latin West, at least in the happier period before 1054; the latest text quoted is from Symeon the New Theologian (d. 1022). The Appendix is thus a kind of fictive document in which all the voices evince a symbolic interpretation of biblical texts. If the first is a selection from Gregory of Nyssa on the creation of a double-natured human race, the divine and human aspects are for de Lubac

53. Susan K. Wood, *Spiritual Exegesis and the Church in the Theology of Henri de Lubac* (Grand Rapids: Eerdmans, 2008), pp. 130-31.
54. Wood, *Spiritual Exegesis and the Church,* p. 175.

a response to the "separated theology" he would later criticize in *The Mystery of the Supernatural;* if the last is a selection from a Holy Week sermon by pseudo-John Chrysostom on Christ as the Cosmic Tree, de Lubac intends to show by it the paradox of the divine-human Incarnation that secures the nature of humanity. Thus the Appendix is an example of the remedial use of patristic and medieval allegorical interpretation. De Lubac placed great hope in the potential of this cure for the ills of modernity. He shows himself to have been inspired by the rhetoric of certain early Christian preachers and biblical interpreters; in the following decades, such rhetoric was, as O'Malley has shown, influential at the Second Vatican Council as well. It remains to be seen whether that rhetoric has had the hoped-for medicinal effect upon subsequent generations.

John O'Malley has described the rhetoric of the conciliar documents as epideictic, and has traced the origin of their style, and much of their content, to the pioneers of *ressourcement* in the first half of the twentieth century. Of these men, themselves dependent upon earlier explorers of the forgotten lands of patristic sources, de Lubac is one of the most important, for his eloquent descriptions of those sources and his evocative call to human unity and fellowship against darker — irreligious or nontheistic — appeals to European humanity in the 1940s. Like an explorer in a new world, he wrote glowingly of the riches of his rediscovered world, and the wealth that could be restored to Europe, and to the Church. Yet de Lubac reported selectively the world of the *Patrologia,* and chose not to portray its shadows and omissions. De Lubac's portrayal of patristic unity helped to supplant an exhausted scholasticism, and it appealed to those elements in a European church in search of theological revival and a kind of European union after the destruction of the Second World War. A historian would exercise caution in judging the effects of this revival for the Roman Catholic Church over the long term. Nicholas Boyle has written to defend (against its detractors) the continuing usefulness of *Gaudium et Spes,* a document in part dependent upon de Lubac's work in *Catholicism* and elsewhere. Yet provisionally, the historian can also observe that more than one of *ressourcement*'s own architects came to regret the effects of the very council their work helped to stimulate, as in the development of recent Catholic theology and culture, patristic "inspiration" was left far behind and some of *ressourcement*'s defenders were forced to take rearguard action and emphasize the "hermeneutic of continuity."[55]

55. See "A Proper Hermeneutic for the Second Vatican Council," by Pope Benedict XVI,

De Lubac himself famously came to regret the excesses of the postconciliar period. He was in a position to observe that the patristic revival — *ressourcement* to its adherents, *la nouvelle théologie* to its former detractors — had been largely sidelined by the church as a whole. Particularly in its rituals and in its catechetical efforts — just those places where a religious culture lives and renews itself — the Church had, in the view of de Lubac and others, abandoned its venerable traditions for contemporary styles and opinions. Furthermore, the late-medieval distinction between the natural and the supernatural, arguably the central problem of de Lubac's work and the inspiration for his return to patristic theology, was overcome not by *ressourcement,* or the efforts of the *Communio* band of theologians loyal to it, but by the late-capitalist materialism that seemed to have become the religion of the West. In other words, theological and "spiritual" harmony did not arrive thanks to the patristic revival. A centralized church could command dismantling, but it could not bring about a harmonious adherence to a past and alleged synthesis. Reform permitted variety and contentiousness as Catholics took the interpretation of Vatican II into their own contemporary hands; a nostalgic reappropriation of the past was not on the agenda of those who took seriously the brief of *aggiorniamento.* It is unsurprising that de Lubac failed to anticipate this.

But then, as any historian of the sixteenth century (or the early twentieth) in Europe would have known, well-meaning, moderate, and institutionally loyal reforms seem to put in motion forces unseen by their proponents, and are often carried to lengths further than those of which they would have approved. Martin Luther was surprised by Thomas Müntzer, but Müntzer was one of many in the period who took portions of Luther's views beyond the reformer's intentions. Perhaps de Lubac's fabrication of a patristic theology for the purposes of renewal actually failed the renewal it envisioned because it could not anticipate or give space to the discordant elements that have comprised Christianity from its beginnings, elements

---

in *Vatican II: Renewal within Tradition,* ed. Matthew L. Lamb and Matthew Levering (New York: Oxford University Press, 2008), pp. ix-xv: "The question arises: Why has the implementation of the council, in large parts of the Church, thus far been so difficult?" Benedict contrasts the "hermeneutic of discontinuity and rupture" associated with "the mass media . . . and one trend of modern theology." On the other hand, "the hermeneutic of reform" reflects the "continuity of the one subject Church . . . [who] increases in time and develops; yet always remaining the same, the one subject of the journeying people of God." See also, in the same volume, "Nature, Mission and Structure of the Church," by Avery Cardinal Dulles, S.J., pp. 25-36, for a similar judgment.

that seem to take the lead whenever reform is the order of the day. De Lubac was a theologian, not a historian. Lacking the skeptical perspective of the latter trade, he may have expected too much of his theological reconstruction — it could excite theologians, but not return the church to its golden age of mystery.[56]

56. Others who take up de Lubac's ecclesiology as a program for reform, or re-reform, of their own churches may be similarly surprised at the results of translating a creative theological ecclesiology into an action agenda. Theory often falls before practical self-interest. For a good, recent Protestant Evangelical appreciation of de Lubac's work, see Hans Boersma, *Nouvelle Théologie and Sacramental Ontology: A Return to Mystery* (Oxford: Oxford University Press, 2001).

# Interpreting the Council and Its Consequences: Concluding Reflections

*Joseph A. Komonchak*

John O'Malley's book *What Happened at Vatican II* appears at a time when the achievements and value of the Second Vatican Council are again the subject of a conflict of interpretations. Some twenty years ago, I proposed that views of the council fell into three ideal-types.[1] A *progressive* interpretation works with a sharp dichotomy between the pre- and postconciliar Church, with the former being criticized very severely and the council praised for reforms of or departures from many Church attitudes, activities, and structures and for long-overdue accommodations to the modern world. Serious church-reform and updating had been resisted by Church leaders right up through the reign of Pope Pius XII (1939-1958), so that when the council set the Church on the path of the renewal and updating that Pope John XXIII proposed as goals of the council, it was natural that change and newness would be emphasized. Unfortunately, when the council ended and the bishops returned to their dioceses, the leaders of the Roman Curia remained in place — men who had looked with suspicion on the preconciliar movements of renewal and had resisted the council's new orientations. Unsympathetic to the spirit of the council, they used their authority to narrow and weaken the course of permanent reform and renewal to which the council had called the Church.

Perhaps not so oddly, a *traditionalist* interpretation of Vatican II works with the same sharp dichotomy, only the polarities are reversed. Preconciliar Catholicism had responded appropriately to the successive challenges represented by the Reformation, the Enlightenment, and the so-

---

1. See Joseph A. Komonchak, "Interpreting the Second Vatican Council," *Landas: Journal of Loyola School of Theology* 1 (1987): 81-90.

cial, cultural, and political revolutions of the nineteenth and twentieth centuries, a long genealogy of decline. In its teachings and in the reforms that it authorized, Vatican II called into question the attitudes, practices, and structures that the Church had developed in response to the challenges of modernity and, as the postconciliar chaos demonstrated, it left the Church powerless to maintain its traditional integrity or to pursue its apostolic mission to an apostate world. It was the council itself that was responsible for this capitulation before a modernity that had rightly been resisted before.

Between these opposing tendencies stands a *reformist* interpretation. It refuses the sharp dichotomy of before Vatican II and after and tends, therefore, to stress elements of continuity in the conciliar teachings and reforms. It argues that the popes and bishops of Vatican II never intended revolution but rather reform and especially spiritual renewal. If there has been confusion since the council, the fault lies not with the council itself, but with progressives whose "spirit of Vatican II" went far beyond and even contrary to the wishes of the council as set out in its sixteen documents, which are, however, the touchstones of the council's "spirit."

The third of these interpretations, of course, is the one that the present pope has been proposing for at least twenty-five years, and that he proposed again in his speech to the Roman Curia in December 2005. In his 1984 interview with Vittorio Messori, the then-Cardinal Ratzinger commented:

> There is no "pre-" or "post-" conciliar Church; there is but one, unique Church that walks the path toward the Lord, ever deepening and ever better understanding the treasure of faith that he himself has entrusted to her. There are no leaps in this history, there are no fractures, and there is no break in continuity.[2]

This view led him, in the 2005 speech, to offer his own typology of opposed interpretations of the council, a "hermeneutic of discontinuity" that ought to be resisted and a "hermeneutic of reform" that alone is adequate and accurate. This schema collapses my three interpretations into two and makes continuity into the sole, or at least, the principal criterion of differentiation; it passes over in silence the differences between the progressive and traditionalist evaluations of the aspects of discontinuity. Against both,

---

2. *The Ratzinger Report: An Exclusive Report on the State of the Church* (San Francisco: Ignatius, 1985), p. 35.

the claim is repeated that the Church is a "single subject . . . that grows in time and develops, while always remaining the same single subject, the People of God on its journey," and that for this reason one may not speak of "ruptures" or "breaks" in the Church's life.[3]

Pope Benedict's view has been oversimplified into a contrast between a hermeneutic of discontinuity and one of continuity and interpreted as a rejection of any approach that would speak of the council as a difference-making event in any sense other than spiritual. Continuity was so emphasized that John O'Malley was moved to title one of his essays "Did Anything Happen at Vatican II?"[4]

Whether the council must be considered an "event," and, if so, in what sense, remains a subject of considerable debate in which theological and historical approaches often disagree. Historians, of course, are occupationally interested in change, or at least historians who are not content to inventory *la longue durée*. Narrative history tells a story that unfolds within a plot, and it is hard to imagine a plot in which nothing happens! An *event* is an incident or happening, or a set of them, that is noteworthy, and usually noteworthy because it breaks with routine by its mere occurrence or because it does not leave things the way they were before. An event, in other words, means difference.

Difference, of course, can be discerned only against "a backdrop of uniformity,"[5] that is, when placed within a series, plotted between moments prior and subsequent. If there is difference, it can only be as a change from what had been before, and for occurrences to constitute an "event," the changes must endure; an event has a *Wirkungsgeschichte*. (On this view, Vatican II would be considered an "event," while the Roman Synod of 1962 would not be.)

It is not necessary that such an event be perceived as such by contemporary participants or protagonists; but even when it is so perceived by

---

3. The speech may be found in six languages at http://www.vatican.va/holy_father/ benedict_xvi/speeches/2005/december/documents/hf_ben_xvi_spe_20051222_roman-curia _en.html.

4. The essay is reprinted, along with essays by three others, in *Vatican II: Did Anything Happen?* ed. David G. Schultenover (New York: Continuum, 2007). I have analyzed the pope's speech in "Benedict XVI and the Interpretation of Vatican II," *Cristianesimo nella Storia* 28 (2007): 323-37; in shorter form in "Novelty in Continuity: Pope Benedict's Interpretation of Vatican II," *America* 200 (2 February 2009): 10-16.

5. Paul Veyne, *Writing History: Essay on Epistemology,* trans. Mina Moore-Rinvolucri (Middletown, CT: Wesleyan University Press, 1984), pp. 7 and 5.

them, the historian's judgment about it will not depend solely on what contemporaries perceived, intended, or desired. A first step in a complete history is indeed the reconstruction of a historical moment of human interaction as discernible through the traces it has left, but this reconstruction of the contemporary intentions and decisions does not suffice for a determination of whether something event-ful was going on and, if so, what it was that was going on. There is such a thing as the law of unintended consequences! A dramatic change may be intended and not take place, that is, not have consequences; and decisions thought and intended to be mere reforms may turn out to be revolutionary in their effects.

Do these considerations, which I take to be commonplace among historians, apply in the case of the Church? The two quotations given above from the present pope could suggest that historic events are not to be expected, at least none that suggest rupture or break, that is, discontinuity. The Church, he claims, is a single historical subject, and its journey is one of continuous progress toward deeper understanding of the faith; it is not marked by fractures or breaks, or by leaps either.

This theological claim is one that not only historians but many theologians, too, will find very puzzling. Their first question will be about the relationship between the Church so described and the actual communities of believers who have constituted the Church in the past and constitute it today. They will wonder, for example, whether it was all progress when the Church ceased to be persecuted and became established; whether the Church did not change significantly when the Roman Empire collapsed; whether the Gregorian Reform did not represent a break from the Church of the ninth and tenth centuries; whether the necessities of polemic did not narrow the Church's theological vision in the second Christian millennium; whether modern circumstances did not require the Church to look differently at the questions of Church and State and religious freedom.

I put the last of these questions in that form because to it Joseph Ratzinger has consistently given a positive answer. He once made the general point that one never encounters a "world-less Church," that is, a Church without specific reference to the world in which it lives and which itself changes as that relationship changes.[6] Later he spoke of such texts of

---

6. "Christianity has never existed in a purely world-less state. Because it exists in men, whose behavior is 'the world,' it never appears concretely except in a relationship to the world. This interweaving with the world may mean that in an apparent clash between faith and world, it is not Christianity that is being defended against the world, but only a particular form of its relationship to the world that is being defended against another form. For ex-

Vatican II as *Gaudium et Spes, Dignitatis Humanae,* and *Nostra Aetate* as a "counter-Syllabus."[7] Most recently he devoted a great deal of his speech on the interpretation of Vatican II to the argument that the Church had to re-think its multiple relationships with the modern world, and that the re-sults of this reconsideration were changes that not only advanced some earlier positions of the Church but also corrected others of them.

The abstract description of a Church that never leaps forward and never has to break with its past is in some tension with the concrete de-scription of a Church that has had to correct its attitude toward the mod-ern world. The latter is the Church with which historians are familiar; the former seems to be floating off somewhere in the ether, describing a Church with no human beings in it. If this tension, unresolved in the pope's writings on the council, is not noticed, the danger will be to greatly oversimplify his views and to read him as suggesting that one has to choose between continuity and discontinuity in interpreting Vatican II. In his speech to the Curia, however, the pope did not contrast discontinuity and continuity, but discontinuity and *reform,* and he devoted the largest part of his talk to establishing and illustrating that reform means "continuity *and discontinuity* on different levels" (my emphasis).

Lastly, the question of continuity or discontinuity refers to a more or less proximate past. Perhaps the most common referent is to an immediate past that one wishes to continue as it was or from which one wishes to de-part. In the latter case, one may wish to rejoin an earlier past from which the most recent past itself represented a departure; in this case, discontinu-ity might be for the sake of continuity. For example, Pope Benedict said, in his speech on the interpretation of Vatican II, that in its *Declaration on Re-ligious Freedom,* the council "recognized and made its own an essential principle of the modern state and at the same time recovered the deepest patrimony of the Church. By so doing she can be conscious of being in full harmony with the teaching of Jesus himself (cf. Mt 22:21), as well as with the Church of the martyrs of all time." Here the deepest patrimony of the Church is something that had to be recovered, and full harmony with the teaching of Jesus and with the Church of the martyrs something achieved

---

ample, what may seem to be a conflict between faith and world may really be a conflict be-tween the thirteenth century and the twentieth, because the thirteenth century's polarizing of Christian existence is being identified with the faith itself." Joseph Ratzinger, "Der Christ und die Welt von heute," in *Dogma und Verkündigung* (München: Wewel, 1977), p. 187.

7. Joseph Ratzinger, *Principles of Catholic Theology: Building Stones for a Fundamental Theology* (San Francisco: Ignatius, 1987), pp. 381-82.

while adopting an essential principle of the modern state. Discontinuity with the Church's modern defense of the ideal of a state religion, then, enabled a recovery of a deeper harmony.

John O'Malley's writings on Vatican II have always been alert to these elements in a historical interpretation of the council. It is worth noting that he has approached the council primarily as a historian, not as a theologian. Particularly in his book on the council, he has sought to make the event of Vatican II intelligible by placing it within a series of earlier moments in the history of the Catholic Church. Two streams in that history are especially important for the plot O'Malley follows. The first is the series of previous ecumenical councils, which provides a point of contrast with Vatican II, a council that departed in important respects from the pattern of earlier councils. The second context is what O'Malley calls "the long nineteenth century," extending to the end of the reign of Pope Pius XII, which provides the backdrop against which the drama of the council is described. It is in terms of these two contexts that the question of continuity and discontinuity, at different levels, is addressed.

While he makes use of the scholarly resources that have become available in recent decades, O'Malley's book does not consider developments in the Church after Vatican II. He has been mainly interested in recapturing the contemporary experience of the council and of identifying distinctive elements of its teaching. But like any good historian, he has not undertaken his task as if history stopped with the close of the Second Vatican Council. What has happened in the five decades since it was announced surely has influenced the kinds of questions he has asked and alerted him to dimensions of the experience of the council that might have passed unperceived by participants in the event. In any event, it is clear that an appreciation of Vatican II cannot prescind from what happened after it and, in varying degrees, because of it.

The essays collected in this volume were commissioned as a set of reflections on O'Malley's book. They may be usefully described by locating them in terms of three moments of a total history of Vatican II: conciliar context, conciliar experience, and conciliar consequences. Although almost all of the essays say something about all three of these moments, some focus more on one or another of them.

Robin Darling Young's essay reflects on Henri de Lubac's theological project, exemplified in his very influential book *Catholicism,* one of the major contributions to the *ressourcement* that made Vatican II possible. Setting that work in a context larger than that of many studies of the

French Jesuit, Darling Young argues that its romantic evocation of a patristic Church united around the mystery of Christ failed to take into account the "sea of conflict" and "bitter polemics" that marked early Christianity. To what degree de Lubac's views influenced the texts of Vatican II has not been studied in adequate detail, but Darling Young's thesis is that his incomplete vision failed to prepare proponents of *ressourcement* for "the rancorous conflict" that followed Vatican II. The thesis suggests the need for studies on the limitations of the conciliar documents, and of their adequacy for dealing with postconciliar developments both in Church and in world.

In his essay John Connelly spans all three moments of a history of Vatican II. He throws new light on the process that resulted in the section on the Jews in the council's *Declaration on Non-Christian Religions (Nostra Aetate)*. The process is personalized in the figure of John Oesterreicher, one of the architects of that section, and in the two conversions he underwent, from Jew to Catholic and from a proponent of a mission to Jews to an advocate on their behalf. In this essay, too, postconciliar developments prompt questions about what precisely was achieved by Vatican II and about the permanency of its effects.

Both Cathleen Kaveny and Darlene Fozard Weaver remark in their essays how little attention was given in the texts of Vatican II to moral theology, a fact that, as far as I know, has not really been explored or explained. Each essay offers a description of preconciliar moral theology as developed primarily to prepare priests to administer the sacrament of reconciliation. To the emphases of that tradition Fozard Weaver's essay contrasts the theological anthropology that can be educed from the council's stress on the common call to holiness and on the responsibility and freedom of conscience. The developments and controversies in moral theology that followed the council are briefly sketched, along with some predictions for the future. This essay shows the need of a historical study of debates in Catholic moral theology before the council as well as of the decision to drop already-prepared texts on fundamental moral theology and on sexual ethics from the conciliar agenda.

Kaveny argues that because Vatican II said so little about moral theology, Catholic moralists, if they are to understand "the council's tremendous impact on the field of moral theology," have to turn to the "spirit" of the council. A merit of the essay is that it makes this notoriously vague term more precise by reference to the three issues that O'Malley has identified as underlying the texts of Vatican II: continuity and change, center and periphery, and rhetoric and style. After a description of the orientations and emphases of preconciliar moral theology and of controversies in the field since the council, Kaveny argues that Pope John Paul II's encyclical on moral matters, *Evangelium Vitae*, when placed within O'Malley's threefold framework, represents "a model of magisterial moral theology done in the spirit of Vatican II."

Treatment of postconciliar developments is also prominent in the remaining two essays. Francis Sullivan's analysis of the doctrine on the salvation of adherents of other religions has the fullest and best-documented discussion of the history of the relevant conciliar texts. Breaking down the question of development into two manageable issues, Sullivan concludes that both in the conciliar teaching itself and in subsequent magisterial documents, a "striking development" has taken place in Catholic thinking about the possibility of salvation for members of other religions, a clear illustration, then, of O'Malley's first underlying issue: "continuity and change."

Massimo Faggioli focuses his essay on the new ecclesial movements that have emerged and flourished in the decades since Vatican II. He argues that they find greater support in the "spirit" of Vatican II than in the letter of its documents, which say little to anticipate the form that these movements would take. The link between the council and the movements is, as Faggioli puts it, more theological than historical. He thinks, however, that in one important respect, the movements run counter to the new emphasis that Vatican II placed on the local Church; they indulge a universalist ecclesiology, focused on the pope, that the council tried to balance in its treatment of the authority of bishops, particularly as heads of local churches. It is the "center-periphery" issue that prevails in this essay.

These essays contribute to the effort to elaborate a full interpretation of the Second Vatican Council both as an achievement in itself and in the consequences it has had on the life of the Catholic Church. Similar studies need to be done on the other documents of the council in order for a full appreciation of the council's work and its impact to be possible.

Meanwhile, of course, the life of the Church continues, and as Fr. Congar pointed out ten years after the council closed: "It would be absurd to think that things have to remain in the state at which you find them at the end of the council, December 8, 1965."[8] The council had accomplished

---

8. *Une vie pour la vérité. Jean Puyo interroge le Père Congar* (Paris: Le Centurion, 1975), pp. 131-32.

far more than he had dared to dream when it was first announced and when it first began to meet. Even so, Congar thought that the council's work of renewing and reforming the Church had been left "at the half-way point," in part at least because Pope Paul VI sought as full a consensus as would be possible. It would be the life of the Church that would spell out the implications of the council's accomplishment at every level.

That work, what technically is called the "reception" of the council, is still under way, of course. The Council of Trent did not reveal all its reforming force until centuries after its close, and there is no reason to think that Vatican II has exhausted its power to renew and reform the Church in a mere half-century. The contemporary debates about the history and the consequences of the Second Vatican Council are important and need to be pursued; but a full appreciation of this dramatic moment in the life of the Catholic Church will also have to wait until the council has deployed all its virtualities in the life of the Church. We — all of us — are even now determining "what happened at Vatican II."

# Contributors

JOHN CONNELLY has taught the history of East Central Europe at the University of California at Berkeley since 1994. He received a BSFS from Georgetown University (1982), MA (in Russian and East European Studies) from the University of Michigan (1987), and PhD from Harvard University (1995). He has published *Captive University: The Sovietization of East German, Czech and Polish Higher Education* (Chapel Hill: University of North Carolina Press, 2000), which won the 2001 George Beer Award of the American Historical Association, and edited with Michael Gruettner *Universities Under Dictatorship* (Penn State University Press, 2005). Other work has appeared in *Minerva, East European Politics and Societies, Geschichte und Gesellschaft, The Journal of Modern History, Slavic Review, The Nation*, the *London Review of Books,* and *Commonweal.* Connelly is currently working on a study of the evolution of Catholic thinking on the Jewish people from 1933 to 1965.

DR. MASSIMO FAGGIOLI was a member of the "Istituto per le scienze religiose — Fondazione Giovanni XXIII" in Bologna between 1996 and 2008. Since September 2009, he has been Assistant Professor in the Department of Theology at the University of St. Thomas (St. Paul, MN). His recent publications include *Il vescovo e il concilio. Modello episcopale e aggiornamento al Vaticano II* (Bologna: Il Mulino, 2005); *Breve storia dei movimenti cattolici* (Roma: Carocci, 2008) [Spanish translation, Madrid: PPC, 2011]; *What Are They Saying About Vatican II?* (Mahwah NJ: Paulist, 2012). Books in progress and forthcoming include: *Reforming the Liturgy — Reforming the Church at Vatican II: The Profound Implications of "Sacrosanctum Concilium"* (Collegeville, MN: Liturgical Press, 2013); *Le culture politiche del Vaticano II* [The Political Cultures of Vatican II] (Roma-Bari: Laterza, 2014).

JAMES HEFT (Marianist), a priest of the Society of Mary, spent many years at the University of Dayton, serving as chair of the Theology Department, Provost of the University, and University Professor of Faith and Culture and Chancellor. He left the University of Dayton in 2006 to found the Institute for Advanced Catholic Studies at the University of Southern California in Los Angeles, where he now serves as the Alton Brooks Professor of Religion and President of the Institute for Advanced Catholic Studies. He has written and edited twelve books and over 150 articles and book chapters. Most recently he edited *Intellectual Humility among Jews, Christians and Muslims* (Oxford, 2011), and co-edited *Engineering and the Catholic University* (Notre Dame: University of Notre Dame Press, 2011). He has just finished writing *Catholic High Schools: Facing the New Realities* (Oxford: Oxford University Press, 2011). In 2011, he received the Theodore Hesburgh Award for long and distinguished service to Catholic Higher Education.

M. CATHLEEN KAVENY is the John P. Murphy Foundation Professor of Law and Professor of Theology at the University of Notre Dame. She received both her JD and her PhD from Yale University. A specialist in the relationship of law, religion, and morality, she is completing one book on the pedagogical function of law in a pluralistic society, and another on the role of prophetic discourse in the public square.

JOSEPH A. KOMONCHAK, a priest of the Archdiocese of New York, recently retired after thirty-two years of teaching at the Catholic University of America. Ordained in 1963, he received his Licentiate in Sacred Theology at the Gregorian University, Rome, in 1964 and his doctorate in philosophy at Union Theological Seminary, New York, in 1976. He taught theology at St. Joseph's Seminary, Dunwoodie, from 1967 to 1977, when he joined the faculty of the School of Theology and Religious Studies where he taught courses on ecclesiology, modern theology, the thought of John Courtney Murray, the theology of Joseph Ratzinger, and the history and theology of Vatican II. He has published many articles on these subjects in major journals both scholarly and popular. He was the chief editor of *The New Dictionary of Theology* and the editor of the English-language edition of the five-volume *History of Vatican II*. A collection of his essays was published as *Foundations in Ecclesiology.* His Père Marquette lecture, *Who Are the Church?*, was delivered and published in 2008.

JOHN W. O'MALLEY, S.J., is University Professor in the Theology Department of Georgetown University. He received his doctorate from the History Department of Harvard University, with specialization in the religious culture of early modern Europe. He has lectured widely at home and abroad and has held visiting professorships at Harvard, Oxford, and the University of Michigan. His *Praise and Blame in Renaissance Rome* won the Marraro Prize from the American Historical Association, and his *The First Jesuits* won the Barzun Prize from the American Philosophical Society. John O'Malley is past president of the American Catholic Historical Association and of the Renaissance Society of America. In 2002 he received the Lifetime Achievement Award from the Society for Italian Historical Studies and in 2005 the corresponding award from the Renaissance Society of America. He was elected in 1995 a fellow of the American Academy of Arts and Sciences and in 1998 a member of the American Philosophical Society. He has written extensively on Vatican Council II.

FRANCIS A. SULLIVAN, S.J., was born on May 21, 1922, in Boston. In 1938 he entered the New England Province of the Society of Jesus. He obtained the MA in philosophy at Boston College in 1945, the MA in classics at Fordham University in 1948, and the STL at Weston College in 1952. After obtaining the STD at the Gregorian University in 1956, he taught ecclesiology at the Gregorian for thirty-six years, serving also as dean of the faculty of theology from 1964 to 1970. After being declared *emeritus* of that faculty in 1992, he taught theology at Boston College until 2008. He is the author of eight books, the most recent of which are the following: *Creative Fidelity: Weighing and Interpreting Documents of the Magisterium* (New York/Mahwah: Paulist, 1996) and *From Apostles to Bishops: The Development of the Episcopacy in the Early Church* (New York/Mahwah: Newman Press, 2001).

DARLENE FOZARD WEAVER is Associate Professor of Theology and Director of the Theology Institute at Villanova University. Weaver specializes in moral anthropology and ethical theory, which she extends in work on practical moral problems in sexual, social, and medical ethics. She is the author of *Self Love and Christian Ethics* and the forthcoming *The Acting Person and Christian Moral Life: Involvements with God and Goods,* and editor of and contributor to *The Ethics of Embryo Adoption and the Catholic Tradition* (co-edited with Sarah-Vaughan Brakman). Weaver's essays appear in scholarly journals like the *Journal of Religious Ethics* and in a number of edited collections, including the *Oxford Handbook of Theological Ethics,* as well as journals of opinion such as *Commonweal.* Weaver is invited to lecture around the country and abroad. She serves on the editorial boards of the *Journal of Religious Ethics, Religious Studies Review,* and *Reviews in Religion and Theology.*

ROBIN DARLING YOUNG is a historian of early Christianity specializing in the languages and cultures of the eastern Mediterranean world. She has focused on the literature of early Christian martyrdom and on the development of learned asceticism from the fourth to the seventh centuries. Prof. Darling Young teaches in the Theology Department of the University of Notre Dame. She has taught early and medieval Christianity at Wesley Theological Seminary and the Catholic University of America and has been a visiting professor at the Universities of Chicago and Virginia. She has participated in the official bilateral dialogues between Catholics and Eastern Orthodox as well as Oriental Orthodox.

# Index

Abortion, 35-37, 46, 54, 57, 66; circumstances surrounding, 62; crime or right, 59; intrinsically evil, 62; social context, 60; strictures against, 67

Abraham, the stock of, 112-13

Absolution, 46

*Abusus non tollit usum*, 62

Acceptance, Catholicism and, 29

Acrimony, 41

Actions: evil, 38, 52, 56-57, 62; personal, 37; sinful, 49; social, 65; visions of morality and, 29

Activism: political, 43; service and social, 27

*Ad Gentes* (1965), 78, 80

Adler, Gary, viii-ix

Adoption program, 39

Agendas, political, 43

Aggiornamento, 3, 24, 53, 58, 143, 162

AJC, 105, 108

Alberigo, Giuseppe, xi, xiii

Alienation, 151

Ambrose, 141

America, 54, 118; culture in, 59; pro life and pro–social justice in, 65

American Jewish Committee, 105, 108

Americans, culture wars and, 64

Anathemas, vii

Anglican Church, 141

Anthropology, 154; Christology and, 159; moral theological, 31, 170

Anti-Catholicism, 99

Anti-Semitism, 96, 98-99, 103, 111, 113, 142

Apathy, religious, 134-35

Apostolate: Christian, 8; forms of, 6; to the Jews, 100; lay, 6

*Apostolate to the Jews* (publication), 10

*Apostolicam Actuositatem* (1965), xvi, 6-7, 11

Appreciation, Catholicism and, 29

Appropriation, Catholicism and, 29

Aquinas, Thomas, 4, 26, 53, 56, 64, 139, 141, 143, 147-48; on nature and grace, 138; pure nature in, 153

Arms, call to, 67

Art, morality and, 27

Assisi, meeting in, 84, 88

Association of Prayer for the Conversion of Israel, 98

Associations, Catholic, 6

Atheism, religion and, 153, 159-60

Augustine, 64, 97, 136

Augustinianism, 159

Authority, 28; bishops', 13-16; bureaus and, 45; church, 34, 62; distribution of, 45, 62

B'nai B'rith, 106